T0274957

WELCOME THE WRETCHED

Also by César Cuauhtémoc García Hernández

*Migrating to Prison: America's Obsession
with Locking Up Immigrants*

Crimmigration Law

WELCOME THE WRETCHED

In Defense of the "Criminal Alien"

CÉSAR CUAUHTÉMOC GARCÍA HERNÁNDEZ

THE
NEW
PRESS

NEW YORK
LONDON

Requests for permission to reproduce selections from this book should be made
through our website: https://thenewpress.com/contact.

Published in the United States by The New Press, New York, 2024
Distributed by Two Rivers Distribution

ISBN 978-1-62097-779-8 (hc)
ISBN 978-1-62097-830-6 (ebook)
CIP data is available

The New Press publishes books that promote and enrich public discussion and
understanding of the issues vital to our democracy and to a more equitable world.
These books are made possible by the enthusiasm of our readers; the support of a
committed group of donors, large and small; the collaboration of our many partners
in the independent media and the not-for-profit sector; booksellers, who often
hand-sell New Press books; librarians; and above all by our authors.

www.thenewpress.com

Composition by dix!
This book was set in Garamond Premier Pro

Printed in the United States of America

10   9   8   7   6   5   4   3   2   1

To Lupita, Raúl, Sol-Angel, and Carlos,
who blazed the path that I walk.

Give me your tired, your poor, your huddled masses yearning to breathe free, the wretched refuse of your teeming shore.

—Emma Lazarus, *The New Colossus*

To tell the truth, the proof of success lies in a whole social structure being changed from the bottom up. The extraordinary importance of this change is that it is willed, called for, demanded.

—Frantz Fanon, *The Wretched of the Earth*

CONTENTS

WELCOME THE WRETCHED

INTRODUCTION

In July 2015, forty-five-year-old José Inéz García Zarate was sitting on a bench on San Francisco's Embarcadero—a popular waterfront walkway—when he found a pile of rags. José was living on the streets, like he had many times in his life, so he was used to scrounging. As he picked up the pile, thirty-two-year-old Kate Steinle—a sales professional out for a walk with her father—crossed his path. A bullet flew across the walkway and hit Kate in the back. "Dad, help me, help me," she pleaded with her father as they waited for an ambulance to arrive. By the time the emergency crew got her to the hospital, it was too late. Kate was dead. And José had pulled the trigger.[1]

This might have been just another tragic gun death in the United States, except that José was not just another tourist out for a summertime walk. A Mexican citizen and longtime resident of the United States, he didn't have the government's permission to be here. It's unclear whether he ever had. But live here he had, and there's a long criminal record to prove it. Over two decades he had been deported at least five times and racked up a string of low-level felony convictions. Most were for coming to the United States in violation of immigration law, but a few involved drugs. He probably would have been deported a sixth time that spring, before shooting Kate, had a twenty-year-old arrest warrant not gotten in the way. Instead of handing him over to Immigration and Customs Enforcement after almost four years at a federal prison for violating immigration law in the past, federal prison officials sent him to San Francisco to face charges over a decades-old drug deal involving $20 of marijuana.

But the San Francisco of 2015 was not the San Francisco of 1995. City officials declined to prosecute. Minor drug activity wasn't a priority for prosecutors. California was on its way to legalizing marijuana. Without any criminal charges pending, the Sheriff's Department released him. Ten weeks later, Kate was dead, and José was holding the weapon.[2] In newspapers and on TV, Kate—young, thin, blond—her bright future evident in the smile that radiates from every image, was the hopeful contrast to the aging, laggard José, whose absent stare into the camera suggested there was no room for other people in his heart, his orange prison jumpsuit a signal that we would all be safer with him behind bars.

Tossed onto the blaze of modern immigration politics, a bipartisan chorus quickly erupted around Kate's death, pinning blame on San Francisco for its migrant-friendly policies. In Kate's untimely tragedy, the city's policy of limiting police cooperation with ICE was revealed to be deadly, Democrats and Republicans claimed. Dianne Feinstein, California's Democratic U.S. senator, criticized San Francisco. "We should focus on deporting convicted criminals, not setting them loose on our streets," she wrote to the city's mayor.[3] Hillary Clinton, on her way to becoming the Democratic Party's presidential pick, added, "The city made a mistake not to deport someone that the federal government strongly felt should be deported." [4]

Nothing more than a flashy tabloid celebrity with presidential ambitions at the time, Donald Trump quickly joined in. This was a "senseless and totally preventable act of violence committed by an illegal immigrant," he said. [5] During the next few months, he continued pointing to Kate's death to justify his calls for strong-armed immigration policing. "Beautiful Kate in San Francisco was shot by an illegal," he added. [6] On stage at the Republican National Convention that summer, he paused with practiced sympathy to remember Kate once more. "Where was the sanctuary for Kate Steinle?" he asked. "Where was the sanctuary for all of the other Americans who have been so brutally murdered, and who have suffered so, so horribly?" [7] Angel families, he called them, using their loss to fuel his political rise.

Despite the politicians' outcries, a jury saw José's actions on the San Francisco waterfront differently. José was certainly holding the gun when the bullet leaped from its barrel, but he probably didn't know there was a gun inside the cloth rag he picked up from the sidewalk. In court, the former head of the San Francisco Police Department crime lab testified that the gun was pointed at the ground. He added, "You couldn't do this on purpose." [8] Two years after Kate died, a jury acquitted José of her murder.

Outside the White House, President Trump called the jury's work "disgraceful." Taking their cues from Trump, two years later federal prosecutors tried again to convict José.

"A repeatedly deported, previously convicted felon has no right to possess a firearm under federal law, even if California extends him sanctuary," the U.S. attorney in San Francisco said.[9]

Everyone agrees that the gun belonged to a federal law enforcement officer. Someone stole it from a park ranger's car. No one thinks José was to blame for that. Police never figured out who was. José said he found it under the park bench, and prosecutors never disputed that. It was just bad luck that the pile of rags he reached for had a gun inside it, but bad luck was enough to end Kate's life and make José a target.

For José, possessing a gun meant he would get no harbor in the United States. After Trump left the White House, his lawyers asked Joe Biden's administration to stop going after their client, but prosecutors refused. Years passed while José sat inside a jail. During that time, he was diagnosed as schizophrenic, but received next to no treatment. "That must have been hell," a judge later commented.[10] Seven years after being arrested for Kate's death, still in jail, prosecutors wore him down.

They couldn't nail José for Kate's death, but long after Trump had moved to Florida, they were able to get him to plead guilty to holding the gun, a federal crime for someone with a criminal record and for someone who doesn't have the government's permission to be in the United States. The judge sentenced him to three years of supervised release, plus the time he had already spent in jail, but not a single day more of prison time. It doesn't really matter, though, since not even the judge expected him to serve his sentence. Instead, everyone expected ICE to deport him. The judge even told him to never return to the United States.[11]

As the spring of 2023 approached, José still hadn't left. Prosecutors hadn't let him. After the case wrapped up in California, federal officials sent him to Texas. Federal prosecutors there wanted to punish him yet again. In 2011, four years before that tragic afternoon on the Embarcadero, he'd been convicted of returning to the United States without the government's permission, a federal crime, and was told to stay out of trouble and keep the court up to date on his whereabouts.

People are often released from prison with a long list of requirements. Many fail to meet them. It's hard to deny José is one of them. He was convicted of two crimes for holding the gun, and he almost certainly didn't tell the court that he was living on the streets of San Francisco. Prosecutors weren't required to haul him back to court, but that's the option they chose for José.

After Donald Trump and Hillary Clinton made him famous, it's not surprising that a prosecutor in Texas wanted to bring the law down hard on José. In fact, the official papers that the prosecutor submitted to the court asking for permission to bring José back to Texas mentioned national media reports surrounding Kate's death. In October 2022, the judge sentenced José to another two years of imprisonment, leaving José to do what he has done so many times in his life: pass the days locked inside another federal prison.[12] He's now spent more time inside prisons in the United States than he ever did living in Mexico.

Mental illness and living on the streets are nothing new in

the United States, the country where José has spent most of his life. In the California of 2015, the year José found the rag that led to deadly consequences, there were more than 115,000 people like José who didn't have housing.[13] Twenty percent probably suffered some severe form of mental illness.[14] California is far from alone. All around my Denver, Colorado, home, it's hard to miss my neighbors who make their lives on sidewalks and along the South Platte River, constantly being pushed farther away from the booming downtown and the luxury mid-rises filling old industrial sites and lots where aging bungalows once stood. In raggedy tents and dirty blankets, mental illness and petty crime are on public display there, just as they are somewhere in every major city in the United States.

José isn't a product of his birth in Mexico, the country where he lived as a child but left as he approached young adulthood. He's a product of his time in the United States. In his untreated mental illness and homelessness, José is the picture of the social crevice that politicians have created. In his decades of prison time due to petty criminality, he's the image of politicians' fetishization of policing and prison. In his stumbling onto a loaded weapon, he's a flesh-and-bones reminder of our country's love affair with guns. And in his status as an unauthorized migrant, he's the reflection of immigration laws that have lost touch with reality. To believe that José is someone else's problem foisted onto the United States is to hide from the country we have built.

I wrote most of this book while living in Mexico City. From there, the irony of deporting José to a country I've spent more time in as an adult than he has was especially visible. My life was made possible by the United States, just like his was. Mistreated in jail, punished by the judge, José needed help getting onto his feet. Instead, he sat in yet another prison waiting for yet another prosecutor to claim yet again that he's not worthy of living among those of us who happened to be born north of the border. Donald Trump proved lousy at building the wall he promised, but to cheer on José's deportation is to hope that courts, prosecutors, and immigration police operate like the wall Trump dreams of.

In the United States, immigration law and policy isn't a simple story about upholding the law. It's also not a morality play about right and wrong. It never has been. Immigration law and policy is driven by politics. As with so much else, where Congress and the president see a problem, police, prosecutors, and prisons are their preferred answers.

What were once sleepy corners of the federal government have become generously funded, well-staffed, and impressively equipped law enforcement agencies that leave a stamp on communities around the country. The Department of Homeland Security's two immigration law enforcement agencies, Customs and Border Protection and ICE, count more than 20,000 personnel in each of their ranks. Through its Border Patrol unit, CBP monitors the nation's international boundaries. In reality, that mostly means the Mexican border, where 85 percent of its agents are stationed. Its counterpart, ICE, searches the nation's interior for people who might be deportable, stationing agents inside county jails and partnering with local police forces to identify migrants who land on a cop's radar for anything from a busted taillight to a serious crime.

In a political era plagued by partisan dysfunction in Washington, there is always bipartisan support for lavishly funding immigration policing. In 2023 alone, Congress gave CBP $21 billion and another $9 billion to ICE. That year, the agency that most of us think of as the nation's most important law enforcement unit, the FBI, received $10.7 billion—one-third of what its immigration-focused counterparts got. With this money, CBP pays for holding cells, guns, and surveillance balloons that it flies over communities like the one in South Texas where I grew up. Its agents are looking for immigration scofflaws. When they find them, some are deported, and others are first walked into a federal courtroom to be marked as criminals.

For its part, ICE pays for beds spread across 125 prisons, SWAT-team-style gear, long guns, and contracts with private companies that search through massive quantities of data in an attempt to sniff out who might be deportable. Working with local cops, county jails, and state police, they search for people who run into criminal law problems, but are also ever ready to use their weapons against people who have never come near the criminal legal system.

Through the political process, fear—sifted through the dirty prism of racism—has treated some people as desirable members of our communities and others as dispensable outcasts. Details change over the years, but the basic premise holds firm. Through immigration law, the United States privileges some people and tars others as unworthy of inclusion.

At one time, race did all the work, nakedly and unapologetically. In the late nineteenth century, Congress barred Chinese migrants, then took its aim at most other Asians. A century ago, immigration law welcomed migrants from northern and western Europe, but kept tight limits on Italians, Jews, and other people from southern and eastern Europe. From the 1920s through the middle of the twentieth century, Congress targeted socialists, anarchists, and communists. Later, queer people took their turn receiving the brunt of Congress's ire.

The targets changed, but the basic point has remained constant. Since the late nineteenth century, Congress has used immigration law to sort migrants into two camps: desirable and undesirable. Courts say that telling some migrants they can't live in the United States isn't punishment, even when we're talking about people who have lived here for decades or are sure to leave behind spouses and children. To the law, forcing a migrant to leave is just the process of sorting people into a world divided into hundreds of countries. It's not punishment, so deportation isn't a matter of criminal law. Instead, immigration law is a form of what lawyers call civil administrative law. As a legal matter, the federal government can do that. But as an ethical matter, a look back at the laws that Congress has enacted to sort good migrants from bad migrants makes clear that at every turn it has chosen shameful metrics: race, ideology, sexuality.

For most of the history of the United States, criminal law and immigration law largely existed in separate silos. Fall into problems with the local cops, and you dealt with the local judge. The law usually worked the same for U.S. citizens and migrants. Citizen or not, a life in the United States was possible even with a criminal record. That was true of low-level offenses like traffic violations just as it was true of serious crimes like murder.

By the late 1980s, the marker of undesirability had changed. Gone were the days of open racism. Slurs and taunts were forced to evolve. Instead of the vile epithets of the past, policymakers landed on the cold neutrality of crime. A legal landscape in which criminal law and immigration law rarely intersected became history. During the last half-century, policing, prosecuting, and convicting people have become a pastime in the United States. Through criminal law's power to send people into prisons where they disappear from the rest of us, policymakers take a stand in favor of order and against illegality. That claim makes for good slogans but poor policy. Just beneath the surface of the modern-day criminal legal system in the United States—with its police, guns, prisons, prosecutors, and judges—is the sordid reality of racism in which people of color are overpoliced and underprotected.

Picking up where local police and criminal courts leave off, immigration officials point to criminal records, supposedly to sort good migrants from bad. Sometimes these are crimes committed in the United States, from the most mundane to the most serious. Sometimes they're nothing more than crimes of migration, policed, prosecuted, and celebrated as if the nation's existence depended on it.

Ignoring the racial undertow of modern-day policing, the policymakers who enact these laws and carry out these policies claim that in the outcome of criminal cases they can determine who is worthy of making a life in the United States and who is not. Relying on criminal law's allure, immigration law creates the wretched refuse of today. The political right points to the need to uphold the law, claiming that illegality is illegality and nothing else matters. From the left, liberals add that punishment rightly comes to people who do wrong. Both positions ignore racism's role in pegging some people as undesirable and luck's role in insulating some of us from the pain of immigration law based solely on the fact that we were born in the United States.

In the United States, crime, race, and citizenship embrace in an ugly effort to manage the nation at its most basic level— the people. Policymakers send police to arrest and prosecutors to convict, blissfully blinding themselves of the racial bias that's everywhere in the criminal legal system. The Supreme Court gives police the power "to surveil, to racially profile, to stop-and-frisk, and to kill," writes legal scholar Devon Carbado.[15] Indignities, inconveniences, interruptions, even mistakes, all bathed in the warm glow of law's mythical inherent correctness. Piling immigration consequences onto a criminal law regime doused by racism and poverty only throws fuel onto the fire of a legal system that, on its best days, barely touches justice with the ends of its fingertips. Whiteness, wealth, and citizenship protect some people, while people who are not white, not rich, and not U.S. citizens get two layers of punishment: a criminal conviction followed by deportation.

The refrain that Republicans and Democrats can't agree on immigration policy misses the reality that for a generation both parties have wielded the criminal legal system as a weapon against migrants. In the fevered battles about immigration that regularly rock Washington, Democrats and Republicans agree that the United States should deport migrants convicted of crimes. Overwhelmingly, these are people who aren't white. Almost always, they're people who aren't rich. In every instance, these are aliens, the word that immigration law uses to describe everyone who isn't a U.S. citizen. To politicians, these are criminal aliens, their misbehavior outranked only by their otherworldliness. Back in November 2014, President Barack Obama walked into the East Room of the White House—its red carpet and white columns signaling the event's importance—to announce his administration's new immigration law enforcement priorities. The federal government, he said, would target "felons, not families. Criminals, not children. Gang members, not a mother who's working hard to provide for her kids."

Just over two years later, President Trump renewed the government's focus on criminal activity by migrants. During his first week in office, he signed an executive order declaring that anyone convicted of any crime was a top priority for immigration imprisonment and removal from the United States. Early in his White House tenure, President Biden set his administration's tone. ICE should target anyone convicted of an aggravated felony, a sprawling category of crimes that includes everything from murder to tax fraud, the agency announced in Biden's first month. The administration would later shift its enforcement focus, but even then, it continued using criminal history to gauge whether someone might "threaten America's well-being." [16]

———

Stained with the mark of criminality, migrants who commit crimes have become politicians' favorite piñata. Elected officials take whacks at them while their supporters cheer on, their eyes covered to avoid seeing the damage they cause, uncovered only to revel in the spoils of in-the-moment reverie. Tagged by criminal law as misfits, criminal aliens are imagined as lone figures whose failures are entirely their own and whose lives affect no one but themselves and their victims. Denigrating them rhetorically and targeting them through immigration law and policy, politicians make migrants who commit a crime out to be owed nothing but the harshest edge of modern policing's prowess. In that zeal to be tough on crime, migrants are rounded up, their families and friends are left with a hole in their lives, and the ugly head of racism is ignored.

To imagine migrants as caricatures without a care in the world, whose ordeals ripple nowhere, is to imagine a fantasy world in which deportation solves a problem without creating new ones. Fantasies make us feel good, but law shouldn't revolve around fantasies. Migrants aren't lifeless figurines unmoored from the world. They are real people connected to friends, relatives, jobs, churches, and neighbors, and they behave like it. With pasts and hopes for the future here, many, like José Inéz García Zarate, will come back. If the United States is home, then it will continue to be home. But their return following deportation will be clandestine, a federal crime, making the journey more dangerous and their life in the United States more tenuous.

Others, like Vietnam War veteran José Padilla, will fight all the way to the Supreme Court to stay here. Over four decades in the United States, José Padilla had agreed to die on behalf of the United States. He had married, raised a family, and started a trucking business. The country where he was born, Honduras, was barely a memory. Driving around the United States delivering all sorts of merchandise, in September 2001 José made his way through Kentucky carrying too much weight in his trailer. Traveling just days after the attacks of September 11, 2001, José had nothing to do with terrorism, but with the politics of security swallowing immigration policy, all that mattered was his citizenship status and his cargo. Inspectors at a highway weigh station took a close look at his trailer and found about one thousand pounds of marijuana. José wanted to fight the drug possession charges that prosecutors brought against him, claiming he had no idea what was inside the boxes he was hauling. If he pleaded guilty, prosecutors wouldn't ask for much prison time, his lawyer told him, so he'd be able to go home soon.

José worried that it wouldn't be so easy. He was a lawful permanent resident—a green-card holder—not a U.S. citizen. He could live, work, and die in the United States, but he could also be deported. The lawyer told him not to worry. The Immigration and Naturalization Service, ICE's predecessor, wouldn't go after a Vietnam vet, the lawyer promised. "Because of the stressful condition in which I saw my wife and daughter at the time, I ended up taking the plea bargain," José said years later.

By then immigration agents had proven José's lawyer

wrong. They'd tried to deport José, only to find an adversary who wouldn't give up. José took his case to the Supreme Court and won. His lawyer's promise that he didn't have to worry about deportation wasn't just incorrect; it was unconstitutional. Criminal law is separate from immigration law, but that doesn't mean defense attorneys can invent the law so that they can promise their clients what's pleasing to the ear. Just like they're constitutionally obligated to figure out the criminal law that might lead to their client's conviction, defense attorneys are constitutionally obligated to figure out the immigration law that might lead to their client's deportation. Since José's lawyer didn't do that, the court tossed out his conviction, allowing José to stay in the United States. Eventually he even became a U.S. citizen. But most migrants can't count on getting good news from the Supreme Court. For many migrants with a criminal record, there are few escapes from the immigration prison and deportation pipeline. Once in, it's hard to get out.

Claims by politicians that they make the United States safer and promote the rule of law by targeting criminal aliens overlooks the substantial consequences of immigration laws that target people who commit crimes. Children are routinely left without a parent, and spouses are forced to carry on without a partner and income-earner. At its worst, deporting migrants with checkered backgrounds displaces danger—prioritizing safety in the United States over insecurity elsewhere. Sometimes, deportation even increases risk everywhere. When Congress went after gangs in the 1980s and cops across California followed by going after kids who

were born in Central America, the result was to create a per-
verse migration loop: the gangs hatched in struggling cities
across the United States exported to struggling cities across
Central America. Social disorder here fueled instability there,
which eventually led back here in the form of another round
of migration, this time the children and families fleeing gang
violence since 2014.

Immigration policies, like people, are difficult to corral.
Crime is defined broadly to include coming to the United
States without the government's permission, something that's
common even for people coming in search of asylum. Federal
law is clear that any migrant can request asylum no matter
how they got to the United States or if they received the government's permission to come. What federal law doesn't do is
insulate asylum seekers from criminal prosecution. In a per-
versity born of immigration law's entanglement with criminal
law, the "huddled masses yearning to breathe free" that Emma
Lazarus celebrates in words latched onto the Statue of Liberty
are also criminal aliens.

Politicians' zeal to target the easily maligned criminal alien
has redefined all of immigration law. Tactics justified by fears
of migrant criminality have become standard for all migrants
even if they haven't been convicted of a crime. Trained to see
in migrants existential threats to the nation, Border Patrol
agents and ICE officers view all migrants as potential dangers.
Armed to defend themselves against the greatest risk, they
bring their weapons to every encounter.

Sometimes these practices even hit people who are U.S. citizens. It turns out that citizens are not very good at carrying

proof of their citizenship. Law doesn't require it, nor should it. That just means that most of us rely on a mix of luck and loose stand-ins for our citizenship. Living in neighborhoods that don't have too many migrants, speaking English with some kind of U.S. accent, or worse: skin color and wealth. But luck and outward signals have their limits, sending some U.S. citizens, always people of color, into ICE prisons and onto deportation.

Criminal aliens are easy to tar and hard to defend. But defending criminal aliens' place in the United States is exactly what this book does. Migration should never be criminalized, and evidence of crime should have no place in deciding who gets to live here and who doesn't.

Instead of using the criminal legal system to identify people to imprison and deport, the United States must reconstruct immigration law and reimagine citizenship. Instead of a zero-sum game in which those of us born into our citizenship limit who else can access this all-important tie to the nation, we should think of citizenship as the constantly changing link between ordinary people and the imperfect political community that we've built and rebuilt collectively.

A rightful claim to belonging in the United States has never been determined solely by citizenship, and citizenship has never been static. Time and again, citizenship has been reimagined. Time and again, citizenship has expanded. New generations have changed citizenship's basic features, radically rejuvenating an old concept to give it new relevance. The country has taken steps backward, to be sure, but a clear trend has developed. Over the years, the citizenry has widened to welcome people previously shunned to the margins, decried as dangerous, described as undesirable members of the political community, or declared unfit to hold an equal stake in the experiment in self-governance called the United States of America.

All of us have skeletons in our closet. I'm no exception. My own family's skeletons span two countries, two languages, two legal systems, and many generations. I hear of them in whispers. Murmurs of drugs and rape, prisons and beatings. Violence. Escape. Anger. More violence. Often, these skeletons are revealed only as death approaches. Sometimes there's remorse: a plea for forgiveness in old age or poor health. Always there is sadness.

Learning about these traumas can begin the process of healing wounds. Hearing about my own family's secrets, I've learned to understand better the anger I saw. To make sense of the alienation I felt. To look at old photos and accept the person whose words stomped on my childhood heart. Hearing other people's stories, I realized that my own family's experiences may have been unique, but the buried pain and dysfunction were not.

This is a book about the ordinariness of migrants.

My aunt knows about this ordinariness. Born in Mexico, she spent most of her adult life in South Texas. She raised her kids there. She cleaned rich white people's houses there. And on the side, occasionally she helped people cross the border illegally. There wasn't much money in it. Just a lot of gratitude from the migrants who made it into the United States with her help: people whom she knew from the pueblo or whose parents she knew or whose cousin she knew. And from the rest of us, a lot of respect. Here was a woman who opened doors for others at great personal risk. She could've been prosecuted. She could've been deported. I was just a child then, but I too sensed the selflessness in what she did. An ordinary woman taking extraordinary risks to make life possible for people who in many ways were just like me. But even then, I also knew she was committing a crime. My aunt was a criminal. Fortunately, the law never caught up with her.

The law did catch up with my uncle. Also born in Mexico, he was sent to California to raise himself. Instead, he was raised by alcohol. Drunkenness followed. Violence followed. Police followed. Divorce and isolation followed. A life laying pipes in the United States followed. Now, slower and weaker, a humble future cloaked by the anonymity of impoverished retirement follows. Off and on, he lives with my mom. Roommates of a sort, like when they were little, only back then they had dirt floors and shared a bedroom. I like that he's there keeping my mom company. Politicians would call him a criminal alien. My mom calls him her brother. I call him my tío.

My wife's grandmother knows about this ordinariness. The first of her Italian migrant family to be born in the United States, she was nearing ninety by the time I showed up on the scene. She was struggling with her hearing and her mobility. Her house was filled by the sound of Fox News blasting in the background as her dog yapped and threatened to pee on everyone it didn't like. That included me.

Her stories of life in an immigrant family matched mine.

She was proud of her parents and siblings. I of mine. Only in her view, her family had done things the right way. Mexicans like me not so much. Early on she had warned my wife—at that time the word "girlfriend" would've been a stretch—to get away because our cultures were too different. But by the time grandmom and I were sharing family histories under the blaring sounds of Lou Dobbs and his xenophobic colleagues on Fox News, she enjoyed telling me about how her father came to the United States to work. A brother had come earlier and made sure he had a job lined up in Philadelphia, she explained. I enjoyed telling her about the Contract Labor Act, which made bringing someone here with a job in hand illegal. She liked telling me about the importance of following the law. I liked telling her about how her family violated the law. Meanwhile Lou Dobbs yelled, the dog barked, and our visits ended with a hug, a kiss, and a promise to return soon. Eventually she even told my wife that she liked me. But she never did wrap her mind around the fact that her relatives had violated immigration law just like mine had.

This is a book about families and skeletons. Every family has skeletons. Some of us own up to them. We measure our parents' love against their flaws. We measure our family's joys against our family's tragedies. But many of us hide from the skeletons. We wish they didn't exist, so we pretend they don't. Eventually wishes become reality. The skeletons become lost to history. Romanticization takes over, clouding our memories. We recall a version of the past that existed but forget the messier version that did too. The drunken grandfather becomes just another grandfather—a bit cold, perhaps, but certainly not dangerous and definitely not criminal. Absolutely never imprisoned.

Begin to unlock dusty drawers in our family histories and suddenly skeletons appear. Sometimes they come with criminal records. Sometimes with funerals. Sometimes skeletons are locked away for so long that they turn to dust that blows away with the winds of time. In my own life, I know stories that I've been forbidden to tell. I know other stories that I don't want to tell. All of us do.

We are complex, contradictory people because we come from complicated stock. Each of us does no matter what our family's myths say. Some of us just don't know it.

Immigration law and policy in the United States relies on myths. It turns on a romanticized view of migrants to the United States: the hard-working, ambitious, morally upstanding, self-reliant, up-by-the-bootstraps migrants. And it leaves out everything else. This book focuses on the everything else, beginning with the forgotten features of the story of migration where migrants' complexities and contradictions are to be found.

1

CELEBRATING CRIMINALS

I don't remember when Pati and I met. We were both in
college, living in New England, far from anything we had
known before. I grew up in South Texas. Pati in California's Central Valley. At Brown University, we were just two
poor Mexican kids trying to figure out what we were doing
there. There weren't too many of us, so it felt like we all knew
each other. My best guess, and hers, is that we must have met
through that small group. She was a year ahead of me. A year
older, I like to remind her every time her birthday comes
around.

Now forty-four, Pati looks like the Brooklyn social worker
she's been for sixteen years. Her hair always hangs simply
down her shoulders, her smile welcomes conversation, and
often she's dressed in the colors of Mexico's soccer team. At
the New York public school where she's been the lone social
worker most of the years she's been there, Pati helps teenagers
who have only recently arrived in the United States figure out
their new path in their new home. A new country, a new language, and a new culture—all as teenagers.

Life in New York City is never easy, and these kids feel that every day. Few have the luxury of just being students. Most go from school to work or from work to school. For many, there might as well not be trains and bridges linking Brooklyn to Manhattan. There's no time or money for the glitz of Midtown. Pati's job is to try to keep them from getting overwhelmed. "There's always more need," she says in the understated tone of the committed, experienced social worker that she is.

Pati grew up in California and has made Brooklyn home, but she got started in the Pacific coast town of Mazatlán, Mexico. She was five when all of that changed. Her mom, Doña Francis, recalls the journey with a mix of admiration and sadness. Pati, she says, did exactly what she needed to do: answered honestly when she needed to answer honestly, walked when she needed to walk, lied when she needed to lie, and ran when she needed to run.

Somewhere east of Tijuana, where a wall now rises, Pati and her mom walked across the arid mountains into the United States. Doña Francis had a friend whose brother was a *pollero*—what in other parts is called a coyote—a person who guides migrants into the United States. In recent years, drug cartels have become involved with migration, so smuggling has become more professionalized and, sadly, driven by money, but back in the 1980s when Pati and Doña Francis were trying to get into the United States it was common to rely on friends or friends of friends. Social networks provided guidance and offered safety.

In a group, Pati and her mom stood in the mountains of Tijuana and looked north. They walked quickly and quietly.

The moment they stepped across the border, mother and child committed a federal crime, crossing into the United States without the federal government's permission.

Through tears almost forty years later, Doña Francis remembers the moment someone spotted Border Patrol agents. Pati was near the front of the group. Doña Francis further back. "Migra!" someone yelled, using the pejorative Spanish word for immigration agents. Everyone ran for cover, but it was too late. The agents were onto them.

By the time I asked Doña Francis about that day, I'd known her almost a quarter-century. Her daughter had become almost like a sister to me. And yet I knew I was asking her to relive a moment that she would rather not have lived the first time. Her words slowed and grew quieter while her breaths became deeper and louder. "Eso sí me da mucha tristeza. Las dos sufrimos," she told me. "That makes me very sad. We both suffered."

At the sight of the Border Patrol agents, the group split up. Pati remembers a man who had been walking near her lifting her across a stream. When he put her down, they ran through mud so thick her shoes came off. With a child's innocence, Pati wasn't worried about getting caught. She was worried that her mom was going to be mad at her for losing her shoes.

In reality, Doña Francis was busy yelling at the agents that her daughter was ahead. "My daughter," she shouted. "My daughter. She's up there." She laughs a little at the irony of asking the Border Patrol to get her daughter. Almost immediately, tears replace laughter. "Don't let them take her," she recalls telling the agents. She had no reason to think that the people who Pati raced off with were dangerous. They were just ordinary people like her whose lives came together for the single moment that they trekked through the mountains. It's just that she didn't know them, Pati was five, and suddenly they had been separated.

By the time they saw each other again, Pati and Doña Francis were at the Border Patrol station in a room that looked like a jail cell. "My mom was a mess. I remember walking in and seeing my mom, and she was in the corner crying," Pati said. "She's not going to get after me about my shoes," she remembers thinking. Retelling that part of her experience decades later, she laughs. But she's also clear that these are memories she'll never forget. "It was hard," she added quietly.

Politicians didn't use the phrase back then, but Pati and her mom had become criminal aliens. Entering the United States without the federal government's permission is a federal crime. So is doing that after having previously been deported.

Today, tens of thousands of migrants get convicted of these crimes every year, but in the 1980s, things were different. Illegal entry and illegal reentry were both on the books, but prosecutors hardly used them. If Border Patrol agents caught migrants sneaking their way into the United States, they could've turned them over to prosecutors for criminal charges, but the reality back then was that prosecutors weren't interested. They would rather spend their time, energy, and money on other crimes. That's why Border Patrol agents typically just deported people.

That's what happened to Pati and Doña Francis, just as it

happened to so many others. They were deported, only to try again weeks later. That time, mother and child had more luck. The two reached the Central Valley, Pati started school, and the new life that Doña Francis hoped for began.

Soon President Ronald Reagan would push through Congress a massive shakeup of immigration law. With Republicans in control of Congress, the Immigration Reform and Control Act of 1986 allowed Doña Francis to erase her immigration law violations. For the first time, federal law forced employers to verify that a new hire has the government's permission to work in the United States. It's the reason why starting a new job comes with completing an immigration form and showing up with identification. Penalties are mild: as little as $250 for getting caught knowingly hiring one person without work permission and as much as $10,000 per person for repeat violators.

The federal government has never taken these requirements too seriously. Inspectors rarely come knocking. When they do, pointing to the immigration forms is almost always solid proof of following the law.[1] Supporters claimed that demanding proof of employment authorization would limit how many migrants worked in the United States. That's not what has happened, but in 1986 the claim was enough to convince skeptical members of Congress to vote for a version of the bill that contained a separate provision that made a world of difference for Doña Francis.

The immigration reform law that Reagan signed almost forty years ago is the last time that Congress enacted a sweeping amnesty law. In exchange for employer sanctions and throwing more money at border policing, roughly 2.7 million people went from living in the United States without authorization to living here with the government's permission. Doña Francis was one of those. Reagan's amnesty law let her become a permanent resident—a green-card holder. Like her, most people who benefited from the law were Mexican citizens. Later, Doña Francis became a U.S. citizen and helped her daughter fix her own immigration situation. Today, Pati is also a U.S. citizen with a life grounded in the United States but that reaches back to Mexico.

Pati and her mom were helped by luck. Priorities back then weren't what they are now. But just because they didn't get prosecuted and convicted doesn't mean they didn't commit a federal crime. Two actually. Pati's age would've helped her, but her mom didn't just enter without asking permission. She actively helped Pati sneak in too.

The last time I saw Doña Francis, we were in a Mexican resort town celebrating another friend's wedding. I danced with her that night. We toasted the bride and groom. In a way, we were toasting the remarkable twists that life had taken. What began with a nighttime scamper across the border had led to that evening: an elegant reception overlooking the twinkle of San Miguel de Allende's church towers and rooftops.

But to get there, Pati and her mom first had to commit crimes. They had to become criminal aliens. For their sake, I wish it had been easier. For my sake, I'm glad they did what they did because without that Pati wouldn't have become part of my life.

Rogues, Vagabonds, and Beggars

Long before the United States began to use immigration law to create criminals or to keep them out of the country, it used immigration law to welcome them, celebrating their role in Britain's growing ambitions. For the first 150 years of European colonization on the Atlantic seaboard, criminals were a common presence on ships leaving Europe for North America. Since it first sent settlers to the Atlantic seaboard, Britain had permitted people convicted of crimes to accept freedom as long as it was in one of its newly settled colonies. As early as 1603, James I ordered the removal of "Rogues Vagabonds and Sturdy Beggars" from Great Britain. A few years later, in 1611, the governor of Virginia asked to receive English felons, a request that Parliament made good on. Virginia's governor "seems to have believed that they would prove better than the three hundred profane, diseased and mutinous colonists who had gone on his first voyage," the historian Abbot Emerson Smith writes.[2]

Called "transportation," sending convicted offenders to North America was a win–win practice. The British government could rid itself of criminal offenders while benefiting from their labor in the difficult new terrain that it desperately wanted to populate. In the words of a 1717 statute passed by Parliament, "in many of his Majesty's colonies and plantations in America, there is great want of servants, who by their labour and industry might be the means of improving and making the said colonies and plantations more useful to this nation." For people given the option of being sent to North America, transportation was better than being sent to a workhouse or "burnt in the hand or whipt," the standard punishments for criminal activity that Parliament viewed as alternatives. Instead, the 1717 law let courts sentence people to labor in the colonies. Legal right to their labor was given to whoever paid for their trans-Atlantic passage. Most people ordered into transportation were required to stay in the colonies for seven years, but people convicted of one of two specified crimes—murder and knowingly receiving or buying stolen goods—were sent for fourteen years.

To ensure that people who were transported to North American colonies kept their end of the bargain, Parliament permitted their execution if they went back before completing the period of forced exile.[3] A harsh punishment, perhaps, but for many of these people, death was already on the table. In the Great Britain of that era, execution was Parliament's chosen punishment for approximately three hundred crimes, including stealing anything worth more than a shilling. Compared to court-ordered death, the uncertainty of an ocean voyage combined with forced labor in North America at least allowed the possibility of liberty, making banishment in what would eventually become the United States a lenient punishment.[4]

As happens frequently in immigration policy, the political winds soon shifted. Instead of welcoming convicted offenders, colonists began to resent them. In 1670, Virginia's colonial legislature enacted a law refusing to allow the colony to be on transportation's receiving end, and in 1676 Maryland followed.[5] Midway through the next century, as political tensions fumed between the Crown and the colonists, transportation fit into the budding militants' list of grievances. In a 1751 essay published in the *Pennsylvania Gazette*, Benjamin Franklin suggested that transportees be left in "Places of Pleasure about London."[6] By the time Britain lost its grip on the unhappy colonists, the newly independent states were ready to ban transportation for good. In 1788, the Continental Congress encouraged each state to ban "the transportation of convicted malefactors from foreign countries into the United States."[7]

"How can we get rid of them?"

For most of the next seventy-five years, Congress avoided immigration law. When it returned, its earlier concern about crime was gone. Instead, beginning in 1875, legislators focused squarely on using immigration law to mold the nation's racial stock. Around the time of the Civil War, the United States began to grapple with a dramatic shift among the population. For starters, the Civil War's end meant that Black people could no longer be treated as merchandise to be bought and sold. After the Fourteenth Amendment was forced onto the secessionist states, African Americans, including former slaves, were indisputably citizens.

There weren't many Black people along the West Coast, but racial dynamics were changing there too. From 1850 to 1880, the Chinese population went from a mere 750 or so Chinese citizens spread around the United States to more than 105,000, almost all in the Western states and territories.[8] At first welcomed as miners, lumberjacks, and, most well known, railroad workers, by the middle of the nineteenth century, anti-Chinese racism appeared in prominent newspapers around the country. The *New-York Daily Tribune*, among the most dominant newspapers of the period, declared the Chinese to be "uncivilized, unclean and filthy." [9]

Illustrating the country's long tradition of tying undesirable people to African Americans, a song used at anti-Chinese protests by California craft unions declared, "We have no place among us for the Coolie or the slave, But only for the manly, the enlightened and the brave." [10] Repeating that derogatory term for Chinese workers, the *San Francisco Chronicle* announced, "When the coolie arrives here he is as rigidly under the control of the contractor who brought him as ever an African slave was under his master in South Carolina or Louisiana." [11] One witness at a California State Senate committee hearing sounded the alarm about a Chinese "invasion." Another declared, "The Chinese are upon us. How can we get rid of them?" [12]

Yielding to demands to block Chinese migration, Congress began enacting a series of immigration bans. With little regard to the fact that migrants might want to join relatives already in the United States, prominent critics of Chinese migration concluded that women traveling without a husband or father were almost certainly being forced into prostitution. Echoing this view from his powerful position, President Ulysses S. Grant told Congress in 1874 that when it comes to Chinese women, "Hardly a perceptible percentage of them perform any honorable labor, but they are brought for shameful purposes, to the disgrace of the communities where settled and to the great demoralization of the youth of those localities. If this evil practice can be legislated against, it will be

my pleasure as well as duty to enforce any regulation to secure so desirable an end." [13] The following year Congress responded, enacting a law that, on its face, regulated morality
by banning prostitutes. Known as the Page Act in honor of
its primary congressional promoter, California congressman
Horace Page, the law was clearly aimed at Asian women. Anyone coming from "China, Japan, or any Oriental country," a
phrase that the statute uses twice, for "lewd and immoral purposes" was barred entry. [14]

Not content with keeping out Chinese women, Congress
returned to anti-Chinese legislation a few years later when it
enacted the Chinese Exclusion Act of 1882. Broader in scope
than the Page Act, the new law aimed to do exactly as its name
suggested: keep out the Chinese. Anyone of Chinese descent
pegged as a "laborer" could no longer enter the United States.
If they were already here, they had to register with a government official. The law also blocked any Chinese person from
becoming a naturalized citizen. [15] Six years later, another law
took an even harder approach. Even if they registered, Chinese laborers were barred from returning to the United States
if they left. [16]

While both of those laws were harsh, neither directly answered the question posed to the California legislature: "How
can we get rid of them?" In 1892, Congress responded force-
fully by enacting the Geary Act. Any "person of Chinese descent" could be deported. Plus, Chinese laborers had to get a
certificate of residence, but to get it they needed a "credible
white witness" to testify on their behalf. If they failed to meet
the white-witness requirement or violated immigration law in

any other way, they could be deported.[17] To Fong Yue Ting, Wong Quan, and thousands of other Chinese residents of the United States, the white-witness requirement was one indignity too many. They refused even to apply for a certificate of residence. Others, like a man named Lee Joe, applied, but having only the support of Chinese witnesses, they were denied.

In a test case organized by Chinese community groups, the three men, who had been living in New York, asked the Supreme Court to intervene. The Court did, but not as the Chinese community hoped. Keeping out migrants who want to come and deporting migrants who are already here is "an inherent and inalienable right of every sovereign and independent nation," the Supreme Court declared in *Fong Yue Ting v. United States*.[18]

Like judges often do, Justice Horace Gray's opinion for the majority of the Supreme Court made the law seem clearer than it was. By the late 1800s there were almost seven hundred years of a right to mobility for some people that Gray should have known about. Magna Carta, the 1215 treaty that influenced the U.S. and state constitutions, includes a clause guaranteeing merchants' legal right to enter, leave, or travel within England without asking the Crown's permission.[19]

Instead of faithfully applying well-worn legal principles like he claimed, Justice Gray was selectively reading the past to invent the future he wanted. Emmerich de Vattel, the Swiss legal scholar whose book *The Law of Nations* Justice Gray relies on, claims that "every nation has the right to refuse to admit a foreigner into the country," one of the passages Gray's opinion quotes. The problem with resting the government's right to exclude and deport migrants on Vattel is that an intellectually honest position would also guarantee that anyone, including migrants, has the right to take what they need to survive, including by force, no matter what the government says, a position that Vattel describes just as clearly as the part that Gray quoted. One example in Vattel's book involves Dutch sailors killing Indians to get food. Another is about taking women so that men have someone with whom to reproduce.[20] These aren't just dated ideas; they're repugnantly racist, misogynistic pillars of eighteenth-century European colonialism.

If Justice Gray was familiar with Vattel's embrace of white supremacy and sex slavery, there's no reason to think it would've made him uncomfortable. In *Fong Yue Ting*, he described Chinese migrants as "apparently incapable of assimilating with our people" and quoted approvingly an earlier Supreme Court decision warning of "vast hordes of its people crowding in upon us."[21] Turning to the white-witness requirement that Fong Yue Ting and the others were challenging, Gray didn't see a problem. If Congress wishes to exercise its fundamental right to decide who can live in the United States by conditioning residence on the testimony of a white person, so be it. He described the white-witness requirement as nothing more than a rule of evidence common in all U.S. courts. It "is within the acknowledged power of every legislature to prescribe the evidence which shall be received, and the effect of that evidence," he declared.[22]

Justice Gray was thinking about the effect that evidence has inside courtrooms. But it was outside of courtrooms that his decision had a much larger and troubling effect. Thanks to the Supreme Court's willingness to let Congress enact such a blatantly racist requirement like the white-witness standard, immigration law became a convenient tool for racist policies. Any migrant who couldn't claim the protective shield of whiteness could be targeted for exclusion or deportation—and over the coming decades many would be. What started with a hatred of Chinese migrants would eventually spread to include most of Asia, with migration from Japan almost entirely barred after 1924.

Wielding Violence

For xenophobic zealots, congressional action often proved insufficient. In defense of white supremacy, violence was better. In Truckee, California, a small lumber town tucked into the Sierra Nevada mountains, "Chinatown Holocausted," a headline in the local newspaper, the *Truckee Republican*, announced on May 29, 1875. From one day to the next, most of the Chinese residents' homes and businesses had burned into ash. The newspaper article added that the fire probably started "in a cook-room at the rear end of a row of hovels" in the town's Chinese neighborhood. The newspaper doesn't imply that an anti-Chinese arsonist was to blame, but the next few years in the town's history suggest that if white residents weren't complicit in the 1875 blaze, a sizable portion was at least pleased with the outcome.

The year after the fire, members of a vigilante group called the "Caucasian League" surrounded two rooms full of Chinese workers, set the buildings on fire, and shot at them as they tried to flee. The vigilantes were tried and acquitted.

"Upon learning of the outcome, Truckee's white residents rejoiced, firing a cannon for each exonerated man," historian Adam Goodman writes. Two years later, in 1878, white residents again set fire to Chinatown. When Chinese residents rebuilt, white residents attacked, using axes, hammers, and crowbars to tear down the newly refurbished neighborhood. Within a few days, most of the Chinese residents of Truckee left town.[23]

In the years that followed, Truckee was remembered for its particularly effective use of white vigilante violence. But in their anti-Chinese zeal, there was little unique about the white residents of the California mountain town. Across the West, mobs of white people regularly terrorized their Chinese neighbors. In Rock Springs, Wyoming, white residents, convinced that Chinese mineworkers and railroad workers were willing to work for lower wages, surrounded Chinatown in September 1885. They moved in, beating and murdering Chinese residents and burning their homes and businesses. Similar attacks occurred in Denver, Los Angeles, Salt Lake City, and small towns across the vast region.[24]

Racist, xenophobic violence certainly wasn't limited to attacks on Chinese migrants. Through a gruesome mix of bullets and lynch ropes, the state police force in Texas, the Texas Rangers, acted like vigilantes with badges. Older than Texas itself, they quickly earned a feared and hated reputation among South Texas Mexicans. The most important scholar of South Texas, Américo Paredes, writes that "the Rangers often killed Mexicans who had nothing to do with the criminals they were after."[25] With learned understatement, the historians William Carrigan and Clive Webb say the Rangers "had a deserved reputation for administering the law with blatant racial partiality."[26] More colorfully, the historian Walter Prescott Webb, whose history of the Rangers was celebrated for decades as much as it celebrated the Rangers, credited the Rangers with an "orgy of bloodshed" against Texas Mexicans.[27]

Indeed, by the 1840s, when Texas joined the United States and the newly emboldened pair invaded Mexico, Texas Mexicans referred to the Rangers as "los Tejanos sangrientos," or, as one historian put it, "los diablos Tejanos"—the bloody Texans or the Texas devils. Even the soldier who would later try to destroy the United States in favor of the slave-holding Confederacy, Robert E. Lee, didn't like the Rangers. Deployed to Texas during the war between the United States and Mexico, Lee once commented that, as the Rangers searched for an armed rebel from South Texas named Juan Cortina, "those spared by Cortina have been burned by the Texans." Future president Zachary Taylor described the Rangers as "a lawless set" and complained that "the mounted men from Texas had scarcely made an expedition without unwarrantably killing a Mexican."[28]

The rinches, as the Rangers are known in South Texas even today, had few boundaries. "Le echaron cincuenta galones de gasolina, y vivo lo quemaron," one oral history unearthed by historian Monica Muñoz Martínez recounts. In it, an unnamed resident of South Texas describes the Rangers capturing Tomás Garza in 1915. "The rinches grabbed him, tied him to a mesquite tree with a chain, and then they poured fifty gallons of gasoline on him, and they burned him alive." [29]

White people in the nineteenth century weren't just willing to commit crime to preserve the country's racial order. Their criminality was celebrated. It still is. Today, most people know the Texas Rangers as a baseball team. These days, there are a few plaques hidden away in cities like Denver and Salt Lake reminding the occasional reader of the crime that occurred there some generations back against Chinese residents. Mostly, though, no one stops to read these signs. Small and unremarkable, they are designed almost as if to be overlooked. It's a way of honoring the past without having to remember it. That means we can celebrate the criminals who came before us without having to grapple with their crimes.

Imprisonment at Hard Labor

The targeted people changed, but for most of the nineteenth and twentieth centuries, race held the lead role in distinguishing which migrants were welcomed into the United States and which were not. Through the same series of blatantly racist laws that Congress adopted in the late 1800s, the federal government tried to turn migrants into actual criminals. The Geary Act of 1892's white-witness requirement for a certificate of residence proved too much for many Chinese in the United States. Just two months after the witness requirement went into effect, Wong Wing, Lee Poy, Lee Yong Tong, and Chan Wah Dong were arrested in Detroit. Where they claimed citizenship is unclear. Writing to the Supreme Court, their lawyer claimed that the four "may be citizens of Canada."[30] But that point was largely irrelevant. The anti-Chinese laws of the late nineteenth century didn't focus on citizenship; they tracked race. And here there was no question that everyone considered Wong Wing and the others arrested in Detroit that day as "Chinese persons" who didn't have the residence certificates that the law demanded. For local customs officers, that was good enough to raise suspicions.

After a short hearing in which none were given a jury trial, nothing unusual at the time, they were found to have violated the Geary Act by being "unlawfully within the United States." Under the new law, the group could have been sentenced to prison for one year. Maybe out of a sense of leniency or maybe just because the law was so new, Wong Wing, Lee Poy, Lee Yong Tong, and Chan Wah Dong were each sentenced to sixty days at hard labor in the Detroit House of Correction. Afterward, they were to be sent to China.[31] A grey fortress of a building surrounded by a waist-high fence that today would sit near towering stadiums for the city's revered baseball and football teams, the city-owned jail was known for housing inmates from throughout Michigan.[32] It was no surprise that Wong Wing and his co-defendants would find themselves there.

Challenging their imprisonment all the way to the U.S. Supreme Court, the group claimed that they couldn't be punished by imprisonment without the trappings of criminal proceedings. It was unconstitutional. The Fifth Amendment, their lawyer F.H. Canfield argued, requires prosecutors to indict them. The Sixth Amendment, he added, guarantees them a jury trial. And if by some twist of logic the justices conclude that they are not being punished for a crime, the requirement that they work while at the Detroit House of Correction means they are enslaved, a violation of the still new Thirteenth Amendment, added to the Constitution after the Civil War.[33]

The government's lawyer, Jacob M. Dickinson, a former Confederate soldier and future secretary of war, pushed back.[34] Rather than go head-to-head with Canfield on the constitutional arguments, Dickinson defended the 1892 law by claiming that the Constitution simply didn't apply to Wong Wing and the three other men because they were in the United States in violation of federal law. Summarizing a string of court decisions recognizing that Chinese migrants have some constitutional protections, Dickinson argued, "None of these cases decided that an alien could sneak or force his way into the United States against their will, and stand under the protection of the Constitution."[35]

Distinguishing a client's situation from past cases is a common tool for lawyers, but Dickinson, like any well-trained advocate, didn't stop there. Borrowing an argument that had already convinced the Supreme Court in other cases, Dickinson added that only Congress gets to decide which migrants can remain in the United States and under what conditions. The 1892 law was only one among several that clearly showed Congress's desire to ban Chinese laborers. Wong Wing and the others don't have to like the laws that Congress passes, but surely the Supreme Court could agree that Congress was empowered to make them, Dickinson's legal brief went on.

If China is unhappy, it can use diplomatic channels to complain to the United States. Fitting for a future secretary of war, Dickinson even suggested that the only alternative that China had to diplomacy was "appeal to arms."[36]

Whatever option China chose, it was not up to the Supreme Court to second guess the conditions that Congress imposed on migrants. "This is a political question, and under the Constitution of the United States, its determination is entrusted exclusively to the legislative department, and its conclusions are necessarily binding upon the judiciary and all of the departments and officers of the United States," Dickinson argued.[37] In effect, Dickinson was telling the Supreme Court to stay out of immigration law. Deciding who to allow into the United States and with what strings attached was a question for Congress and the president, not the courts.

In a decision that laid the legal foundation for today's mass criminalization of migration, the justices split the difference. Siding with the government, the Court announced that imprisonment without the standard features of criminal prosecutions is permissible "to give effect to" immigration law goals like deportation. Detaining migrants while immigration enforcement officers or immigration judges decide if they will be allowed to stay in the United States fits this description—what lawyers call civil immigration detention.

Locking up Wong Wing while officials decide if he's the kind of person Congress banned is one thing. But sending him to the Detroit House of Correction to perform hard labor is another. Conceding that Congress can choose the sentence that goes along with a federal crime, Canfield had asked: "If Congress can constitutionally provide that an alien who is found by a commissioner to be unlawfully within this country may be punished by the order of such commissioner by imprisonment at hard labor, why may it not also provide that he shall suffer the death penalty under such an order?"

This time siding with Wong Wing, the justices described hard labor as "infamous punishment." Just like lawyer Canfield argued, the Court concluded that imprisonment at hard labor is constitutionally allowable as punishment for violating immigration law only "if such offense were to be established by a judicial trial." The Geary Act's attempt to have it both ways ran afoul of these constitutional principles. To punish migrants with imprisonment, Congress "must provide for a judicial trial to establish the guilt of the accused," the Supreme Court wrote.[38] Congress had not done that, so the government had no right to keep them locked up in Detroit.

It was a minor victory for migrants. The Supreme Court gave its blessing to a blatantly racist law, setting a depressingly low bar for immigration laws to come. And it described the roadmap for punishing migrants through the criminal legal system that Congress would eventually follow.

2

MAKING CRIMINALS

Walking around South Carolina's capital, Columbia, today, it's hard to spot evidence of Coleman Livingston Blease, a state legislator, governor, and the state's U.S. senator from 1925 to 1931. At the State House, Corinthian columns overlook Jefferson Davis Highway. On the carefully manicured lawn, there's a monument remembering the Civil War and another celebrating the state's most influential politician, Strom Thurmond. When I was there in the summer of 2021, cheerleaders, music, and a large crowd celebrated a college basketball championship. In the middle of the mass stood a statue of Ben Tillman, Blease's political nemesis. But Blease's name wasn't visible anywhere.

Things were different a century ago. A wily politician who fashioned himself as an up-by-the-bootstraps underdog, Blease was a man full of ambition and self-confidence. Despite his comfortable upbringing as an innkeeper's son and a Georgetown graduate, he told South Carolina legislators that he "was born without a silver spoon in his mouth." Nonetheless, "this boy, by hard struggles, by hard fighting, and by devotion to his friends" climbed to the top of South Carolina politics, he claimed.[1] With a thick head of dark hair and matching mustache, "dark fierce eyes," and a penchant for ostentatious attire—wool hats and the insignia of the many fraternal societies he had joined on his way to political power—Blease was easy to spot.[2]

He was just as hard to ignore. Blease attacked just about every symbol of authority—from political opponents and critical newspaper reporters to administrators at Clemson College, the state's powerhouse public university only a few decades old then.[3] And he did so with flair. Journalists were a "dirty set of liars," he claimed, and he complimented a political ally put on trial for killing a newspaper reporter.

But it was his outsized ego, powerful oratory, and sharp sense of political opportunity that led him to the governor's mansion, then the U.S. Senate. During his single term there, Blease made his mark on history. With the support of Congressman Albert Johnson and Secretary of Labor James Davis, Blease transformed the common act of moving across the U.S. border without the government's permission into a federal crime.

Rooted in the ugly social order of his day, "Coley" read the politics of class and race division like a fortune teller divining his own future. As the governor of South Carolina, he once told a crowd where his sympathies lay: "Whenever the constitution of my state steps between me and the defense of the virtue of the white woman, then I say to hell with the Constitution."[4] A popular magazine of his era claimed that Blease once "declared that he would never order out the militia to quell uprisings of people who threatened the life of a black man who had laid his hands upon a white woman."[5] Explaining to the state legislature why he decided to pardon a white man convicted of attempting to rape a Black woman, Blease wrote, "I have heretofore stated that I do not believe that a white man would commit rape on a negro, and I certainly see no necessity for it, by which he runs a risk of being sentenced to the Penitentiary or possibly to the electric chair for possibly what he could usually get from prices ranging from 25 cents to $1."[6]

Even in the Jim Crow South, Blease's racism stood out. When lynching was widespread, Blease endorsed mob violence at the end of a rope so vigorously that some Southerners thought he went too far.[7] At one point, Alabama's governor spearheaded a resolution condemning his South Carolina colleague.[8] And in an era when monuments to the Confederate cause were popping up throughout the South, Blease embraced the glorification with zeal and showmanship. During a debate in the 1910 gubernatorial race, one of his opponents proudly told an audience that he had voted to support public financing of a monument to the women of the Confederacy. In response, Blease criticized him for doing nothing more than pushing through legislation. Like a magician, he reached into his pocket and pulled out a receipt for his own private donation. No one single individual in the state contributed more than he did, he declared to enthusiastic cheers.[9]

Fear of Foreign Hordes

For a wily, deep-in-the-bones white supremacist like Blease, anti-Black racism didn't have to crowd out other targets. His was a well-rounded bigotry. Whenever he thought it would help his political ambitions, he would wield his rigid vision of the proper racial hierarchy against other people. White Protestants were always on top. Everyone else was a threat. During one political campaign, he attacked an opponent for being part Jewish.[10] He didn't much like Catholics either. "We want men who recognize God as their adviser and the Bible as their creed, and no priest or no minister!" he declared in 1915 while he was governor.[11]

Migrants were no better. With ease, he slotted them into the southern racial hierarchy alongside Black and mixed-race people. Running for governor in 1908, he criticized a proposal to bring migrant workers into South Carolina, claiming the migrants would be "worse than negroes" who would "underbid our people."[12] In a subtle reference to a newspaper owned by the Gonzales family whose patriarch arrived in Columbia, South Carolina, from Cuba, Blease defended lynching. "This is a white man's country and will continue to be ruled by the white man, regardless of the opinions or editorials of quarter or half breeds or foreigners."[13]

After he set the Senate as his new political goal, migrant tarring became even more important. Campaigning in 1914 against an incumbent, Ellison Smith, Blease needed a way of distinguishing himself. Both were Democrats and staunch racists who defended lynching. Unlike Blease, Smith didn't spring into power poking the wealthy. Instead, just before winning his first of six elections to the U.S. Senate, he had been a top official with the Southern Cotton Association, a powerful industry group. When he arrived in Washington, he pushed the federal government to adopt policies that favored cotton growers, eventually earning the nickname "Cotton Ed" Smith.[14] The senator's alliance with the powerful, wealthy growers made for easy criticism from Blease.

To increase the likelihood of beating the incumbent Smith in 1914, Blease added an anti-migrant barb to his attack. On the campaign trail, "Blease campaigned on 100 percent Americanism," historian Kelly Lytle Hernández writes.[15] He didn't just oppose migration. As far as he was concerned, migrants were worse than native South Carolinians and reliable pawns for corporate capitalists. If elected, he promised "to stay this tide of riffraff that's crowding in from Europe—people who work cheaper than you can, and as soon as they pocket a little money, put back home." The "corporations and trusts" were to blame, he claimed, for "bringing them here."[16] When Smith had a chance to benefit the state's small farmers by holding up a bill that would've restricted migration, he caved to pressure from Woodrow Wilson's administration, giving Blease an opportunity to pounce.[17] Elect him to the Senate and he'd put a stop to the deluge of low-paid foreigners crowding out native-born South Carolinians by targeting the big business interests that encouraged them to come.

The South Carolina of Blease's day is rightfully thought of as a pillar of Jim Crow racism, but just like now, Blease's South Carolina didn't exist in a vacuum. The politics of one region of the world didn't pass the state by, and Blease knew that. In 1910, war started in Mexico, beginning the century's first large migration of Mexicans into the United States. Four years later, the assassination of Austrian archduke Franz Ferdinand pushed Europe into violence. Eventually the United States and Japan would also participate, giving the first World War its global name.

As war touched most corners of the world, the humans who dared escape brought fears of migrant newcomers to South Carolina. With war to the nation's south and across the Atlantic, a business group called The Southern Commercial Congress announced a conference intended to craft an immigration policy for the South. Organizers promised that the gathering, to be held in Washington, DC, in December 1914, would address "methods of caring for the horde of foreigners that will probably come to this country at the close of the European conflict." This goal caught Blease's eye. He accepted the invitation and headed to Washington.[18]

Held at the Willard Hotel, a block from the White House, the conference began with an address by President Woodrow Wilson's secretary of labor, William Wilson. The first secretary of labor in the country's history, Wilson was a Scottish migrant who had risen to the top of the United Mine Workers union. At the helm of the new Department of Labor, which was responsible for immigration matters back then, Wilson didn't like it when migrants were penalized simply for the company they kept. Staying true to his labor union background, he opposed attempts to deport migrants simply because they joined unions.[19] But when it came to people who wanted to alter basic features of life in the United States, Wilson had no patience. "Any alien who comes to the United States and advocates the overthrow of our Government by force is an invading enemy, who is treated with leniency when he is simply deported," Wilson wrote several years after the conference Blease attended.[20]

After Wilson came Terence Powderly, a longtime labor leader who was then serving as chief of the Bureau of Immigration, later to be renamed the Immigration and Naturalization Service. The son of Irish migrants, Powderly became famous as a leader of the Knights of Labor. At the peak of its influence, the Knights were a powerful force for the eight-hour workday. Less nobly, they were also a powerful force of racist xenophobia, embracing attacks against Chinese workers. With Powderly among its top officials, the Knights endorsed the Chinese Exclusion Act of 1882 and Contract Labor Act of 1885. The 1885 law didn't list its racist goal in the title, but it, too, fit neatly into Blease's white supremacist, xenophobic sensibilities. "American capitalists and corporations have imported and shipped into this country, as so many cattle, large numbers of degraded, ignorant, brutal Italians and Hungarian laborers," the bill's main sponsor, Ohio's Martin Foran, told his colleagues in Congress. Emphasizing the racially undesirable character of these Italians and Hungarians decades before they were considered white, Foran compared them to Chinese migrants and Black slaves, and he worried aloud about the impact that these "cheap men, ignorant, degraded, dangerous," would have on the racial stock of the United States.[21] Powderly agreed. In a letter describing "the evils of Hungarian labor," he explained, "If it were possible to make good and useful citizens of these men, I would never raise any voice against them, but that seems impossible." The United States, he added, should be reserved for "a race of freemen."[22]

Finally, Anthony Caminetti, Wilson's commissioner general of immigration, capped off the trio of high-ranking government officials. Also from a migrant family, Caminetti often complained about the limits of immigration law. He wanted to use immigration law as a tool to rid the United States of leftists: the socialists and anarchists who were common among migrant communities then.

When it came his turn to speak, Blease left no question that he was aligned with the marquee names. He stood firmly for fewer migrants, he told the immigration conference audience. Just as important was the type of people who came. He had no interest in just anyone. He wanted people who were like the South Carolinians who were already there—and already willing to support his political ambitions. "We want a good Christian people," Blease said. "We will furnish them something to live on, we will put them on the farms, and we will stock the farms," he added. Taking a swipe against proposals to add education requirements to immigration law—efforts that would lead to a literacy test two years later—the governor added that education was not the measure of worth. A lot of education wasn't necessary for the "laboring citizenship" he wanted in South Carolina. "If you will apply that test, a good many that we have got might have to migrate to some other country!" he declared.[23]

In 1914, sitting in the same room with powerful men, all of whom had risen to fame through a mix of anti-corporate nativist racism, probably felt right to the ambitious Blease. An evening reception at the White House with President Wilson in attendance couldn't have hurt. Blease saw himself climbing ever higher in prominence, and the immigration conference offered him an example of a means to win the stardom he wanted.

Blease wasn't able to win the Senate race that year, but eventually he got there. When he did, he embraced the anti-migrant position of the nationally known figures already in Washington.

Legislating Racism

The Senate of the 1920s was just the place for someone whose dislike of big business had proved politically advantageous and whose hatred of people of color had no limits. The previous decade, Democrat Woodrow Wilson had vetoed a bill that would have barred migrants from most Asian countries and imposed a literacy test on hopeful migrants. The literacy test was "a penalty for lack of opportunity" rather than "a test of character, of quality, or of personal fitness," Wilson wrote to Congress in his 1917 veto message.[24] A few days later, Congress overrode Wilson's veto.[25]

Nativists were only getting started. They wanted to tie the country's future to its past and weren't about to let one legislative loss stop them. In 1920, Congress sent Wilson a proposal that would have set quotas on the number of migrants who could come to the United States, tying the annual cap from each country to census records from 1910. Every year, each country could send to the United States 3 percent of the foreign-born residents who were already here in 1910. Wilson again vetoed it. Instead of meeting to override Wilson's veto,

Congress waited him out. Soon he was gone from the White House and Warren Harding was the new president.

In early 1921, Congress sent Harding a version of the law that the new president quickly signed. The Immigration Act of 1921 capped the number of new migrants who could come in any year at 3 percent of the number of citizens of that country who were in the United States in 1910, a period when most people in the United States traced their roots to northern and western Europe. That law was temporary, so in 1924 Congress returned to immigration legislation. This time Congress made the quotas permanent, lowered the ratio to 2 percent of the foreign-born population, and tied it to the 1890 census. By anchoring future arrivals to the number of people who lived in the United States in 1890, the bill's sponsors cemented into law the country's racial composition in the late nineteenth century, years before the number of people coming to the United States from southern and eastern Europe began to increase.

Equally significant, the new law didn't calculate the percentage based only on the number of migrants from a particular country. Instead, the law tied migration to "national origin." To do that, it traced everyone, including U.S. citizens, back to their country of origin, meaning that the pool of people whose families stemmed from northern and western Europe increased substantially. Italians were left with four thousand slots, Poles with six thousand, and Greeks with a mere one hundred.[26]

The 1924 bill's lead sponsor in the Senate, Pennsylvania's

David Reed, was the same senator who led the override of
Wilson's veto in 1917. Reed was a well-known nativist who
embraced eugenics, the pseudo-scientific theory that had
taken hold in the most elite academic institutions in the
United States and in the influential policy circles of Washington, DC. Eugenicists claimed that intelligence was in-
extricably tied to biological races, and it could be measured
objectively. The 1924 law was meant to ensure that newcomers
"be of the same race as those of us who are already here," Reed
wrote in the *New York Times* under the headline "America of
the Melting Pot Comes to End."[27] By tying new migration
to the entire population, including citizens, in 1890, the Immigration Act of 1924 "does away with all this unfairness"
toward citizens.

What Reed's celebratory article in the *Times* ignored is
that the 1924 law didn't touch migration from other nations
in the Western Hemisphere.[28] The law simply didn't apply to
any of those countries. Agricultural interests were too strong
for Congress to muster the votes needed to enact a similarly
deep cut, especially to Mexican migration.[29] Members of
Congress didn't miss this. Fiorello La Guardia, the towering
Republican congressman from New York whose name now
graces one of the city's major airports, pointedly accused the
bill's primary sponsor of favoring Mexicans. "If you want to
reduce immigration, why let the doors open at the Mexican
border?" La Guardia asked the bill's primary booster in the
House, Representative Albert Johnson, the accusatory tone
of La Guardia's question dripping from each word. With a
pedigree in the popular racism of the day that was as strong as

Reed's, Johnson didn't push back. Instead, he responded that more legislation was on the way.[30] All that was needed was patience.

It would take four years, but eventually nativists would be ready to target Mexicans just like Johnson promised. By then, Blease was in the Senate, ready to help. Johnson had already failed to criminalize migration three times: in 1925, 1926, and 1928.[31] Finally, on December 22, 1928, Blease, a member of the Senate's Committee on Immigration, introduced the bill that eventually would become law. As originally written, the bill said nothing about merely entering the United States without the government's permission. Instead, Blease's proposal would've punished with up to two years of imprisonment only people who were deported, then got caught returning illegally—what is today called illegal reentry.[32] It's not clear why Blease's bill initially went after illegal reentry while leaving the initial clandestine entry untouched. Maybe Blease worried about finding enough votes for a more aggressive version. Perhaps he realized that his bill, even focused narrowly on illegal reentry, would require a massive financial investment in immigration policing if the law was going to carry a bite. Whatever the reason, the bill remained this way even after Blease brought it up for debate in the Senate.[33]

Without the years of congressional service that David Reed or Albert Johnson could claim, Blease couldn't round up the attention for his bill that had helped his colleagues push their anti-migrant proposals through Congress earlier in the decade. In his short time in the Senate, Blease had tried to bar the U.S. government from hiring migrants and had even tried to cut back voting rights for people who became U.S. citizens through the naturalization process. Both attempts failed to become law, but they succeeded in signaling that his hatred of migrants hadn't withered. He was still the unrepentant racist migrant-hater that South Carolinians had backed time and again.[34]

With Reed and Johnson on his side, Blease's bill quickly received an important endorsement. James J. Davis, the secretary of labor, who historians think may have written the draft legislation, gave the criminalization proposal much-needed attention by backing the bill early on, and lent Blease credibility.[35] Born in Wales and raised in Pennsylvania, Davis recalled moving quickly through the immigration station at Castle Garden in New York in 1881. His father had gone before the rest of the family, but when James was eight years old, he, his five siblings, and their mother followed. "Having passed the immigrant tests, we found ourselves set out on the dock, free to go where we pleased," he later wrote in his memoir. "Now we were in America hungry and penniless, and hard was the bed that we should lie on."

Like so many migrants, James's parents hoped that in the United States they could give their children lives unavailable in their native communities. But as soon as mother and children stepped off the ship, things got tough. They quickly realized that someone else had made off with their luggage. Worse, in the chaos of getting off the ship only to discover their bags had gone missing, James's mother lost two of her children, four- and six-year-old Walter and David. Two days later, she found them at a rescue home for children.

Her troubles didn't end there, though. The children were back, but the luggage was permanently gone and the hotel bill for those unanticipated nights in New York remained. By some good grace, a fellow Welsh migrant covered the cost of the hotel.[36] After a few days in New York City, mother and children headed west. They thought they would meet their father in Pittsburgh, but after the mill where he had been working shut down, he moved to Hubbard, Ohio, near the Pennsylvania border, where his brother lived. Unemployed and relying on his brother's support, James's father waited for the rest of the family. "Now he was out of a job, and we were coming to him without as much as a bag of buns in our hands," James later recalled.[37]

Poverty was common among the migrants of the late nineteenth century, so in that way there is nothing remarkable about the Davis family's situation. When James and his family landed in Manhattan in April 1881, there were few federal laws limiting who could enter the country. The Alien Enemy Act of 1798 let the president bar anyone who presented a threat to the United States, but that didn't apply to young James. Neither did the Page Act, enacted in 1875 just a few years before James left Wales. That law applied only to "any subject of China, Japan, or any Oriental country."[38] Between then and James's arrival, Congress didn't weigh in on immigration with new laws. Racism and luck were on James's side because the year after he stepped foot in New York, Congress enacted two sweeping immigration laws, although the first, the Chinese Exclusion Act, wouldn't have applied to him. But if James had arrived just sixteen months after he did, he would have been barred by the second immigration law Congress passed in 1882: "Any person unable to take care of himself or herself without becoming a public charge . . . shall not be permitted to land." The law went into effect on August 3, 1882.[39] It's hard to see how James's mother wouldn't have fit that description.

In an era where the federal government was only beginning to enact laws regulating cross-border movement, state laws might have been a bigger problem for the Davis family had Ohio officials cared to enforce them. It sounds odd today, but during the country's first one hundred years, states often enacted laws barring certain people from becoming residents, and poor people were a popular target. By the time James and his family moved to Ohio, the state had almost a century's experience excluding poor migrants from settling there.[40] A law enacted in 1865, which the legislature affirmed in 1876, just five years before James arrived, declared it unlawful to bring "any poor or indigent person" into the state with the idea of seeking public assistance.[41] Plus "any person becoming a charge" who hadn't lived in Ohio for at least one year could be removed to another state.[42]

No matter how closely young James and his family came to clashing with state or federal laws controlling the movement of people just like him, as an adult he found ways of distinguishing himself from the next generation of migrants. "The people that came to this country in the early days were of the beaver type and they built up America because it was in their nature to build. Then the rat-people began coming here, to house under the roof that others built," he wrote in his memoir. "Beware of breeding rats in America."[43]

As Davis rose through the political ranks, he became a tireless supporter of laws favoring northern and western Europeans—the "beavers" who built the United States—and an equally strong opponent of migration from the rest of the world. In a 1925 book that he published while serving as secretary of labor, Davis argued for "the wisdom of a definite, selective policy in immigration" that would distinguish between the "bad and good stock, weak and strong blood." Davis wholeheartedly celebrated the laws enacted earlier in the decade. "Let us thank the literacy test, let us thank our 2 per cent quota law, let us thank our faithful immigration officials for what each has done toward saving us from the results of that last great wave of immigration to threaten our shores," he wrote.[44] More influentially, as the person who followed William Wilson as head of the Department of Labor, Davis oversaw the federal government's immigration law enforcement responsibilities. Under Davis, the Labor Department launched the Border Patrol in 1924, which in its earliest days focused on Chinese migrants entering the United States through Canadian British Columbia.

For an arch-restrictionist like Davis, laws in place toward the end of the 1920s left the United States at risk. By excluding countries of the Western Hemisphere—especially Mexico—from the national origins quotas enacted in 1924, Congress had left the United States open to the Mexican migrants whom nativists decried as backward. "Our experience exempting British North America, Mexico, Central and South America from all quota limitation has proved disastrous. It has had the effect of closing the front door to immigration and leaving the back door wide open," Davis wrote. Previewing his later support for Blease's bill, he added, "It has practically put a premium on illegal entry into the United States. Under it nearly sixty-five thousand Mexicans entered this country in one year, bringing into American communities lower standards of living."[45] During a period when migration often topped 1 million people per year, 65,000 Mexicans represented only a small fraction, but, to Davis, it was too large a fraction.[46]

Congressman Albert Johnson was likewise unhappy about the exemption for Mexicans. From his perch as publisher of *Grays Harbor Washingtonian*, a small newspaper based in the Pacific coast community of Hoquiam, Washington, southwest of Seattle, Johnson launched his political career on the strength of his attacks on migrants. There was an especially dark place in his heart for the Chinese migrants entering the United States from Canada.[47] A Republican first elected to the House of Representatives in 1912, he would stay there for twenty years. A racist firebrand, Johnson saw in immigration policy a tool for defending white supremacy. As early as August 1913, only a few months into his congressional career, he embraced "the union of the white race," called for "the early union of the white nations," and warned of the impending "yellow flood"—all in a single speech.[48]

Six years later, in 1919, Johnson took over as chair of the House Committee on Immigration and stayed in that role for most of the next two decades. For someone who cared more about limiting migration than anything else, this was a powerful position. As chair, he could influence the bills that got his colleagues' attention, with Mexicans high on his list. In 1926, for example, he shared with the House Committee on Immigration and Naturalization a letter describing Mexicans as "racially not assimilable" and "undesirable from an economic point of view."[49] Many Mexicans were turned back at the border under immigration law's public charge provision—the bar against poor people enacted in 1882—but Johnson suspected that many others entered clandestinely. In his view, only wholesale exclusion of new migrants would fix what he thought of as an immigration problem.

Where his heart pointed, his political instincts told him his votes couldn't follow. A complex mix of southwestern agribusiness, northern industrialists, and State Department diplomat-types protected Mexicans from falling under the 1924 quota regime. Big farms in the Southwest relied heavily on cheap Mexican labor. So did steel manufacturing and meatpacking in the Midwest. Diplomats worried about appearing unneighborly to Mexico and Canada. Each of these interests had many friends in Congress, including Johnson's main partner in the push to enact the 1924 legislation, Pennsylvania's David Reed, who embraced the concern about souring relations with Mexico or Canada.[50]

Blease's Law

Compared to South Carolina's capital, Washington, DC, proved a much more difficult place for Blease to make an impression. The "demagogic Senator" from South Carolina, as one newspaper editorial board described him in 1929, "exerted little influence in Washington," according to a biographer.[51] This account of Blease's political career overlooks his impact on criminal law's reach into migration. Loud-mouthed and uncouth, Blease received a lot of attention from journalists of his era. Almost none, though, seem to have noticed his interest in migration. One of the few reports about his efforts to amend immigration law describes "a very dangerous bill" that Blease introduced. But the article, appearing in *The Nation*, isn't talking about the illegal entry and reentry bill that criminalized migration. It focused on a registration requirement for migrants that Blease promoted at the same time.[52]

By the end of the decade, Davis and Johnson were ready to team up to fix the hole in immigration policy that they saw when they looked south. In the new senator from South Carolina, they found a willing ally who might be able to push through a bill that would punish Mexicans without upsetting big business interests.

Blease might have been new to Washington, but he wasn't new to Washington powerbrokers. He came with a nationwide reputation as a gifted politician who wasn't afraid of a fight and who was committed to a white racial order. In James Davis, he also found a fellow moose, members of an oddly named whites-only fraternal organization called the Loyal Order of Moose. By the time Blease was elected to the Senate, he'd served as his local chapter's "dictator," while Davis had been the national organization's director-general. Blease was a well-known dabbler in fraternal organizations, but Davis was a committed Moose, often traveling to tout the racist group, once even visiting Europe for this purpose.[53]

Kindred in their animosity toward migrants, the two Moose men found purpose in collaborating on a bill targeting Mexicans. Trying to ban all Mexican migration, as Congress had essentially done with the Chinese, or to limit it, as Congress had done to southern and eastern Europeans, was sure to lead to a quick legislative death. Rather than pitch Blease's proposal as a curb on Mexican migration generally, "it was introduced into Congress as a measure to control and punish unlawful Mexican immigrants, in particular," historian Kelly Lytle Hernández writes.[54] Criminal law was the legal path they chose.

It was a politically savvy move. In early 1929, Davis wholeheartedly endorsed the bill that Blease was promoting. Existing immigration law failed to provide "any difficulties or embarrassment" beyond simple deportation. That wasn't enough, Davis claimed, and Blease's proposal would rightly ratchet up the cost of violating immigration law.[55] In a separate memo, the Department of Labor added that a law like Blease's proposal "would be of material aid in enforcing our immigration laws."[56] The powerful business lobby that had stopped earlier attempts to curtail Mexican migration saw value in Blease's bill. Businesses wanted Mexicans to come to the United States when work was available, but they were more than happy for the government to deport them as soon as crops were picked.[57]

With the endorsement of the nation's top immigration law enforcement official and support from key business groups, the bill quickly passed out of the Senate and headed to the House.[58] There Albert Johnson had his own plans for the proposal.

A racist firebrand, Johnson was an equal-opportunity migrant-hater who saw in immigration policy a tool for protecting white supremacy. As the congressman who had pushed the 1924 immigration law through the chamber, Johnson was a veteran of congressional policy battles. He'd promised Fiorello La Guardia that Mexicans were on his radar, and now he was ready to make good on his promise. Johnson was an unapologetic, unreformed racist like Blease, only more sophisticated. Instead of vividly embracing lynching, he wrapped himself in eugenics.

From his position as chair of the House's immigration committee, he brought eugenics into the policymaking mainstream. In 1926, for example, he expressed his "pleasure" at sharing with the committee a letter from Madison Grant, the leader of the Immigration Restriction League, whose book *The Passing of the Great Race* made the case for northern European superiority. Years later, Adolf Hitler would borrow from Grant's book for his own *Mein Kampf* and, in a private letter, reportedly declared it to be his "Bible."[59] In the 1926 letter that Johnson shared with the committee, Grant endorsed "an effective and stringent deportation measure" and warned of opposition from civil liberties groups and "alien blocs."[60]

Two years later, Johnson welcomed to a committee hearing Harry Laughlin, arguably the most prominent eugenicist of the era. Laughlin's impact on immigration policy in the 1920s was possible in no small part because Johnson's committee had tasked him with studying the laws that existed and how Congress might change them to create the population's ideal racial composition.[61] A frequent witness in front of Johnson's immigration committee, on this occasion, Laughlin told the congressmen that exclusion was "the first line of defense" and deportation "the last line of defense against contamination of American family stocks by alien hereditary degenerates."[62]

When Blease's bill reached Johnson's committee in the House, the congressman was ready to boost the first line of defense that Laughlin touted and was wary of the opposition that Grant warned about. Under Johnson's leadership, the Committee on Immigration and Naturalization amended Blease's proposal to boost its impact. Instead of limiting the bill to people who returned to the United States after an earlier deportation, the House committee also went after anyone who entered without the government's permission. Called illegal entry, the House's amendment promised up to one year imprisonment for doing this.[63] Just like Grant predicted, the ACLU balked. To the civil liberties group, "there is no need whatever" for the "far more sweeping" House version. Criminalizing illegal entry "is especially objectionable" because "it is one thing to deport a person for coming here illegally; it is quite another thing to imprison for a year or fine him a thousand dollars."[64]

The opposition proved no match. Within days, the amended bill had moved out of the House. Now it was up to Blease in the Senate, Johnson in the House, and their colleagues to resolve differences between the two versions. Johnson immediately made his position clear. As he asked his colleagues to agree to a conference with the Senate—and to appoint him to negotiate on their behalf—he promised to "insist on the House amendment."[65] It didn't appear he had to insist too hard. Within two weeks, Blease, Reed, and the three other senators representing the Senate agreed to the House's version.[66] The bill, with Johnson's amendment, headed to the White House, where on March 2, 1929, in one of his final acts in office, President Calvin Coolidge signed it.[67] Blease's bill had become law. The Mexican loophole that Fiorello La Guardia had complained about five years earlier had been closed.

Illegal Entry and Reentry Today

In 1929, illegal entry and illegal reentry became crimes, and migrants were made into criminals. For illegal entry, the law threatened migrants with up to one year in prison. For illegal reentry, Congress authorized up to two years imprisonment.[68] The United States has changed dramatically since 1929, with policing back then being hardly recognizable today. But what hasn't changed much is the language of Blease's law. Today, the two crimes remain part of federal law. Illegal entry is now punishable by six months imprisonment for a first-time offense, but illegal reentry is punishable by up to twenty years in a federal prison, a jaw-dropping length that, admittedly, no judge I'm aware of has ever imposed.[69]

It would take many decades, but eventually Blease's law would dominate federal courthouses. Starting with the last few years of George W. Bush's tenure in the White House, illegal entry and illegal reentry, together, have topped the annual list of most prosecuted federal crimes, or come close. Every year since then, prosecutors using Blease's law have made tens of thousands of migrants into criminals in the most technical sense of the word. In fiscal year 2010, for example, 28,503 illegal entry and reentry cases were prosecuted in federal district courts nationwide, with 27,689 ending in a conviction. Almost all were against Mexicans. Most of the rest came from Central America, then the Caribbean.[70] Imagined as a way of punishing Mexicans, the law is doing exactly that. Thanks to the law that Blease, Johnson, and Davis pushed through Congress in 1929, today, almost a century later, migrants are routinely escorted into federal criminal courts in handcuffs and shackles for prosecution. In places like Tucson, Arizona, and McAllen, Texas, these cases fill courtrooms day after day, turning Latin American migrants into criminals. In row after row of courtroom seats, migrants are pronounced guilty, a migrant turned into a criminal alien with the bang of a gavel.

To move tens of thousands of migrants through federal courts year after year, prosecutors and court officials teamed up in Del Rio, Texas, to launch Operation Streamline in December 2005. The goal was to raise the stakes for migrants who violated immigration law by wielding the power of criminal law. For decades, Border Patrol agents in Del Rio, just like everywhere else, had used deportation as their go-to tool. When they ran across someone who they thought had only recently entered the United States and didn't have permission to do so, agents would usually drive them to the nearest border crossing point and point them toward Mexico.

Under Operation Streamline, Border Patrol officers in the

Del Rio area instead began flagging single adults for federal prosecutors. Trained to spot criminal activity, federal prosecutors did exactly that, charging migrants with illegal entry or illegal reentry, the federal crimes that Blease had ushered into law. Not content with letting courts run their course slowly, Streamline twisted regular criminal proceedings into something out of an authoritarian show-trial. Gone was a hearing in which a defendant could stand in court alongside a defense attorney, hear the prosecutor's evidence, push back on its weakness, and get the undivided attention of a judge. Instead, dozens of migrants were brought into the courtroom—walking slowly and awkwardly as shackles announced the metallic ring of criminalization—after having had only a few minutes to talk with a lawyer. There, a judge would go through questions for everyone at the same time. Do you understand that you're being charged with a crime? Do you understand that you can remain silent?

In a normal hearing, judges go through each question, wait for an answer, then move on. When one person's hearing ends, another's begins. But Operation Streamline isn't normal. Instead, the judge asks a question of the entire group and listens for a jumbled murmur in response. Written court transcripts often describe a "general yes answer."[71]

Streamline ramped up immigration crime convictions, but even that wasn't enough for the Trump administration. Standing in front of a group of Border Patrol agents in 2017, Jeff Sessions, at the time Trump's attorney general, demanded that prosecutors prioritize illegal entry and reentry cases. And so they did. Two years later, before the Covid-19 pandemic brought the world to a standstill, the 31,495 immigration cases filed in district courts made up 34 percent of all new criminal cases—the largest category of criminal cases pursued that year nationwide.[72]

Remarkable though it is, explaining that immigration crimes occupied the top spot in federal district courts is actually an understatement. Most immigration cases don't show up in district courts. Instead, they're filed in what's called a "magistrate" court because they're overseen by judges who are hired as long-term judicial employees rather than being nominated by the president and confirmed by the Senate. The idea is that magistrates can dispose of minor matters like prosecutions for low-level crimes. There are so many immigration cases in federal courts these days that if we don't look at magistrate courts, we'll miss most immigration crime prosecutions. In the same period that the 31,495 immigration cases represented the largest category of prosecutions in district courts, magistrate courts dealt with another 91,466 immigration cases.[73] That means that in 2019 alone, federal courts handled almost 123,000 immigration crime cases. Since Blease's day, Congress has criminalized other migration activity, but the vast majority of immigration crime cases are for illegal entry or reentry. Prosecutions for these offenses have gone down under Biden, but even during this administration twenty thousand or so people are targeted for immigration crimes every year, not far off from the Bush era, when prosecutors began to dust off Blease's law.

The pace of immigration crime prosecutions is so intense that one judge described his courtroom as "a factory putting out a mold."[74] The raw materials that are manhandled are people whose hands are cuffed and legs are chained because they reached the United States without the government's permission. The judges and lawyers who toil mindlessly repeat their labor hour after hour, day after day. Their quickly manufactured good is a conviction that is followed by another, then another. At the end of the process, convictions are lumped together and sold at market to the segment of the public that imagines immigration crime prosecutions as the solution to some problem. Justice has been commodified. A less romantic description of the criminal legal system isn't possible.

Coleman Blease died in 1942, thirteen years after his most significant accomplishment in the Senate became law. If he was still alive today, he would certainly be smiling. He has never been more important. In the tens of thousands of people who are marked as criminals, imprisoned, and deported every year, his racism and xenophobia live on.

3

IMAGINING ALIENS

Thanks to the law that Coleman Blease pushed through Congress in 1929, sometimes crime finds migrants, turning the courageous act of leaving one home in search of another into a crucible. Other times, migrants find crime, freezing their lives at their worst moment, the details of that instance in the past becoming a ghost that haunts the future.

For Wynnie Goodwin, the worst moment came on May 29, 1993. Passing by a restaurant in Orange County, California, she and a group of friends stopped when they saw some other kids they didn't like. Things quickly worsened. Shouting started, a gun came out, shots were fired. Two girls ended up in the hospital.

"I unlawfully attempted to kill Nhung Luu and Saythong Thongprachanh with malice aforethought," Wynnie wrote on the guilty-plea form she signed and submitted to the court. Twenty years later, she says it didn't happen that way. "Absolutely not true," she told me when I read the words back to her. "The way it's written it's like I planned and plotted the crime, which is not true. And that I did it with intent, which is not true."

She doesn't deny that she wrote the sentence. She just says that her lawyer told her what to write. "I would not have come up with that language."

I believe her. *Malice aforethought* is a legal term that means the premeditated intent to harm or, worse, kill. This isn't a phrase that rolls off the tongue, especially not a teenager's. At the time, Wynnie was seventeen. She'd spent most of her life in coastal Louisiana, but in the summer of 1988 her family relocated to Orange County. There they moved in with her father's older brother and his children.

That's when things started getting bad. One cousin was older, another the same age. While the parents hustled to survive in Southern California, the kids got into trouble. The police say that Wynnie was in a gang. On the plea form, she agreed. Looking back on it, Wynnie says that's overblown. "It was just a bunch of teenagers that had no positive influence," she told me. "As children, we came together to be part of something because I didn't fit in anywhere."

There's nothing unusual about Wynnie's teenage years. Gangs certainly weren't new to Southern California in the late 1980s and early 1990s, but they were becoming more common. More important than what was happening on the streets of Orange County was what was happening in Washington. Wynnie's teenage years coincided with a period when Republicans and Democrats were going after each other as being weak on crime. The year that Wynnie arrived in California, 1988, President Ronald Reagan announced "Crime Victims Week," declaring "the responsibility for crime lies with those who commit them." [1] That fall, allies of Reagan's vice president, George H.W. Bush, attacked the Democratic nominee for president, Massachusetts governor Michael Dukakis, for his position on releasing prisoners. Describing the stabbing and rape of a white couple by a convicted Black man, Willie Horton, who had received temporary release from a Massachusetts prison, Republicans orchestrated a brutal ad campaign, branding Dukakis's position as dangerous. Launched by Lee Atwater, a political operative who got his start in politics as an aide to the unabashedly racist Strom Thurmond, South Carolina's longtime senator, the TV spot added an unspoken racial element to the Democrat's dangerousness: Black men were a threat to white people.

Credited with carrying Bush to the presidency, the Willie Horton ad is a lesson in the power of the media to fan fears of crime. Over and over again, TV news broadcasts flashed menacing images of Horton—a mug shot, an image of him looming over cops, a scary close-up—often pairing them with photos of the white people he had attacked.[2] California wasn't immune to what was happening at the national level. That winter, the *New York Times* announced, "Gang Violence Shocks Los Angeles."[3] A year later, the *Los Angeles Times* reported a record-high number of gang murders even as the police said the number of homicides was down.[4]

Democrats learned a lesson. Four years after the Willie Horton ad pushed Bush into the White House, the incumbent president's Democratic opponent, Arkansas governor Bill Clinton, was ready to take the offensive on crime. On the campaign trail, Clinton blasted Bush as weak on crime. "He's talked a lot about drugs, but he hasn't helped people on the front line to wage that war on drugs and crime. But I will," Clinton promised as he accepted his party's nomination for president.[5] After Clinton's victory, his allies in Congress were ready to make good on that promise. Delaware senator Joe Biden stood on the floor of the U.S. Senate in 1993 to bemoan young people "without any conscience developing." Speaking the same year that Wynnie was arrested, Biden added, "We have predators on our streets."[6]

Biden could've been talking about Wynnie. Gang or not, Wynnie and her friends were up to no good that night. Decades later, she doesn't deny that. She was there, in the middle of the argument, when shots were fired and two people were hit. Fortunately, neither died. Cops tried to get her to snitch on her friends, but she refused. She was afraid that the other kids would go after her family. Besides, "that's just something you didn't do," she told me.

Convicted of two counts of attempted murder, plus a sentencing boost for gang involvement, Wynnie got twelve years in the state prison system. She served six, with the first two-and-a-half at a juvenile detention facility. Wynnie had lived in the United States for all but the first month or so of her life, and the government knew it. In fact, she'd entered as a refugee. She was born in Vietnam just before her parents fled because of the war. In those chaotic last days of the conflict, she didn't so much leave Vietnam as she was taken out. She was a newborn carried onto her family's fishing boat in her parents' arms. The first place she saw in the United States—though she was too young to remember it—was Fort Chaffee, Arkansas, a major entry point for Vietnamese refugees in 1975. Like

Wynnie's father, most of the people brought there had been involved with the defeated South Vietnamese military.[7] Talking about whether she remembers the country of her birth doesn't make much sense. She was so young when she left that it would have been impossible. Wynnie is a product of the United States, flaws and all. In the words of her criminal defense attorney, she's "American through and through." As a refugee, Wynnie had permission to stay in the United States for the rest of her life. She knew she was a permanent resident, not a U.S. citizen, but to a teenager that distinction doesn't much matter.

To immigration law, that's the only distinction that does matter. Permanent residency is the highest form of immigration status. It comes with the right to live and work in the United States indefinitely, but it's not citizenship. And only U.S. citizens are protected from deportation. With two attempted murder convictions on her record, Wynnie was deportable, and immigration officers knew where to find her: Valley State Prison in Chowchilla, California. Watching the people around her, she realized that wasn't the future she wanted. Passing the days in Chowchilla, she also knew she wouldn't be free at the end of her time in state custody. Agents with the Immigration and Naturalization Service, predecessor of today's Immigration and Customs Enforcement agency, had already told her they'd pick her up. "That's when I realized I'm in trouble," she told me. She was afraid she'd be deported.

As promised, California prison officials handed Wynnie over to the INS. They took her to a county-owned immigration prison that she describes as "inhumane," and she sat there for several months until the INS transferred her closer to the San Francisco immigration court where an immigration judge was considering the INS's deportation case against her. In early 2000, the immigration judge agreed with the government, signing her deportation order. Wynnie should be sent back to the country where she had been born but had never known.

Only the INS couldn't deport her. No country, not even the United States, can dump people in another country without that government's permission. Since the mid-twentieth century, Cuba has been the most important example of a government that routinely refuses to accept its citizens whom the United States doesn't want. But there are others. China, India, Russia, and ten other countries all made it so difficult for the United States to deport their citizens that in 2020 the U.S. State Department declared them "recalcitrant" countries. Vietnam was at risk of non-compliance with U.S. deportation goals along with another sixteen countries, according to the State Department.[8]

Two decades earlier, in 2000, when an immigration judge issued Wynnie's deportation order, relations between the governments of the United States and Vietnam were still feeling the hangover of the U.S. invasion. Diplomatic relations had been restored in 1995, but the two countries didn't have a deportation agreement through which the United States could deport the roughly 6,200 people like Wynnie who had been ordered deported despite having lived here for years.[9]

The war that drove Wynnie's family out of Vietnam kept her away once more. The INS had nowhere to send her except home: Orange County. Returned to the community she knew best, she jumped off the troubled path she'd been on as a teenager and threw her energy into education. She wanted to become a lawyer, but she worried that she couldn't get into law school with a serious felony record. She got her bachelor's degree, then two master's degrees instead. Now she oversees a thirty-person human resources department at a 2,000-person company. She's married, raising four U.S. citizen kids, and keeps busy volunteering with survivors of domestic violence.

In the meantime, California changed its criminal laws, making it possible for a judge to revisit Wynnie's convictions. Everyone thought she was eighteen when her friends attacked the other kids at the restaurant, but they were wrong. She was seventeen. No one caught this because her immigration documents listed her birthdate as January 1, 1975, which would've made her eighteen when the shooting happened in May 1993. Only she wasn't born in January. Wynnie doesn't know exactly when she was born, but in October of that year, a military doctor at Fort Chaffee wrote that she appeared to be one month old. This was "too young for shots," a handwritten note on a medical exam record says.

For people like Wynnie who were born in the Vietnamese countryside, it wasn't unusual not to know their exact birthdate. Many were born at home without birth certificates. Plus, in the middle of a warzone there were other things occupying her parents' attention. When they arrived in the United States, government officials often made things easier on themselves by picking the same birthdate: January 1. In reality, she was probably born in late June or early July of 1975.

That means she wasn't quite eighteen years old when her friend shot those kids, so she shouldn't have been prosecuted as an adult. This was a fatal error, a judge concluded in December 2021, vacating her convictions—an odd legal term that just means a court wipes away old convictions. The following year, the immigration courts erased her deportation order and a few months later she took the citizenship oath. Forty-seven years after arriving in the United States, Wynnie Goodwin became a U.S. citizen.

The Politics of Migrant Criminality

Teenaged Wynnie didn't know it, but her worst moment came at the worst time. In the late 1980s and early 1990s, the United States was in the middle of a criminalization revolution, and migrants were one of the chosen targets.

A couple of decades after the civil rights era, white supremacy wasn't gone, but the legal and cultural foundation had shifted. Racism that in the 1950s and 1960s was best illustrated by white police officers and vigilantes attacking Black civil rights activists across the South was no longer legally or culturally permissible. Instead, appeals to white racism began to substitute crime for race using a dog-whistle tactic in which government officials rarely mentioned race but everyone understood that's what they were talking about. As early as 1956, the Border Patrol, which two years earlier had launched a nationwide roundup of Mexicans called Operation Wetback, now advised agents to "use the words, 'criminal alien.'"[10] Intent on winning the support of disaffected white voters, Republican Barry Goldwater launched the "Southern

Strategy" the following decade, using crime as a thinly veiled cover for racism. It didn't get him very far. He carried all of one state outside the Deep South, his home state of Arizona.

But with a little finesse, the subtle pitch that government policies hurt white people to help people of color soon took hold. Richard Nixon pointed to drug use. Ronald Reagan added welfare. "In Chicago, they found a woman who holds the record. She used 80 names, 30 addresses, 15 telephone numbers to collect food stamps, Social Security, veterans' benefits for four nonexistent deceased veteran husbands," Reagan said at a 1976 campaign rally. The claim was probably more fiction than fact, but it caught on all the same. Reagan didn't snatch the Republican nomination from sitting President Gerald Ford, but four years later he won the nomination and then the presidency.[11]

What began with Republicans stoking fears of African American violence and immorality soon found another bogeyman to target: migrants from Latin America and the Caribbean. In the late 1970s, Haitians fleeing the dictatorial regime of François Duvalier began making their way to the United States. In South Florida, where many Haitians were heading, immigration officials worried that letting poor Haitians into the United States "could produce a flood of economic refugees from all over the Caribbean," Edward Sweeney, the top INS official in Miami, told reporters. "It could conceivably also apply to Mexicans who illegally cross the border," he added.[12] Florida senator Paula Hawkins claimed that "Haitian arrivals are infected with parasites" and "infiltrated with subversive groups." But worse than disease and political subversion was the crime problem that Haitians brought, Hawkins claimed. "The greatest concern to Floridians is the increase in crime that has accompanied the arrival of the Cubans and the Haitians in this latest influx," Hawkins told senators in 1981.[13]

Around the same time, Cubans resumed a familiar pattern: seeking refuge in the United States. They were also met with hostility. "Among the tens of thousands of people fleeing oppression in Cuba and seeking to reunite with their families in the United States, Fidel Castro has very cynically thrown in several hundred hardened criminals from Cuban jails," a White House statement claimed in 1980.[14] Cuban officials were forcing boat captains to transport "persons released from a variety of institutions, many with criminal records," the U.S. State Department added.[15] Once in the United States, they were sent to Fort Chaffee in Arkansas, Fort Indiantown Gap in Pennsylvania, and even Miami's Orange Bowl football stadium.[16]

Sitting in the governor's mansion in Little Rock at the time, the future president Bill Clinton had a front-row seat to the Carter administration's ad hoc response. That spring, federal officials began flying around some of the 125,000 Cubans who reached the United States. Almost 20,000 would eventually wind up at the Arkansas military base near the Ozark mountains, the very same place Wynnie and her parents had been just a few years earlier. For a while, everything was fine. In the first group of Cubans to arrive, some shouted "victoria"—victory. One asked for a trumpet so that he could play "The Star-Spangled Banner."[17]

The euphoria didn't last long. There was little to do at the camp. "They tell you that it improves chances of being sponsored out if you work every day," Juan González Dominguez told a reporter. "I don't believe them anymore. I just work to keep from going crazy."[18] Few were being released.

Officials were just trying to keep the Cubans in and local residents out. If they remained separated, maybe there would be fewer misunderstandings.[19] By early summer of 1980, migrants had become frustrated that they had nothing to do and little prospect of getting out. Some began protesting. "Today, conditions at Fort Chaffee are not unlike those at the internment camps in which the United States held many Japanese-Americans during World War II," a reporter for the *New York Times* would later write.[20] In May, about three hundred walked out of the camp. They were peaceful, but military police rounded them up and sent them back. "The situation has gotten utterly ridiculous," Clinton said at a press conference the next day, soon after deploying sixty-five state National Guard troops to boost the government's control of the facility. "President Carter needs to make it plain to the refugees that if they are going to come here they are going to have to obey the law," he added.[21]

That was just the beginning. Things soon got a lot worse at Fort Chaffee. In early June, almost one thousand migrants burned down several buildings and pushed through the military installation's front gate, where they were met by state police officers who fired live rounds above the crowd, then hit them with clubs and tear gas. The migrants responded with rocks and bottles. Two hours later, one Cuban was dead and forty were injured. So were fifteen state troopers. "Hardened criminals exported to the United States by Fidel Castro" were to blame, the White House press secretary said the following day.[22] Clinton blamed "a few serious agitators."[23] Violence occasionally popped up again in the following months as Cubans, including children, resisted their detention.

For Clinton, Fort Chaffee spelled political defeat. In the middle of a reelection campaign for governor, Clinton found himself between a president of his own party—a Southern Baptist just like him whom he supported—and a public ready to be done with Cuban refugees. Republican Frank White pounced. He splashed ads on local TV stations showing Cubans trying to escape Fort Chaffee. "Cubans and Car Tags" became his campaign catchphrase, a constant reminder to potential voters of Fort Chaffee and a fee hike on car transfers that happened under Clinton's watch.[24] The tactic worked. White beat the incumbent, handing Clinton the only major election loss of his career. In Clinton's mind, the Cubans at Fort Chaffee were a big part of the reason.[25] He wouldn't forget it.

Reconstructing Immigration Law

As Haitians and Cubans dominated news cycles, legislators' concern about migrant criminality soon transformed into a full-blown reconstruction of immigration law. Instead of scattered laws targeting migrants who committed crimes, the Reagan administration launched a sweeping punishment agenda. Made famous by the "Just Say No" mantra that First Lady Nancy Reagan popularized as part of Reagan's "War on Drugs," the administration popularized fears of illicit drug activity in U.S. cities. Before then, few people in the United States reported much worry about drug use. But with Reagan officials taking to the airwaves to decry urban drug activity, public opinion soon began to change. From April to the end of August 1986, the number of people in the United States saying that drugs were the nation's most pressing issue jumped from 3 percent to 13 percent—a staggering 333 percent increase in just four months.

What happened in that short time span? Reagan delivered multiple nationally televised speeches focused directly on what he declared to be a drug problem. The *New York Times* ran dozens of stories about drug use. *Time* magazine said crack was "the issue of the year." *Newsweek* went even further, declaring crack the biggest thing since Vietnam. When college basketball star Len Bias collapsed onto the floor of a dorm room at the University of Maryland, rumors quickly spread blaming crack. The All-American's end came courtesy of cocaine, but that detail didn't much matter in the era's anti-drug hysteria. The scene was set for Congress to launch a massive legislative attack on drug users. "As individuals, they are responsible," Reagan said in one of his 1986 TV addresses. "The rest of us must be clear that we will no longer tolerate drug use by anyone," he added.[26]

In short order, Congress raised the stakes for people involved with illicit drugs. To make sure that the new laws would carry a strong bite, Congress opened the federal government's purse strings to state and local law enforcement agencies. The Anti-Drug Abuse Act of 1986 made its intentions known in its very name. To finance the federal government's new policing emphasis, the law authorized the Justice Department to seize drug industry assets.[27] Revealing the racist undertones that pushed the law through Congress, the ADAA punished a drug associated with Black users like Len Bias, crack, far worse than a virtually identical drug associated with white users, cocaine. Possessing 1 gram of crack was treated the same as possessing 100 grams of cocaine.[28] That 100-to-1 disparity would remain the law until 2009, when Congress amended it. But even then, crack and cocaine wouldn't get the same treatment, as the disparity was reduced to 18-to-1.[29]

In 1988, Congress sent Reagan's successor, George H.W. Bush, another key step in the budding "War on Drugs" campaign. Reflecting either an unusual lack of creativity or a desire to reiterate Congress's anti-drug messaging, the new law was called the Anti-Drug Abuse Act of 1988. Cementing anti-drug policy as a core political objective, the ADAA of 1988 created an Office of National Drug Control Policy within the White House responsible for coordinating a national anti-drug strategy and administering newly created federal grant programs.[30]

As they spread fears of crack, cocaine, and marijuana, policymakers found an ideal villain in migrants arriving in the United States from Latin America and the Caribbean. The Cubans who arrived in the late 1970s and early 1980s were the "dregs" of Cuba's prisons that Fidel Castro unleashed onto the United States, Hollywood claimed in *Scarface*, the 1982 hit starring young Al Pacino and Michelle Pfeiffer. "Of the 125,000 refugees that landed in Florida, 25,000 had criminal records," the film's opening scene explains, before following Pacino's character as he kills his way to the top of South Florida's drug trade. This was a wild overstatement, but at least the movie didn't claim to be telling the truth. By contrast, the same year, a Miami grand jury issued a sixty-page report tying Haitian and Cuban migrants to an increase in crime, specifically blaming drug traffickers. "Who were these people and where were they coming from?" the grand jurors asked of recent arrivals.[31] Meanwhile, legislators in Washington also pegged drug use to Black migrants, this time from Jamaica.[32]

While it was busy building Reagan's War on Drugs, Congress was also busy ratchetting up the consequences for migrants. Many of the very same laws that increased prison time for involvement with drugs also made it easier to fall into the immigration prison and deportation pipeline. The ADAA of 1988, for example, added the concept of the "aggravated felony" to immigration law. Thanks to that law, immigration officials are required to detain anyone convicted of an aggravated felony, and those so detained are barred from the most charitable form of relief from removal. An immigration judge cannot even consider individual circumstances that might justify releasing them. Perhaps because the stakes are high, the 1988 law listed a mere three crimes as falling under the aggravated felony rubric: murder, drug trafficking, and firearms trafficking.

Over the decade that followed, that list would get much longer, and it would come to include crimes that most people don't consider severe. Forging a passport, skipping a court date, and some kinds of shoplifting are all included. Today, the list of aggravated felonies is so sprawling that it includes crimes that aren't felonies. It's even possible for Congress to reach into the past, spontaneously turning a crime that wasn't an aggravated felony into one that is even if it was committed long before. Normally backdating a crime like this violates the Constitution, but when it comes to adding deportation to the list of consequences for a crime, the Supreme Court says there isn't a problem. In the four decades since Bush and a Congress on an anti-crime war march put the country on this path, the stakes have become higher and yet the consequences remain exactly how Congress set them in 1988: mandatory confinement and almost certain removal from the United States.

In 2000, when Wynnie Goodwin stood in front of an immigration judge, it was clear that attempted murder was an aggravated felony. That's why it wasn't hard for the immigration judge to sign her deportation order. Wynnie was able to get out of an immigration prison and avoid deportation only because of the poor relationship that the United States had with Vietnam in those days. That had nothing to do with Wynnie and everything to do with politics.

By 1992, a dozen years after Frank White tarred him with the images of supposedly dangerous Cubans storming out of Fort Chaffee, Bill Clinton had more than simply resurfaced. He'd won back the governorship from White and then claimed the Democratic Party's mantle. The so-called Comeback Kid moved into the White House with a win over the incumbent George H.W. Bush, ready to deploy the lessons he'd learned in Arkansas. Smooth-talking and charismatic,

Clinton continued to speak about welcoming migrants, but he hadn't forgotten about the treachery of immigration politics.

Not to be outmaneuvered by Republican claims to be tough on crime, in 1994 a young Justice Department lawyer named Ron Klain, who would become President Joe Biden's first chief of staff twenty-seven years later, wrote to Clinton's attorney general, Janet Reno, and top advisors outlining the administration's response. "We generally support" Republican efforts to expand deportation powers through a proposed crime bill, Klain explained, but warned that the politics could tilt against Democrats if they didn't launch their own anti-crime rhetoric.[33] That year, with Clinton's support, Congress sent the president the mammoth Violent Crime Control and Law Enforcement Act. Usually called the 1994 Crime Bill, the law raised the stakes for illegal reentry, boosting prison time to where it remains today: up to twenty years for people convicted of an aggravated felony and ten years for people convicted of any drug crime.[34]

Democrats weren't done. The following year a young Chuck Schumer told his colleagues in the U.S. House of Representatives, "Noncitizens do not—and, in my judgment, should not—have the same rights as citizens."[35] Soon Congress would make sure that Schumer's judgment became law. In 1996, a Republican-controlled Congress sent Clinton a pair of bills that cemented immigration law's emphasis on criminal activity. In April, Clinton signed the Anti-Terrorism and Effective Death Penalty Act, making it easier for federal officials to detain and deport migrants with criminal histories. It added to the definition of aggravated felony yet again and expanded a fast-track deportation procedure for people serving time in jail or prison to include people convicted of a large variety of crimes.[36] The anti-terrorism law's greatest irony is that it wasn't migrants committing crime that led to its passage. Instead, Congress enacted AEDPA after Timothy McVeigh and Terry Nichols, two white U.S. citizens, blew up a federal building in Oklahoma City, killing 168 people, including 19 children.

AEDPA also made it more difficult for migrants to avoid deportation by limiting a type of pardon power that immigration officers had been able to tap for almost eighty years. In 1917, Congress gave immigration officers the power to decide whether to allow into the United States migrants whose criminal records meant they could be excluded from the country.[37] In effect, Congress trusted immigration officers with deciding which transgressions should be forgiven. In 1952, Congress moved this authority into section 212(c) of federal immigration law, so it became known as 212(c) relief. Other than that, the discretion to waive a crime's impact on a migrant's ability to enter the United States didn't change much until 1976, when the federal government's top immigration appeals court decided that 212(c) relief should apply equally to people asking to enter the United States as to people who were already here and wanted to avoid deportation.[38] Two decades later, fully in the spirit of Congress's tough-on-crime goals, AEDPA blocked immigration officers from using 212(c) relief to help a long list of people: migrants convicted of a drug crime, any crime that fit the expanding definition of aggravated felony, or multiple convictions for crimes involving moral turpitude.[39]

That fall, Congress and Clinton outdid themselves. Debating the Illegal Immigration Reform and Immigrant Responsibility Act (IIRIRA), members of Congress unleashed a rhetorical attack against migrants. In the Senate, only one senator said anything positive about migrants' contributions to U.S. culture while the bill was being debated. By contrast, two senators said migrants negatively affect culture, twelve claimed migrants have a negative economic impact, and fourteen said they made crime worse. Alan Simpson, a Wyoming Republican, claimed, "Criminal aliens are obviously a serious problem in the country." California's Senator Dianne Feinstein described her goals in the clearest of terms. "It is especially imperative that unlawful aliens involved in illegal drug smuggling and manufacture be put out of business," she urged her colleagues. Representing the Clinton administration, INS Commissioner Doris Meissner added, "Aliens who commit crimes in the United States must know they will be prosecuted, convicted, and removed from the United States."[40]

The idea that migrants are happy to break the law—they're drug dealers and murderers—also dominated debate in the House.[41] Republican representative Edward Royce of California pointed to a migrant who allegedly had killed a police officer. "How many more crimes have to be committed?" he asked. His Florida colleague Bill McCollum, also a Republican, added, "I ask the local police about aliens. They tell me they don't ever bother calling up an INS office to report an illegal alien."[42]

Congress wanted action, and Clinton was ready to join them. In September 1996, Clinton signed IIRIRA. Out of character, he vastly undersold the monumental impact the law would have. Signing the bill, he declared, "It strengthens the rule of law by cracking down on illegal immigration at the border, in the workplace, and in the criminal justice system—without punishing those living in the United States legally." [43]

IIRIRA would do so much more. For starters, the new law hit people who did have the government's permission to be here. Hyung Joon Kim, for example, was a lawful permanent resident who had lived in the United States since he was six. When he was eighteen, he was convicted of burglary and a year later of petty theft. The INS claimed that, under IIRIRA, they had no choice but to detain him while the immigration courts decided if he'd be deported. Congress had the power to enact this law, and it was the agency's responsibility to enforce it, the government's lawyers argued. The Supreme Court agreed. In the process, Chief Justice William Rehnquist echoed Schumer's vision of a two-tiered legal system. "Congress regularly makes rules that would be unacceptable if applied to citizens," Rehnquist wrote for the majority of the Court. [44]

IIRIRA also transformed the relationship between federal immigration officials and local police and sheriff's departments. Through a change to section 287(g) of the Immigration and Nationality Act, the federal law governing immigration, IIRIRA gave the INS (now ICE) the power to partner with state and local law enforcement agencies. By letting immigration enforcement tap the staff and budgets of any police or sheriff's department that wants to work with it, Congress obliterated for migrants any meaningful distinction between criminal police forces and immigration enforcement. It would take a few years for these partnerships to spread, but once they did, interacting with police operating under a 287(g) agreement meant getting funneled into the immigration prison and deportation pipeline. Once there, migrants could no longer count on 212(c) relief to avoid deportation because of their criminal history. IIRIRA finished what AEDPA began by eliminating 212(c) relief entirely.[45]

By century's end, the punitive trend that had begun in a quickly improvised fashion when Haitian migrants surprised the Carter administration had matured. By the time Clinton left the White House in January 2001, immigration law and policy had been thoroughly reconstructed. Criminal activity had become immigration law and policy's central operating principle. People convicted of an ever-growing list of crimes could be imprisoned and deported, with fewer options to escape the immigration prison and deportation pipeline. "These changes to our immigration law have dramatically raised the stakes of a noncitizen's criminal conviction," the Supreme Court wrote in José Padilla's case.[46]

Defending the Homeland

For a brief moment in the early years of Republican George W. Bush's administration, the policies that Carter launched, Reagan expanded, and Clinton cemented seemed like they might give way. For his first state visit, Bush invited his Mexican counterpart, Vicente Fox, to Washington. At a White House press conference, the two leaders spoke of the "special friend-ship" between their countries. On the same day, the White House congratulated the Senate for passing legislation that would welcome more migrants. That was September 6, 2001.

President Fox had hardly touched down in Mexico City when the world suddenly changed. Images from New York, Washington, and rural Pennsylvania showed a nation under attack. Buildings had toppled and thousands died. In an instant, political priorities shifted, and political possibilities had been turned upside down.

In the new fight against terrorism, everything was on the table, and everyone was suspect. Migrants were no exception, with immigration law high on the list of tools preferred by law enforcement officers. "Let the terrorists among us be warned: If you overstay your visa—even by one day—we will arrest you. If you violate a local law, you will be put in jail and kept in custody as long as possible," Bush's attorney general, John Ashcroft, said the following month. "We will use every available statute." [47] A few days later, Bush ordered the Justice Department and CIA to work together to boost the INS's ability "to identify, locate, detain, prosecute or deport" migrants suspected of terrorism. [48]

After two decades of congressional willingness to tie immigration law to the criminal legal process, Ashcroft and his team at the Justice Department had a lot to work with. Thanks to the 287(g) agreements that IIRIRA created, state and local police could use their resources to throw ICE's power to arrest and deport migrants into overdrive. Unlike ICE, state and local cops patrol the streets of every city and town in the United

States daily. They are the boots on the ground that police and arrest people much more than ICE ever could. Partnering with ICE under a 287(g) agreement, those same officers can now spot and arrest migrants, then hand them over to ICE. As a result, any minor interaction with a cop operating under a 287(g) agreement could become the entry point into the immigration detention and deportation pipeline.

Though they were never used before the attacks of September 11, the 287(g) agreements that Clinton signed into law quickly became popular after the attacks. In 2002, the INS launched the first agreement with the Florida Department of Law Enforcement. The following year, Alabama came on board. By 2008, Bush's final year in office, there were thirty 287(g) partnerships in place and more spread across the country during the Obama and Trump years.[49] They continue to have an important role under President Biden, with 137 agreements operating in July 2023, more than two years into his presidency.[50]

The 287(g) agreements were never limited to preventing attacks like the horror of September 11. True to their origin, they impact people suspected of violating the law in far more ordinary ways. Back in 2018, a 287(g) agreement almost turned Sara Aleman Medrano's life upside down, though no one could accuse her of anything like terrorism. A grandmother and mother whose family lived in Frederick, Maryland, Medrano left home one night with her daughter and grandkids. They didn't make it far before a sheriff's deputy pulled them over. At the time, the Frederick County Sheriff's Office was under its second 287(g) agreement. The first was signed in George W. Bush's final year in office, but had expired. The second agreement went into effect in August 2016 while Barack Obama was president. By its terms, the 287(g) agreement in place two years later when Medrano and her family left home shouldn't have mattered. The contract between ICE and the sheriff clearly stated that sheriff's deputies could only ask about immigration status while working at the county jail. In practice, though, officers felt free to do much more, Medrano and her lawyers claimed. They felt fine questioning people like Medrano wherever they stumbled onto them.

Just a few years earlier, when the county's first 287(g) agreement was in place, Frederick County deputies had arrested a different woman while she was on break from work. That was unconstitutional, a federal court concluded. The Fourth Amendment lets police question, even arrest, people if they think the person committed a crime. That's not what deputies were doing. They couldn't go around arresting people who they didn't suspect of having committed a crime. Illegal though it was, the officers couldn't be held liable. As police officers, they were immune from ordinary violations of the Fourth Amendment.[51] In the name of public safety, cops can violate the Constitution and get away with it. For their illegal arrest, they won't get fined or lose a job. And if in the course of flouting the law they learn that the migrant they have targeted is violating immigration law, immigration judges can consider the evidence. Driven by a desire to push along immigration cases, the Supreme Court explained, "An illegal arrest has no bearing on a subsequent deportation proceeding."[52]

On the side of the road that evening in 2018 with her daughter and two young grandchildren, Medrano was scared. This might be the last time she saw her family, she thought. Understanding English poorly and facing a deputy who didn't speak Spanish, Medrano didn't know why she had been pulled over until a Spanish-speaking officer arrived and told her the car had a bad tail light. This was news to her at the time because she'd never had trouble with the car's lights. It was surprising later that evening when she and her daughter confirmed that the lights were working fine. But in that moment, Medrano and her family were stuck in the car as the officers waited for ICE. They waited for almost an hour, but ICE, it turns out, wasn't interested in them. The officers eventually let Medrano leave, but the fear they put into her that evening over a simple traffic violation—that may or may not have been real—didn't go away so quickly. A year later, she was still suffering from anxiety.[53]

Combined with heavy-handed policing that's common in communities of color across the United States, immigration law has a way of making things very messy, very fast. Nothing better illustrates this than the Bush administration's roundup of Muslims. The Clinton-era IIRIRA included a directive that the INS create an easily accessible electronic database of people entering or leaving the United States.[54] By the time New York and Washington were attacked in 2001, five years had passed and nothing much had come from this requirement. Now, in the name of national security, Congress told immigration officials to get on it "with all deliberate speed," the same phrase that the Supreme Court used in *Brown v.*

Board of Education when it ordered that public schools be desegregated.[55]

Within months of Congress invoking the language of racial progress, the INS launched the National Entry-Exit Registration System, a massive Muslim surveillance initiative. Starting in the summer of 2002, roughly eighty thousand migrants living lawfully in the United States were required to register with the government and submit to an interview with immigration officers. Almost all were citizens of Muslim-majority countries. By the following fall, 13,799 of those people had been put into immigration proceedings and 2,870 detained.[56] Few of those had any criminal history, but all of them faced the possibility of creating one if they didn't comply with the program's requirements.[57] Almost no one was actually prosecuted for anything related to terrorism.[58] The registration system was just a ruse that let the INS use the threat of criminal prosecution to ferret out people who had done nothing worse than stay in the United States after they were supposed to have left.

Immigration officials may have had plenty of tools available under the laws that existed before September 11, but the attacks of that day changed everything. Most meaningful of all was the creation of a massive new cabinet-level department, the Department of Homeland Security. In his pitch to Congress, Bush called it "the most significant transformation of the U.S. government in over a half-century." Approved by Congress in 2002 and launched in 2003, the mission that Congress gave the new department under the Homeland Security Act says nothing about immigration. Its primary purpose is to "prevent terrorist attacks." It's also supposed to respond to emergencies and deal with drug trafficking.[59]

Still, the department was always designed with immigration in mind. In the tragedy's aftermath, news quickly spread that the attackers were not U.S. citizens. Despite dying in September, two received notices in March 2002 that the INS had approved changes to their visas. They'd asked for approval to take flight training courses. Journalists incorrectly suggested that their visa applications had been approved after the attacks, and President Bush expressed outrage. In fact, it was only the notices that had been mailed after the attacks. The changes had been approved months earlier.[60] By then, a political storm had erupted, and DHS was born in it.

Hatched in this political climate, immigration law enforcement would occupy a key role at the new department. "Immediately after last fall's attack, the President took decisive steps to protect America—from hardening cockpits and stockpiling vaccines to tightening our borders," the White House announced. By creating DHS, Congress would take an enormous step "to secure our borders."[61] According to Bush, DHS would take "functions that are not directly related to securing the homeland against terrorism," like the INS's immigration law responsibilities and its 39,000 employees.[62]

Replacing the INS were ICE and CBP, both housed within DHS. The duties of the old agencies would survive, but all would now fall under the banner of homeland security. ICE polices immigration law in cities throughout the country. Primarily through the Border Patrol unit that it inherited from the INS, CBP focuses on the border. The agency claims to be concerned about all the nation's borders equally, but in reality, almost all of its agents are deployed along the border with Mexico. At both agencies, fears of migrant criminality dominate. ICE claims that it targets "cross-border crime and illegal immigration." As "guardians of our Nation's borders," CBP also claims to combat transnational crime and protect against immigration law violations.[63]

Today, the idea that migrants present a threat to the United States isn't just overblown rhetoric by over-the-top politicians like Donald Trump. It's actual laws turned into concrete policies carried out every day in real neighborhoods and courtrooms where questions about life and death, of the ability to keep living in the place a migrant calls home, are put into action.

The irony is that migrants commit less crime than people born in the United States. Reams of evidence going back decades show this. As early as 1911, the congressionally created U.S. Immigration Commission concluded that the available statistics "indicate that immigrants are less prone to commit crime than are native Americans," by which they did not mean Indigenous peoples.[64] Its key workhorse, W. Jett Lauck, pushed back against claims that migrants brought "crime, vice, insanity, or pauperism," writing in a Richmond newspaper that the commission's findings "do not justify these contentions."[65]

A century later, migrant populations are different, and researchers have more data to work with, but the bottom line is the same. The 945-page *Oxford Handbook of Ethnicity,*

Crime and Immigration—bedside reading compared to the Immigration Commission's forty-two volumes—summarizes the situation in the United States: Latine immigration "is credited with contributing significantly to the decline in American crime rates since 1991," the book's editor writes.[66] It's not quite true that migrants make cities safer. There isn't a straightforward cause-and-effect relationship. One more migrant isn't guaranteed to lead to one fewer crime. Still, it is true that communities with many migrants tend to be the safest communities in the United States.

But to say that migrants commit less crime than people born in the United States isn't to say that migrants are angelic. They are not. Migrants are simply people. Like all people, migrants are complicated and contradictory. Instead of viewing migrants in their totality, immigration law focuses on their worst moments. For many migrants, immigration law emphasizes their crimes while undervaluing their deep ties to the United States. Wynnie Goodwin is a daughter and corporate executive, but she was also hanging out with friends when shots were fired, and two kids hit. José Padilla is a Vietnam veteran, a father, husband, and long-haul truck driver, but he also got caught with one thousand pounds of marijuana in his trailer. These are the flaws that mark them as people. But to immigration law, these are also the flaws that mark them as undesirable: ripe for exclusion, fit for punishment.

4

POLICING WITHOUT BOUNDARIES

Sandra Castañeda was twenty years old on the day her life changed. She'd been driving a group of friends through Los Angeles in the spring of 2002 when they passed members of a rival gang. Sandra had been around gangs most of her life, but she had never had trouble with the police. That changed in an instant when one of her friends suddenly aimed a gun out the car window and opened fire toward their rivals. Soon one person was dead and another injured. There was never any evidence that Sandra shot a gun. There wasn't even evidence that she knew her friend had a gun in the car. Still, she was convicted of murder and attempted murder and sentenced to forty years to life in prison, just as if she'd been the one to aim the gun and pull the trigger. Back then, criminal law in California let prosecutors bring a murder charge against someone involved with a crime that led to death even if no one thought that person actually killed anyone. Called felony murder, this was the rule in most states.

Fifteen years later, the California legislature made it easier for courts to vacate a felony murder conviction, legally erasing old convictions. Thanks to that change, a judge could treat

Sandra, who had just been driving the car, differently from the shooter. The judge vacated Sandra's murder conviction and replaced it with a conviction for a much more minor offense, accessory after the fact, which basically involves helping someone after they've committed a crime. A few months later the judge revisited her case again. Now all that was left on her criminal record was a conviction for disturbing the peace, a low-level offense.

Sandra ended up spending eighteen years behind bars. She'd never get back that time, but what she did get back was the ability to say she didn't have a murder conviction on her record. As far as California is concerned, she wasn't a convicted murderer.

She'd be able to return to L.A., the place she calls home. Finally. "I didn't believe it. It was surreal to me," she remembers thinking. "I was in shock."

The day she was freed, she was forty years old. Her family was waiting to take her back to L.A. She had a nonprofit group lined up ready to help her readjust to life on the outside. The head of the state's prison system had said Sandra was ready "to successfully transition back into society." California's governor had praised her transformation, describing her as "a productive citizen."

But to Immigration and Customs Enforcement, it didn't matter that the governor and the judge were on Sandra's side—none of it mattered. Once a criminal, always a criminal. Sandra didn't step outside the prison. ICE showed up for her just inside the door. "I found you a spot," an ICE officer told her. "You're going to Atlanta."

ICE doesn't let go of the past easily. The ICE officer who told her she'd be heading to Atlanta claimed the agency never received proof that her murder conviction had been wiped away. "She's sending me somewhere where I'm going to be screwed," Sandra said. There was no one and nothing for her in Georgia.

In the U.S. legal system, criminal law and immigration law are technically separate. "Deportation is not a punishment for a crime," the Supreme Court announced in Fong Yue Ting's 1893 case.[1] To the justices, it's nothing more than moving people around the face of the Earth. Some people belong on this side of the border. Others belong on that side. As far as immigration law is concerned, it's as simple as that.

Except that Sandra's life isn't simple. "I was devastated. I was devastated," she told me, the second time her voice shaking as she pushed her memories back to that day. Instead of the freedom she had expected to feel, she was getting an ankle bracelet and a seat on a flight to ICE's Stewart Detention Center in Lumpkin, Georgia, where she would spend the next thirteen months. "I was just crying on the plane, thinking, 'What am I going to do?'" she remembers. "Here I am now facing deportation."

With the help of her lawyers, Sandra was able to convince a judge that she should be let free while the immigration court process unfolds. She's back in L.A. living with her family and working with Homeboy Industries, a nonprofit with a storied history of helping young people whose lives have become entangled with gangs. "Most of my memories are in L.A.," she told me. "This is where I live." She was starting slowly. Soon she hoped to begin mentoring young people. "It's my turn to give to the community," she says. "I'm trying to do better."

Even now, while she's back in the only place she's ever called home, ICE continues to try to deport her. Sandra's "murder conviction is still a conviction for immigration purposes," government lawyers told a court in September 2021.[2] They lost their attempts to block Wynnie Goodwin from moving on, and maybe they'll lose this time too. But until the immigration courts decide Sandra's case, there's still the possibility that she won't be able to stay in the United States. Every day she lives in fear. "It was very hard for me to wrap my mind around the fact that I was not going to be able to stay here with my family," she remembers thinking. She wondered whether more time in prison would've been better. "Why am I even out? I should've just stayed there," she said.

In the case that José Padilla took to the Supreme Court, the justices seemed to understand this. All the changes that Congress made to federal law beginning in the Reagan years had flipped punishment on its head. After the death penalty, most of us think of prison time as the worst consequence that can come from a criminal conviction. Migrants often make a different calculation. As the number of crimes that can result in deportation has grown and it's become more difficult to escape from the immigration prison and deportation pipeline, deportation has become "an integral part—indeed, sometimes the most important part—of the penalty" that comes from a criminal conviction, the Court wrote in Padilla's case.[3]

Born in Mexicali, Baja California, Sandra spent all but her first nine years in California, living, evading, and finally falling prey to the gang violence of South Central L.A. and the government's relentless law enforcement tactics.[4] If Sandra had been born in Calexico, California, instead of Mexicali, she could turn her attention to doing better. If she had been born a few miles north, she would be a U.S. citizen. Her past would be behind her. That evening in L.A. when she was nineteen wouldn't be the moment that continues to hang over her head. But the facts are what they are: Sandra was born in Mexico, not the United States, so she's not a U.S. citizen.

Emphasizing their mandate to enforce immigration law, ICE and Customs and Border Protection regularly ignore the human consequences of the legal authority that Congress has given them. Pointing to concerns about migrant criminality, their policing tactics receive a lot of support and very little pushback. No matter how wide their dragnet or how severe the consequences of their focus on policing migrants, there are few limits on their policing activities to act as guardrails against their indiscretion.

To ICE, it's not Sandra's commitment to helping her community that matters. It's her citizenship. To ICE, it's not her hopes for the future that matter, it's her past. To ICE, it's the conviction in 2003 that sets the course for the future, not the judge's intervention in 2021.

To ICE, there's no moving on. Sandra is still a murderer. She's still a criminal alien.

Tactics

Consumed by the idea that they are what stands between the United States' existence and the migrants endangering us,

ICE and CBP agents will do almost anything to detain and deport just about anyone whose past reveals the dark stain of criminality. During the Trump years, for example, ICE routinely visited state courthouses to arrest people who it thought might have violated immigration law. In Denver, ICE agents wrestled a man to the ground at the literal courthouse door. As the man yelled "No!," "My hand," and "Why?" in Spanish, building guards ordered onlookers to stay away. The violent arrest continued while the man's girlfriend filmed the scene, shouting at the officers that her partner had a lawyer. The following month, ICE agents arrested another man at the same courthouse. This time the lawyer was there. On a cellphone video that his colleague took, the lawyer can be heard asking agents if they have an arrest warrant. "Yes, sir," one responds. "Can I see it?" the lawyer follows up. "No, sir."

To ICE under Trump, courthouse arrests were sound policy. Since everyone inside a courthouse has gone through a security screening, these arrests "reduce safety risks," ICE announced in a formal policy released in early 2018.[5] When courts in Oregon and Washington were on the verge of banning ICE from arresting people inside their courthouses, the heads of DHS and the Justice Department wrote that this would be "dangerous and unlawful." State laws in Oregon and Washington were "endangering the public" by allowing migrants to go free after committing crimes, they claimed. Barring ICE from state courthouses "would make the situation worse." For good measure, the pair added that the Constitution would let ICE agents ignore any policy that the state court systems adopted.[6] In a similar letter to California's top judge, Trump officials earlier had claimed barring ICE arrests from California courthouses "threaten[s] public safety."[7]

Clearly, ICE during the Trump era had little concern about scaring migrants and their families away from courthouses. To further their goal of arresting migrants, they were happy to swallow the possibility that they might push people to avoid courthouses at all costs.

ICE claimed that they went after people who were dangerous. But even putting aside the fact that not everyone who commits a crime is dangerous, there are a lot of people at courthouses who haven't been convicted of anything. Some people will get prosecuted, but not convicted. Others are at courthouses to pay fines or deal with legal problems that have nothing to do with crime. Other people go to courthouses to help prosecutors as witnesses to crime. Turning courthouses into arrest zones sends the message that paying a fine, requesting protection from a violent partner, or simply doing as a judge demands might mean never going home again. For migrants, it's an easy calculation: stay away. For the rest of us, ICE's narrow pursuit of public safety is also troubling because without witnesses, defendants, and victims, it's next to impossible for the legal system to operate.

Unconventional law enforcement practices wielded against migrants aren't unique to ICE. A few years ago, CBP tried to make a criminal out of an activist. Scott Daniel Warren gave "food, water, beds, and clean clothes" to two men whom he encountered in the blazing Arizona desert early in 2018, federal prosecutors claimed in a court filing. They were tired and he was volunteering at a remote desert shelter with beds. They were hungry and he had food. They were thirsty and he had water. They were dirty and he had soap. To me, Warren's conduct could've come out of the New Testament, but to Jeff Sessions, Trump's attorney general at the time, it was treasonous.

A few months before prosecutors lodged their accusations against Warren, Sessions had visited Arizona, lamenting "that criminal aliens and the coyotes and the document-forgers seek to overthrow our system of lawful immigration." He promised "to combat this attack on our national security and sovereignty." Speaking to a crowd of CBP agents, he declared, "It is here, on this sliver of land, where we first take our stand against this filth."[8] Hollywood screenwriters couldn't have been more melodramatic. Federal prosecutors were only too happy to do Sessions's bidding, charging Warren with harboring migrants, a crime punishable by up to twenty years in prison. Two jury trials later, federal prosecutors finally gave up. Locals were unwilling to convict.

The immigration officials overseeing Warren's arrest and prosecution ignored the risks of their head-first jump into a policing chasm. To the CBP officers and federal prosecutors involved in his case, their power to enforce immigration law outweighed Warren's humanitarianism. Like their ICE colleagues who were willing to scare people away from courthouses, the CBP officials and prosecutors who went after Warren saw risk in mundane activities and used the full force of their legal authority to target people they viewed as dangerous.

From Police to ICE

To pay for their no-boundaries policing practices, ICE and CBP count on huge budgets. Back in 2005, Congress gave ICE $3.8 billion and CBP $6.4 billion.[9] By 2023, ICE could tap $9 billion and CBP another $21 billion. Pockets this deep have made DHS the biggest federal government unit after the Department of Defense. Collectively, the two immigration agencies employ a small city's worth of people: 21,000 at ICE and 60,000 at CBP.[10]

Despite skyrocketing budgets, both agencies eventually run up against what they can do on their own. They repeatedly point out that they don't have enough money to track down, arrest, imprison, and deport everyone who might be violating immigration law. In 2011, Obama's head of ICE explained that the agency "only has resources to remove approximately 400,000 aliens per year, less than 4 percent of the estimated illegal alien population in the United States."[11] For this reason, immigration officials prioritize targeting some migrants over others—with criminal history a typical calling card in recent decades. Called "discretion," targeted enforcement is such a common part of immigration decision making that in 2012 the Supreme Court described it as "a principal feature" of immigration policy.[12]

To do more than what their own massive budgets allow, immigration officials rely heavily on police agencies around the United States to boost their reach. ICE often refers to local cops and prison officials as "force multipliers." They add to ICE's power but without costing the federal government much or anything. Instead, the cities and counties that pay for the bulk of policing in the United States pick up the tab for the cops who arrest and jail people. The section of immigration law that authorizes 287(g) agreements—those state and local partnerships with ICE in which local cops double as immigration agents—puts the financial relationship simply. Local governments can work hand-in-hand with federal immigration officials, but it has to come "at the expense of the State," federal law says. Other programs rely on city police or county sheriff's deputies to arrest people suspected of criminal activity, then they tap jail guards paid by county or state governments to sift through the people who are arrested. That's how ICE caught up with Sandra as she waited in the custody of California prison guards. Without cities, counties, and states opening up their pocketbooks, federal immigration officials could never reach into every city and town in the United States.

Police to ICE, Texas-Style

Sometimes states go out of their way to expand ICE and CBP's reach. Since 2017, Texans have had to deal with a state law that blurs the distinction between state and local cops and federal immigration officials. In May of that year, the state legislature passed a law that forces state and local government agencies, including law enforcement officers, to flag people for possible removal from the United States. Called Senate Bill 4, the law is audacious. It turned employees of the state's many cities and counties into an infinite number of eyes and ears for ICE. One section blocks government employees from doing anything to make ICE's work more difficult. Another provision forces police to abide by ICE's requests to continue to detain people so that the federal agency can decide if it wants to take them into custody. Most frighteningly, S.B. 4 empowers police to ask anyone, including a crime victim or witness, about their immigration status.

As the bill made its way through the state legislature, thousands of Texans protested. Chiefs of police from the state's largest cities, joined by the executive director of the Texas Police Chiefs Association, published an op-ed predicting that S.B. 4 would "strain the relationship" between cops and the communities they serve. That worsened relationship, the chiefs added, "will make our communities more dangerous for all."[13] Despite the police chiefs' plea, the state legislature passed it on a party-line vote: Republicans in favor, Democrats opposed. Governor Greg Abbott signed the bill into law on May 7, 2017.

Soon advocates sued, challenging the law's immense reach. Ten months later, one of the most right-wing federal appellate courts in the country backed Texas. Just about every directive in the new law was constitutional. The one exception: a provision telling elected officials that they couldn't speak in favor of laws limiting state and local cooperation with ICE or Border Patrol.[14] After the courts weighed in, police chiefs in Texas could continue writing op-eds criticizing S.B. 4, but they had no choice but to enforce every one of its other commands.

Across the state, encounters with police suddenly became much more dangerous, just as police feared and S.B. 4's Republican backers hoped. Back in the Río Grande Valley, researchers tried to measure the new reality in this region where cross-border ties are a defining feature of daily life. In the Valley, most people aren't fully insulated by U.S. citizenship. For people like me who were born in this part of the United States, it doesn't take much effort to find migrants on the family tree. Like with me, often they're parents or grandparents. Perhaps siblings or spouses.

A survey of over two hundred adults conducted in the summer of 2018 uncovered a widespread fear that minor encounters with local police could quickly erupt into life-altering entanglements with ICE or Border Patrol. Almost two-thirds of the study participants who identified as unauthorized migrants told researchers that they feared driving because of their immigration status, a threat made all the more real by the fact that one-fifth said they had actually been detained or deported after a traffic stop. This isn't surprising given that unauthorized migrants aren't allowed to get a driver's license in Texas. But lawful permanent residents and people with DACA are, and yet 26 percent of those said they also worried about driving. Though researchers didn't ask why, 16 percent of U.S. citizens also said they worried that driving around town could lead to immigration problems.[15]

Digital Policing

As life becomes increasingly digitized, ICE is rapidly retooling its enforcement toolkit in light of its no-boundaries policing philosophy. On top of its panoply of traditional powers to police, arrest, and deport, the agency has added innovative efforts to gather and sort through vast amounts of digital data. It's immigration policing for the era of Big Data. Trying to make sense of what ICE knows, how it knows it, and what it does with that information reminds me of the science fiction writer Arthur C. Clarke's "Third Law," which he initially proposed in 1973: "Any sufficiently advanced technology is indistinguishable from magic," Clarke wrote in his characteristic mix of outlandishness that later proved prescient.[16]

ICE's data surveillance strategy isn't quite magic, but it is fast, sophisticated, and remarkably massive. It's also an opaque, largely unregulated arena controlled by a handful of private corporations that profit handsomely from contracts with ICE. In 2021 alone, the agency spent $388 million on its surveillance programs. Some of this pays for license plate scans at toll roads and parking garages. Other contracts access databases of social media profiles.[17] Two companies in particular, LexisNexis and Palantir, have carved out key niches for themselves in the immigration data surveillance labyrinth.

Lexis is best known for its impressive academic research databases. As an undergraduate, I learned to rely on it to quickly search through newspapers. Today, I use it to keep up to date on the law. For lawyers, it's an essential—and expensive—research tool. My law school teaches students how to use it just like every law school I know does. I tell the young social-justice advocates training to be lawyers whom I teach that Lexis's legal research databases are indispensable tools to keep people out of ICE's hands. What I didn't know until a few years ago was that ICE also thinks of Lexis as a vital tool in its attempts to round up and deport migrants. In 2021, ICE turned to the company's databases on 1.5 million occasions, combing through driving records, phone logs, and jail arrest data.[18]

Tapping Lexis's databases, ICE's National Crime Analysis and Targeting Center (NCATC) powers through millions of investigations. In one year alone, 2020, NCATC staff investigated almost 8.5 million people.[19] Despite the unit's unmistakable suggestion that it focuses on crime, in reality it's a massive clearinghouse of all kinds of data that relies heavily on Lexis's resources.[20] The NCATC helps ICE officers sort through everything from criminal history files to the names and addresses of employers or relatives who filed an immigration application for a migrant. Two sources NCATC relies on are actually examples of people who are complying with immigration law: DHS's main database of visa applications and its repository of naturalization applications.

Plus, as a hub of the government's immigration law enforcement agencies, it's easy to assume that NCATC only accesses information about people who are not U.S. citizens. Even ICE doesn't pretend that's true. Information fed into the NCATC about federal prisoners, for example, lists where they were born, but it doesn't say anything about whether someone born outside the United States became a U.S. citizen after birth.[21] This might be a small wrinkle if it weren't for the fact that lots of people are naturalized citizens: more than half a million people have naturalized every year since 1996 except twice.[22] And ICE isn't beyond going after those people either. Through Operation Janus and Operation Second Look, names clearly meant to inspire suspicion of ill-will, the agency led efforts to strip naturalized U.S. citizens of their citizenship.[23] The first word in ICE's name may be "immigration," but that doesn't mean that the 18 million people who have become U.S. citizens since 1996 can breathe freely.

ICE claims that NCATC helps it capture people who pose a danger to the rest of us. But using Lexis's own legal research service, it's easy to find examples disproving the agency's claim. In 2016, for example, ICE agents in New Mexico arrested Maximo Olivas-Perea and charged him with illegal reentry. He'd been deported in 2005 and had obviously returned to the United States. He'd had a few run-ins with the police over the years, including an old conviction for possession of marijuana, but that's not what brought him to ICE's attention. Instead, the NCATC got wind of Olivas-Perea when he renewed his driver's license.[24] Similarly, ICE arrested Juan Carlos Valadez-Muñoz in 2017 and charged him with illegal reentry. Valadez-Muñoz had been deported a few times, most recently in 2005, but had returned to California. There he renewed a driver's license in 2010 and again in 2015. NCATC received information about the 2015 renewal a few months later, but it would take the agency two years to review the information.[25] During that time, Valadez-Muñoz appears to have stayed out of trouble just as he had since 2003, the one period prosecutors say he was involved in crime other than illegal entry or reentry.[26]

Another company, Palantir, is just as important to ICE's digital surveillance prowess, but it operates under a thick blanket of secrecy. It's named after the palantíri, J.R.R. Tolkien's seven spherical stones that "watch from afar," according to the popular fantasy writer's description.[27] Created by benign beings, the stones wind up in the hands of evil. In Tolkien's popular *Lord of the Rings* series, the evil wizard Saruman uses the palantíri to do his master's bidding. Together, Saruman and the sorcerer Sauron wield the palantíri's power of omniscience to manipulate mental weakness. The company's CEO, Alex Karp, told the *New York Times* that he and the company's founder, Peter Thiel, wanted to reflect that a single tool can be dangerous, but it can also be used for good.[28]

A lot can be described that way. To Karp and Thiel, it's up to them and their customers to decide what's dangerous and what is good. "The engineering elite of Silicon Valley may know more than most about building software. But they do not know more about how society should be organized or what justice requires," Karp wrote in a 2020 letter to the Securities and Exchange Commission. "We have chosen sides, and we know that our partners value our commitment. We stand by them when it is convenient, and when it is not."[29] The list of Palantir's customers is a who's-who of federal government agencies and giant multinational corporations. The CIA was an early backer. These days, it works with the U.S. Army, the Department of Health and Human Services, Credit Suisse, and pharmaceutical manufacturer Merck. It also contracts with ICE. After receiving $187 million from ICE between 2008 and 2021, it's easy to see why the company's loyalties lie with the immigration policing agency.[30]

But there's also an ideological commitment. Karp is a unique character. He's the company's CEO, a workaholic with a law degree and a Ph.D. in social theory who studied under the influential German philosopher Jürgen Habermas until the two had a falling out. He likes using words like "monoculture" to describe Silicon Valley and he embraces New Hampshire–style libertarianism, saying he likes "living free" as he works from a fancy barn.[31]

What Karp possesses in eccentricity, Thiel has in Trumpian dogma. Friends since their days at Stanford Law School, Thiel is also a self-described libertarian who has no problem making millions from government contracts. He was an early investor in Facebook and Tesla and helped found PayPal. He made out well from those investments.

Perhaps the most lucrative early bet that he made is Donald Trump. Thiel supported the future president when he was little more than a bombastic reality TV celebrity with an overactive Twitter account. That bet paid off. After Trump's 2016 victory, Thiel was named to the president-elect's transition team, where he was supposed to help vet candidates for senior political appointments, a task he appears not to have been very good at, though he doesn't seem to have tried too hard. "This wasn't really the game Thiel was in. Mainly it was just for show. What he wanted was to get close to government contracts," political theorist David Runciman writes.[32] It's those contracts, after all, that fuel Palantir.

Unlike a traditional private company that contracts with a government agency, Palantir doesn't sell a product. Instead, it sells what the Big Data world calls "data integration." Basically, Palantir charges ICE for access to a homegrown portal through which ICE can sift through vast amounts of data quickly and efficiently. Its Falcon product lets customers search through all the information Palantir pools. ICE claims that only agents who are part of its Homeland Security Investigation unit are allowed to access Falcon. In a flashy promotional video accompanied by music better suited for a national security thriller with too much adrenaline, HSI shows heavily armed agents exiting helicopters, a scantily clad woman behind the label "Investigating: sex trafficking," a muscular agent outfitted in a bulletproof vest and seemingly no shirt tackling someone who is presumably up to no good, and a lot of captured drugs. "Today, America is safer thanks to the agents of HSI," the agency touts.[33]

A lot of the information Palantir packages is already available publicly through government agencies or for a fee from private companies. The company's Integrated Case Management system takes property records from county governments and driver's license and vehicle registration records from state DMVs. Though it and ICE claim their partnership protects the public, much of the information Palantir makes accessible has nothing to do with crime. ICE's HSI agents rely on information about "family relationships, employment, military service, education, and other background information," the agency disclosed in 2016 and again in 2021. All of this, and much more, is fed into Palantir's Falcon system from government files in ICE's main database of migrants detained or removed from the United States. But Falcon also taps private databases like CLEAR, a product sold by Lexis competitor Thomson Reuters, that accesses cellphone records, license plate files, and criminal records.[34]

Claiming to target international gangs, in 2017 HSI launched an initiative called Operation Matador, supposedly to target Mara Salvatrucha 13, the widespread gang that started in Los Angeles then expanded to Central America when the United States began deporting its members. Through Operation Matador, HSI agents wrote memos that ICE lawyers then used in immigration court to show that a migrant was involved with gangs. Often, these claims relied on the thinnest of proof: wearing shoes associated with MS-13 members, being seen talking to a gang member, or sporting certain "apparel including Chicago Bulls Hat," as one HSI report alleged.[35]

Migrants' rights advocates strongly oppose the unrestrained policing practices that programs like these represent. In recent years, they have targeted companies that partner with ICE, informing the public about practices that few of us knew about before. Now when I talk with students about the fantastic legal research capabilities that Lexis offers, I also tell them about the company's ties to ICE. When Palantir moved its headquarters to Denver, locals staged an "unwelcome party" outside its offices.

Activists have also pushed Democrats in many of the nation's largest cities, as well as a handful of states, to adopt laws or policies that limit how much help ICE gets from officials at the city, county, and state levels. Sometimes billed as "sanctuary" laws, other times described simply as efforts to welcome migrants, these types of laws aren't unusual. Under Trump, they thrived. For a while it seemed like cities and states controlled by Democrats were competing against each other to enact the latest pro-migrant law as a way of ingratiating themselves to the groundswell of anti-Trump voters.

Always interested in removing any limits to its enforcement efforts, ICE found an effective path around sanctuary laws by contracting with third-party data brokers. In Oregon, for example, legislators ended state disclosure to ICE only to later learn that the state department of motor vehicles signed agreements with Lexis and its competitor Thomson Reuters to sell driver's license data to those companies.[36] After Colorado legislators enacted a law barring state and local police from sharing identification information with ICE absent a warrant, ICE began accessing the very same information through Lexis and another data broker, Appriss, itself owned by the credit-reporting giant Equifax.[37] In California, CBP skirted laws limiting how much information local governments could give it by contracting with the San Diego Association of Governments, an organization that has significant ties to city and county governments in Southern California but that's formally structured as an independent nonprofit.[38]

There's nothing illegal about ICE or CBP's buying software packages and database access from third parties. So long as Congress and DHS leaders are fine with it, both agencies can contract with whomever they want. But just because it's not illegal doesn't mean it's not troubling. By circumventing the spirit of recently enacted state laws, they undercut the value of democratic participation. What's the point of organizing communities to support city council candidates or of showing up to testify at the state house if the federal government will just buy its way around anything you accomplish? Instead of respecting the outcome of democratic governance, ICE and CBP's willingness to pay for the very information that state and local officials don't want it to get suggests that the agency is willing to buy itself out of the headaches that democracy brings. Oversight might be a feature of democratic governance, but, to ICE and CBP, it's an annoyance to be skirted.

Sometimes, though, it's easier just to tinker with the formula. In a quest to justify locking up more people, researchers found that ICE altered the algorithm that its computers used. Reviewing ICE's practices in 2013 at its Baltimore field office, researchers Mark Noferi and Robert Koulish found that ICE's computerized risk assessment system recommended all of 1 percent of people for release.[39] Apparently, even that was too many. A few years later, Koulish and a different colleague, Kate Evans, found that ICE actually retooled its risk assessment system to tag more people as dangerous. After years of suing ICE to get access to its risk algorithm, Koulish and Evans discovered that the agency rewrote its computer program so that characteristics that in the past would've been deemed a low risk of danger were now weighed more heavily.[40] The higher someone landed on the Obama administration's list of immigration law enforcement priorities—nothing more than a list of politically palatable targets—the higher the score that ICE's program gave them. Nothing changed about the people. But with a tweak to the computer program, ICE declared them more dangerous and, like that, had an easier time justifying their confinement.

"ICE cannot currently be trusted"

Once in ICE's prisons, as Sandra found out, it's hard to get out. Like with her, it usually requires a solid legal argument plus a lot of luck matching good lawyers with sympathetic judges. Almost always, ICE insists that a migrant locked in its prisons is a migrant too dangerous for release. It almost never matters what else is going on—even when the world suddenly turns upside down, like in the spring of 2020.

Early in the Covid-19 pandemic, many counties reduced their jail populations in the name of public safety and national security. But ICE continued with business as usual. In a period when Covid-19 was so dangerous that refrigerated trailers began appearing outside of overflowing morgues, ICE refused to consider releasing migrants locked in its prison archipelago. To agency leaders, the migrants who were detained deserved it. Congress requires that ICE hold people in its custody who have been convicted of one of a long list of crimes. When a migrant doesn't fall into one of those categories of so-called mandatory detention, ICE agents and immigration judges can still send a migrant into the agency's network of hundreds of prisons, but only if they decide the migrant poses a danger to the community or won't show up for court dates.

Normally deferential federal judges quickly became skeptical that migrants pose a danger to the community. Within weeks of the World Health Organization's declaring Covid-19 a pandemic, federal courts from California to Massachusetts ordered migrants released from ICE's prisons. ICE resisted. In its view, altering course would mean reneging on its duty and endangering the public. "We're not going to do a jail break," Acting Secretary of Homeland Security Chad Wolf said in a Fox News interview in July 2020. For months, ICE's website listed the number of people courts had forced it to release from its prison network. Some of these people "pose a potential public safety threat," the agency claimed.[41]

Soon ICE's facilities—never known as models of health care access—started to see illness spread through their cramped quarters. During those early months when schools shut down and people who could afford to do so stayed home, migrants detained at California's Mesa Verde Detention Center were still required to sleep in rooms with beds lined up like a barracks, arms-length apart. "Invariably, ICE argues that the detainee in question should not be released because they pose a danger to the community or are a flight risk," one court explained. Seventy-eight-year-old José Luis López-Guevara, who had heart surgery in March 2020 but had been convicted of murder in 1980, shouldn't be released despite the California parole board's recent decision that he should go live with his son. Neither should Jennifer Lara Plascencia, the mother of a twenty-month-old child, who had been convicted of wire fraud after using her company's credit card without permission. The agency refused to budge. ICE was acting "downright irrational, not to mention inhumane," the court added.

After migrants sued, ICE reduced the number of people held at Mesa Verde by about half, giving everyone a bit more space. But at every turn, the federal court explained, ICE showed "disinterest" and "obstinance" about the need to adjust to the global health crisis. An ICE officer at the facility told the court that every new arrival was quarantined for fourteen days. When lawyers for detained migrants called the agency out on this claim, the officer admitted that it was "inadvertently inaccurate." By this point, the court was fed up with ICE's antics. "ICE cannot currently be trusted," the court concluded.[42]

This wasn't the only court to catch ICE in its lies. Migrants detained at the 1,400-person Adelanto Immigration and Customs Enforcement Processing Center, also in California, sued DHS over the conditions they were forced to live in. By late September 2020, dozens of detained migrants had contracted Covid, as had a handful of staff, yet it remained unclear whether ICE or GEO Group, the private company that runs the facility, was requiring staff or visitors to wear masks. When the company informed ICE that it was ready to launch a universal testing regimen at Adelanto, the ICE officer in charge of operations there said no. There was money and staff available. Testing supplies were stocked. The CDC said it was a good idea, but to Officer Gabriel Váldez, it was better that no one be tested because some might opt out. "I had my reservations based on the—the plan as written and the fact that the tests were not mandatory, they were optional, they were voluntary," Váldez later told the court.

Váldez's baseless safety declarations didn't stop there. To figure out the number of people who could be held there while allowing for six feet of physical distancing, Váldez acted as if he had a superhero's mental abilities. Standing in a room, he "imagined in his head that every detainee had a sphere around their body that measured three feet in every direction," the court explained. "Váldez did not measure any common room, did not measure any cell, did not measure any bed, did not measure any table, did not measure any hallway, and did not measure any other area," the court added.[43]

Policing Begets Illegality

Immigration policing practices focused on what the government can do rather than what the government should do frequently create the very illegality that politicians complain about. When the Trump administration launched a pair of policies that work in tandem to block asylum-seekers, the Remain in Mexico initiative and Title 42, it became common for people to bounce from a port-of-entry to the river. Why wouldn't they? People who request asylum are fleeing for their lives, but these policies kept migrants from asking for a form of legal protection that's been part of U.S. law for decades. Remain in Mexico forced people to wait in Mexico while U.S. immigration officials decided if they would be allowed to enter the United States. The initiative's official name, the Migrant Protection Protocols, was a cruel joke. Instead of safety, it resulted in the creation of refugee shantytowns in Mexican border cities that the U.S. State Department says are too dangerous for U.S. citizens to visit.

"They say here in this country, where we are, they kidnap a lot of people," a migrant named David says he told U.S. immigration agents as they pointed him back toward Nuevo Laredo, a Mexican border city famous for the sophistication of its kidnapping operations. His protest made no difference. Instead of reuniting with his sister, who already lived in the United States, within minutes of reaching the United States, David and his child were sent back across the border by CBP officials. Five hours later, the pair were in the hands of the cartel operatives whom they feared. Under the banner of Remain in Mexico, U.S. officials fed the cartel beast that they claim to despise. After they were ejected from the United States, David and his child were terrorized by kidnappers, who demanded cash from David's relatives in the United States.[44]

For its part, Title 42 quickly rejected people fleeing violence. Ignoring federal laws that allow anyone fearing for their safety to request asylum, Title 42 weaponized the Covid-19 pandemic by using public health as an excuse to do what the Trump administration had been trying to do for years: effectively shut the border. As early as 2018, long before anyone had heard of Covid-19, Trump's top immigration advisor Stephen Miller pushed the administration to seal the border to stop the spread of disease. The only problem was he couldn't find the right disease. As Covid-19 spread throughout the world, that obstacle evaporated.[45] The legal strategy Miller had imagined years earlier finally found the disease he had been searching for.

Even though Covid-19 spread just as easily in a U.S. citizen's body, the Trump administration aimed its public-health powers squarely at migrants. On March 20, 2020, the Centers for Disease Control and Prevention announced that the United States would be safer if people without the right immigration status were kept out. U.S. citizens and lawful permanent residents could continue coming and going, but everyone else would be ejected as quickly as possible. There would be no legal process. Initially, DHS closed off the United States to everyone hoping to request safe harbor. After the Mexican government balked, U.S. officials relented when it came to families and, later, kids traveling without adult relatives. Many people rejected under Title 42 soon became victims of violence. There were almost ten thousand instances of rape, kidnapping, torture, and other types of violence in its first two years, according to migrants' advocates.[46]

Turned back when they approached the official crossing points, only to find themselves with few options while trying to survive in dangerous border towns, migrants did what anyone watching could've guessed they would do: resume their northward journey. Since they couldn't get across by asking an immigration officer for asylum, many migrants rejected from the safety that the United States promises decided to sneak across. CBP's own statistics show that the number of people crossing and recrossing spiked when Title 42 kicked into gear. In the twelve months that ended on September 31, 2019, the federal government's last fiscal year before Title 42 started, only 7 percent of people caught by CBP had been apprehended before in the previous year. The following year that number jumped to 26 percent and then, a year later, to 27 percent.[47] More than one out of every four people whom CBP caught in the early years of the pandemic had tried repeatedly. Instead of putting people into the legal process that Congress created, Title 42 created the conditions for widespread illegal entry.

It's likely that the repeat-crosser rate was even higher. CBP counts only people who its agents caught more than once in a single fiscal year. Twice, government auditors asked CBP to revamp how it counts, pointing out that it was missing many people who tried multiple times. So far, the agency hasn't budged.[48] Looking more broadly at 1.2 million instances in which Border Patrol agents apprehended someone from

March 20, 2020, to September 30, 2021, the Transactional Records Access Clearinghouse found that 60 percent of people had been caught previously.[49] There's no reason to think that this trend changed much before Title 42 finally ended on May 11, 2023.

It's odd to think that CBP wants to deflate its reports about repeat crossing attempts, but it has an incentive to do that. Since 2011, the agency has deployed a series of strategies supposedly aimed at stopping coyotes, human smugglers, from helping migrants get into the United States without the government's permission. Called the Consequence Delivery System, the basic idea is to raise the cost of violating immigration law for migrants and smugglers alike. Under the CDS, coyotes can be prosecuted criminally for the smuggling. Migrants can also be prosecuted criminally for illegal entry or reentry, as well as be detained and deported by ICE and Border Patrol.

More than a decade into its policy of policing and punishing migrants by ratcheting up the consequences of violating immigration law, CBP would look foolish if it admitted that people kept coming no matter what its Border Patrol agents did. It's harder to justify the government's boundaryless immigration policing and its willingness to ignore the effects of its practices if there's nothing to show for it except more illegality.

5

ILLEGAL ISN'T ILLEGAL

One afternoon in October 1939, in the sliver of New York City where Manhattan stretches north alongside the Bronx, Louis Loftus Repouille sat motionless on his son's bed. The thirteen-year-old boy's face was still covered by a rag when a neighbor climbed through a window into the Repouille family's apartment. His body, limp and warm, was stretched on the bed. Earlier that day, Louis had called in sick to his job as an elevator operator at nearby Columbia-Presbyterian Medical Center. He waited until his wife and daughter had gone shopping, then sent the couple's other two children to a movie.

Only the oldest child, Raymond, was left. Always frail, Raymond became his father's target. Louis "soaked a rag with chloroform," the *New York Times* reported, "and applied it several times to the boy's face." We don't know whether the father hesitated, or the son struggled. But by the time the police arrived, there was no question what had happened. Louis had killed his son.

When word spread of his arrest, Louis's co-workers at the hospital collected money to pay the court-ordered bail.

Talking to the jurors just before asking them to convict the father, the prosecutor acknowledged a soft spot for the man charged with killing a child. "I find it quite difficult to approach the issue in this case when our minds are practically engulfed in the mountain tide of sympathy," prosecutor Alfred Scotti said. He meant sympathy for Louis. Soon a jury would convict him of manslaughter, but, along with their conviction, the jury asked the judge to show "utmost clemency."

Despite having killed his own son, Repouille commanded so much sympathy because his son was ill. It's unclear what health problems Raymond had. News reports use dated language suggesting neurological problems that also prevented him from moving around. "He was just like dead all the time," Repouille told detectives. Whatever was going on with Raymond's body and mind, his father's decision was treated as a form of loving mercy. From his friends to the prosecutor, everyone seemed to agree that it was better—or at least understandable—to kill the boy, than allow him to continue suffering. Raymond's killing aside, Louis "was considered a devoted parent," the judge at Louis's criminal trial said even as he announced Louis's sentence. There was no irony. It was possible to kill one child but be a loving parent to the others.

Less than seven years after that dreadful fall afternoon, Louis would become the newest citizen of the United States. A white man born in the Dutch West Indies, Louis had arrived in his adopted country in 1917.[1] Eventually a court would unravel Louis's claim to citizenship, but not because he killed Raymond. "The pitiable event, now long passed, will not prevent Repouille from taking his place among us as a citizen," explained Judge Billings Learned Hand, one of the most influential judges in the history of the United States. Instead, the court overturned Louis's naturalization for the most technical reason: he hadn't waited long enough to apply. Back then, federal law required five years of good moral character before applying for citizenship. Louis had waited four years, eleven months, and one week. Had he just held off applying for another three weeks, he "would have been admitted without question," Judge Learned Hand wrote.

To the judge and one of his colleagues, older cousin Augustus Hand, Louis didn't display good moral character that October afternoon in 1939. But to their colleague Jerome Frank it wasn't so obvious. Judges are too "cloistered" to "have but vague notions" of public opinion. If killing a child is not good moral character, it should be "our ethical leaders" who tell us, not judges, declared Judge Frank.[2] By the slimmest of margins, Louis's crime was considered so disturbing that he needed to have waited five years before requesting citizenship. Had he just been a bit more patient, all three judges would have left his citizenship untouched. Instead, the appellate judges revoked his citizenship, but suggested that he start over. That's exactly what Louis did. In the meantime, he kept living in the United States, going to work at the hospital, and continuing to raise his other children like the devoted parent that the judge said he was. On April 18, 1949, Louis became a U.S. citizen for the second and final time.

I tell my students that the law isn't a science. It's an art. And like all art, sometimes the law runs in different directions. In the 1930s and 1940s, Chinese migrants couldn't come to the

United States to work, but a white man like Repouille could kill a child in cold blood and be celebrated.

The stain of criminality is powerful, but it does not fall on everyone equally. Race is never far from decisions about who can lawfully make a life in the United States, just as it's always barely beneath the surface of policing practices.

Unequal Legality

Given politicians' never-ending complaints about people crossing the southern border, it's easy to imagine that the only people who violate U.S. immigration law come from Latin America or the Caribbean: Mexicans and Central Americans, increasingly Venezuelans, with a smattering of Haitians. For them, like citizens of most of the world, it's not easy to get into the United States legally. Mexicans, Filipinos, Chinese, and citizens of the many other countries that have longstanding ties to the United States need a visa, and most visa options come through relatives or job prospects that Congress prizes. Through a labyrinth of laws, Congress says which relationships or skills are good enough. U.S. citizens, for example, can bring their spouses to the United States—usually after a months-long wait—but most people hoping to reach the United States aren't married to U.S. citizens. Businesses based in the United States can ask the government to allow in highly educated professionals with graduate degrees, but most people aren't highly educated professionals.

Even when visa options do exist, they're often lousy. U.S. citizens who want their parents to join them in the United States, for example, must wait until they reach twenty-one years old before the federal government will consider letting the parents in. Mexican migrants who become U.S. citizens have to wait even longer if they want to be reunited with married kids who are still in Mexico. As of September 2023, the federal government was considering applications filed before January 15, 1998, a quarter-century earlier. There are many other examples like this, all of which point to the fact that for lots of people from Latin America, Asia, Africa, and the Caribbean, the only viable option for a life in the United States is to enter clandestinely. And thanks to Blease's century-old law, every time that happens, a migrant commits a crime.

Politicians don't often talk about it, but people of color aren't the only ones who violate immigration law. Canadians and Europeans do too. The difference is that for the mostly white citizens of Canada and European countries, Blease's law doesn't apply.

Getting into the United States is straightforward for Canadians and citizens of any European country. From Iceland in the northwest to Greece in the southeast, citizens of every European country, plus Australia and Canada, can reach the United States without a visa. All they need is a valid passport. There are only four countries in Asia and one in Latin America that get similar treatment: Chile, Japan, Singapore, Taiwan, and the not-quite half a million people in Brunei. With no visa requirements to navigate, there's almost no possibility of falling into an illegal entry or illegal reentry conviction.

Yet plenty of them violate immigration law in other ways. Through their visa-free legal access to the United States, they can come for business or pleasure. In practice that usually means visiting family or friends or enjoying a vacation. They can come, but they can't stay. Ninety days later, they are supposed to leave.

Most do. Many don't, especially Canadians. From October 1, 2018, to September 30, 2019, more than 83,000 Canadians didn't leave when they should have. That's about twice as many Mexicans as the Department of Homeland Security thinks overstayed, but half the percentage: 0.8 percent of Canadian visitors compared to 1.5 percent of Mexicans. This account of Canadian immigration law violators is remarkable, but it's probably an undercount. DHS tracks air travelers pretty well, but most Canadians come and go by land and the department admits it doesn't have good data on who leaves by car, bus, or foot. Whatever the actual number of Canadian immigration law violators, it's clear that many Canadians "overstayed" their visas, as this type of immigration law violation is described.

Plenty of Europeans did too. During the same period when 83,000 Canadians overstayed, over 16,000 citizens of the United Kingdom did, as did 11,000 from France, and another 8,000 Germans and Italians each. Tens of thousands more did the same from other countries where visas aren't required. And no, the Muslim monarchy in Brunei isn't to blame. DHS says Bruneians accounted for all of eleven overstays that year.[3]

Every time someone overstays, they violate immigration law. Overstayers can't be convicted of illegal entry or reentry, but they can be imprisoned and deported. With well over 175,000 overstayers in one year alone, immigration prisons and deportation flights could be full of people from Canada and Western Europe, most of whom would almost certainly be white, but they're not.

For this, I'm personally grateful because European countries treat U.S. citizens just as kindly. Several years ago, I moved to Slovenia, a small country northeast of Italy and south of Austria that's part of the European Union. With my U.S. passport in hand, I arrived without a visa. I planned to stay longer than the EU's visa-free travel permitted, so I eventually applied for a residency permit that gave me a few more months of permission. It was a frustrating and slow process, but eventually I got the short-term residency permit. By then, though, I'd made summer travel plans. I'd booked places to stay across Europe. Most important, I'd bought one of those plane tickets that doesn't permit any changes without a steep fee for my return trip to the United States. And then I looked closely at my visa and realized that my permission to stay in Europe might end before my planned trip did. I never got to a clear answer, but the immigration lawyer in me had to admit that one reasonable interpretation was that I would spend the last week or two of my time in Europe as an overstayer.

I could've changed my plans. I didn't. Instead, I planned carefully to avoid border crossings where I knew I'd have to deal with immigration officers. I study immigration law and policing for a living, so I knew that the chances of an immigration official hassling me in Budapest, Vienna, or Ljubljana were slim. I knew I could avoid immigration agents by staying inside the EU's visa-free travel region, which meant I wouldn't deal with anyone who might become suspicious until I was on my way out of the EU. So that's what I did. I enjoyed the summer I'd planned: the symphony in Amsterdam, a hike through German vineyards, an overnight train from Poland to Hungary, a World Cup final in Slovenia cheering on neighboring Croatia. Then I took a deep breath and started my return trip home.

That's when things got dicey. On a layover in Frankfurt, I handed the German immigration officials my passport and visa. They looked at the documents, looked at me, asked where I had been living, and where I was heading. Then they asked me to wait. One immigration officer took my documents, consulted with another, then told me to keep waiting. I remember the ball in my throat as he walked out of the cubicle and headed down the airport hallway with my documents still in his hand. And I remember how it grew when I saw him coming back with a different officer, one who looked older and more in charge than the people who staff the desks at the immigration checkpoint. I was sure they'd done the math too and decided that I was violating EU law. Mentally, I was preparing my argument, a mix of pathetic apologizing and practicality: your life will be easier if you just let me get on that flight to Denver that leaves in an hour.

I lucked out. All they wanted was to keep my residency permit. Apparently, I couldn't go home with it. "Okay, that's fine," I said. "Thank you." The ball in my throat cleared, my heart started beating again, and my feet quickly moved me in the direction of the gate. I've never been happier to get onto a ten-hour flight.

I would like to be able to claim that this was the only time I have violated immigration law. It's not. Each time it's been through some manner of ignorance or entitlement, usually mine. Every time, it's been stressful, but it's never gotten worse. I've always relied on whatever was available. Youthful ignorance worked back when I was in my teens and twenties. Another time a U.S. passport and a plane ticket. When it helps, I rely on English. When necessary, I turn to Spanish. I would like to think that I won't violate immigration law again, but I travel too much to too many places to put money on that hope. At every turn, I'm protected by my U.S. citizenship and U.S. passport and backed up by access to dollars. It's a set of unearned privileges I regularly enjoy, but one that migrants of color to the United States don't.

White Impunity

Just like me, every time someone overstays, they violate immigration law. In the United States, there's only one penalty for overstaying: deportation. It's a blunt tool that Immigration and Customs Enforcement and Customs and Border Protection know how to use. Deportation is also an option when people squeeze through a gap in a border wall or walk across an imaginary line in the Sonoran Desert. Overstaying and clandestine entry are different ways to violate immigration law, but they are immigration law violations all the same.

But the law doesn't enforce itself. Privilege matters, and, in the United States, privilege often comes in the form of race and money. Just like other kinds of policing in the United States, policing migration has a color: white people go free, while people of color go to jail. "We don't arrest many German people," an ICE agent says in the Netflix documentary

Immigration Nation. That's true. They could, but they don't. Instead, they target Mexicans and Guatemalans, Brazilians and Nicaraguans. In the two years leading up to the pandemic, the top ten list of countries whose citizens were locked up by ICE reads like an almanac of Latin America. The only countries to make the list from the rest of the world were India and China.[4]

I don't know if Justin Bieber agrees, but, to me, he's the picture of white privilege in policing migration today. Born in Canada, the singer who always seems to be trying to grow into himself descended on the music scene in 2009. Since then, he's remained popular with the Beliebers, his most committed followers.

He's also become familiar to police and the courts. There was one month in early 2014 when he was arrested on assault charges in Canada and suspected of racing through Miami's streets while high on marijuana and Xanax. On his way to the Super Bowl a week later, police in New Jersey spent hours searching his private airplane for drugs.[5] They didn't find any that time, but he hasn't always managed to escape bigger problems. After a paparazzo in Argentina accused Bieber of telling his bodyguards to beat him up, a judge ordered Bieber to answer the court's questions. When he didn't, the judge issued an arrest warrant.[6] That was in April 2015. In June, a Canadian court found him guilty of those 2014 assault allegations. As if to make sure it was a newsworthy assault, it turns out Bieber hit someone with an ATV that he was driving. For good measure, he was also convicted of careless driving.[7] By that time, he was already on probation in Los Angeles for admitting to having thrown eggs at his neighbor's house. Vandalism, the court concluded.[8] For driving stoned in Miami in 2014, he had already pleaded guilty, enrolled in anger management classes, and agreed to contribute to charity.[9] The list goes on.

Unlike most people, Bieber's crimes aren't hard to spot. They fill celebrity gossip websites like TMZ and venerable news sources like CNN. Often, there are videos and photographs to accompany his antics. Also, unlike most people, Bieber doesn't even try to be inconspicuous. This is not someone who benefits from subtlety. He flies into town on private jets and rolls into giant sports arenas and concert halls under literal neon lights. He has an agent, an entourage, a multi-city tour, and a private airplane that registers with the FAA. Waiting at a supermarket checkout, it's possible to buy a copy of *GQ* and read a cover story in which he admits to using drugs so much that his bodyguards learned to check his pulse at night. "For me, the drugs were a numbing agent to just continue to get through," he says.[10] When police in Canada and the United States want to find him, it's not hard.

Justin Bieber isn't just a pop star with a checkered past. He's also not a U.S. citizen. If ICE doesn't think of Justin Bieber as a criminal alien, that's just because they can't imagine that a white Canadian celebrity could possibly fit the bill. There is no doubt that he's a Canadian citizen. Many people are citizens of multiple countries, but Bieber doesn't appear to be one of them. News reports suggest he applied for U.S. citizenship in 2018 shortly after marrying U.S. citizen Hailey Baldwin. Two years later, in the summer of 2020 runup to that year's presidential election, Bieber encouraged his followers in the United States to vote, writing, "I'm Canadian so I can't vote." Two years after that, there was still no news of naturalization. In all likelihood that's because Bieber's many well-documented crimes pose a problem. His 2015 assault conviction alone means he lacks good moral character. Combined with the vandalism, driving under the influence, reckless driving, and admitted drug use, Bieber's naturalization application is a series of red flags.

Bieber's quest to become a U.S. citizen might be stalled, but his ability to live and work in the United States remains unaffected. In the summer of 2022, he was scheduled to perform in a dozen cities throughout the United States. After a swing through Mexico, he was off to Asia and Europe. As far as immigration law is concerned, any one of these visits abroad could be the last time he sees the Los Angeles home that he and Hailey bought in 2020. Since 1891, immigration officials have been able to bar entry to anyone who has committed a crime involving moral turpitude. That's a tricky phrase made more ambiguous by the fact that Congress has had 130 years to tell us what it means but hasn't bothered to. Left to figure it out themselves, courts tell us that a crime involves moral turpitude if it's "inherently base, vile, or depraved."

But who is to say if something is inherently base, vile, or depraved? Robert Jackson, the Supreme Court justice who took a break from his judicial duties to head up the team of U.S. prosecutors at the Nuremberg Tribunal after World War II, wondered whether we should just guess.[11] In Louis Repouille's case, Judge Learned Hand said that we'd be better off if we polled the public every time one of these cases came up. His colleague Jerome Frank wanted to ask "ethical leaders"—perhaps he had in mind a panel of priests, rabbis, and moral philosophers.[12]

In theory, we can't agree on what constitutes a crime involving moral turpitude. In practice, courts decide all the time. Bieber's crimes could certainly fit the definition they use, but we don't know because ICE doesn't try. For Justin Bieber, life goes on despite his criminal history.

Black Criminality

She'yaa Bin Abraham-Joseph wishes he could say the same. United Kingdom native Abraham-Joseph isn't quite as famous as Bieber, but he's far more than just another British tourist. Better known as 21 Savage, Abraham-Joseph is considered among Atlanta's premier rappers. He wears clothes that are as ostentatious as Bieber's and can count plenty of professional success in his past, including a couple of Grammy nominations and an album that debuted in the top spot.

But what 21 Savage has in fame, he lacks in racial privilege. A Black man who came to the United States as a child, 21 Savage has made a home and a career in a place that won't issue him a passport. His father's work visa, originally good for a temporary stay in the United States, stopped helping Abraham-Joseph long before he rebranded as 21 Savage. When his parents divorced, Abraham-Joseph's permission to be here ended, but his residence didn't. Like my friend Pati, who crossed the Mexican border with her mom, and so many young migrants, 21 Savage violated immigration law because his mother decided that life here was better than life there.

To believe his songs, life wasn't easy. "Came from the bottom, disadvantaged," he sings in "Monster," one of his more popular pieces. And it was violent. In "Lord Forgive," a meditation on gang life, he says, "Moving like I'm John Gotti, 12 gauge n**** shotty. Lord forgive me I'm sorry, I can't help it." All part of the life of gangs, drugs, guns, wealth, and death that appear over and over in his fast-growing catalog. "I'm still loyal to the gang," he says in "Lord Forgive."

Fiction isn't reality. 21 Savage describes conflict and violence, but it's far from clear that he lives the chaos about which he sings. Unlike Bieber, he doesn't have a conviction on his record. He had a problem with the law several years ago—a drug conviction in 2014, according to media reports—but his lawyer Charles Kuck, one of the most respected immigration attorneys in the United States, told me that was cleared awhile back. It's been purged from public records, and Kuck wouldn't tell me anything about it, making me think it was serious. As far as immigration law is concerned, though, it shouldn't matter. A court vacated the conviction, leaving Abraham-Joseph with a clean record. Far cleaner than Bieber's. "He was just an overstayer," Kuck told me, acknowledging that his client didn't have the government's permission to live here.

If the key to avoiding immigration prison is to stay off of ICE's radar, 21 Savage did everything wrong. Appearing on *The Tonight Show* in early 2019, the rapper tweaked the end of his hit song "A Lot" to poke ICE. "Been through some things so I can't imagine my kids stuck at the border," he sang in the days when the Trump administration's policy of separating kids from their parents were still fresh. "People was innocent, couldn't get lawyers."[13]

A few weeks later, in February 2019, ICE would make sure he learned the value of lawyers. For a musician who makes a life out of high-profile performances, there are fewer events bigger than the Grammys. A week before 21 Savage was supposed to walk onto the stage at L.A.'s Staples Center to perform at the music industry's annual showcase, ICE agents arrested him. Through a joint operation with the DeKalb County police, ICE tracked him down as he was leaving an Atlanta nightclub where another young hip-hop artist, Young Nudy, had finished performing. Both rappers detail gang life in their songs, and, according to Kuck, that was enough for the local police to have them on their radar.

Whatever their suspicions, the police didn't bother to arrest 21 Savage when they had the opportunity. Instead, with the DeKalb police standing there, ICE arrested him on the side of the road and took him directly to their offices. He didn't spend even one minute in the local police's custody. Thanks to that old conviction that had been wiped away years earlier, ICE had pegged 21 Savage as a criminal alien. "They claimed they had to detain him, they had to arrest him, they had to do that. He had just been on *The Tonight Show* the night before insulting ICE and their detention of children at the border," Kuck said.

Legally, ICE can only detain migrants if it thinks they threaten the public or if they won't show up for court dates. ICE claimed 21 Savage was too dangerous to be allowed to go

home, but the Atlanta police didn't arrest him, and local prosecutors didn't charge him with any crime. They left it to ICE
to deport him. "If you don't have enough evidence to charge
someone criminally but you think he's illegal, we can make
him disappear," one senior ICE official said in 2008.[14] That
was years before ICE caught up with 21 Savage, but it could've
been the same week.

Instead of joining other music industry celebrities in L.A.,
a day after his arrest 21 Savage was on his way to a nearby immigration prison. While his peers in the music industry celebrated, 21 Savage was stuck in Ocilla, Georgia, home to the
notorious Irwin County Detention Center.[15] "It's a hellhole
in the middle of nowhere," Kuck told me. "What you would
imagine a little southern jail in the Deep South. That's what
it's like."

If ICE wanted to make 21 Savage disappear by sending him
to Irwin, they failed to account for the fact that it's staffed by
young people who listen to Atlanta hip hop. Guards immediately recognized the rapper. There aren't too many people who
have a dagger tattooed onto their foreheads. In the presence of
hip-hop royalty, guards took their duties seriously, Kuck says.
21 Savage never lacked for food, access to phones, or the ability to see his lawyer. These may sound like minor allowances.
In fact, everyone detained at any of ICE's facilities is supposed
to get all of this and more, but that's not how immigration
prisons operate.

And it's certainly not how Irwin usually runs. Owned by
the county government but operated by the private prison

company LaSalle Corrections, problems at Irwin went back years before 21 Savage was sent there. In 2016, a group of advocates told a DHS committee created by Obama's secretary of homeland security, Jeh Johnson, that prison officials regularly failed to provide detained migrants with adequate medical care. One person diagnosed with prostate cancer, they claimed, was denied treatment, then declared free of cancer after having been given the wrong diagnostic test.[16] Despite these accusations, ICE renewed Irwin's contract in 2019, the same year 21 Savage was held inside for a week. For every person held there, ICE agreed to pay LaSalle $71.29 every day. After a week's stay, 21 Savage had earned about $500 for LaSalle. That doesn't sound like much, but in January 2019, days before 21 Savage was locked in there, Irwin held 848 people on an average day.[17] For a single week, the amount of time 21 Savage was held at Irwin, ICE paid LaSalle $2.9 million.

For that price, ICE bought more lousy medical care. In 2020, a nurse who had previously worked at Irwin raised concerns about the large number of hysterectomies performed by a gynecologist who regularly treated women detained at the facility. In a complaint submitted directly to DHS, Nurse Dawn Wooten described the doctor as a "uterus collector," explaining, "Everybody he sees has a hysterectomy—just about everybody."[18] After investigating medical care at Irwin—though not Nurse Wooten's allegations about excessive hysterectomies—DHS concluded that facility staff provided "inadequate" care to chronically ill migrants, people like the person with cancer whose care advocates complained about in 2016.[19] By the time DHS issued its investigative report, ICE had ended its relationship with Irwin so there was no one left to be treated poorly.[20]

Thanks to Kuck's efforts, 21 Savage wasn't at Irwin for very long. As soon as he was able to catch up with his client, Kuck started demanding that ICE release him. They claimed he had a conviction on his record. Kuck pointed out that he didn't. ICE wouldn't budge. "This was the Trump administration. They couldn't give a flying flip who they were holding," he says. ICE had decided 21 Savage was in a gang, and the lack of any gang-related arrests or convictions wasn't going to sway them, Kuck told me.

So, he put them to their proof. The conviction they'd pointed to in the media didn't exist in the courtroom. All they could claim was that he would hurt someone. The immigration judge didn't buy ICE's claims. A bit more than a week after ICE arrested him on an Atlanta street, 21 Savage went home.

21 Savage is no longer ICE's most famous detainee, but that hasn't dampened the agency's interest in deporting him. In late 2021, the DeKalb police dusted off the February 2019 incident outside the Atlanta club. Even though they didn't bother to arrest him then, letting ICE take him down to Irwin instead, more than two years later the DeKalb police arrested him and charged him with illegal possession of a gun and drug possession. They could've made the same claims in 2019, but didn't.

Kuck says it's a sign of desperation because he embarrassed them for claiming his celebrity client had a conviction on his record when court records clearly showed that he didn't. "ICE is clearly trying to get him arrested and convicted so they can have a legitimate reason to deport him," Kuck said. "Even though Biden is now president, they don't care."

In late 2022 when I spoke with Kuck about this case, 21 Savage was still fending off the government's attempt to forcibly remove him.[21] They had a court date set for the following summer, but Kuck wasn't confident that would stick. Immigration court hearings get moved around a lot, and the pending criminal case in Atlanta meant that it didn't make much sense for the immigration court to move forward until the criminal court wrapped things up. Meanwhile, 21 Savage kept busy touring the United States.

"He's a really good guy," Kuck told me, clearly happy that his client was living at home and pursuing his career.

Unequal Illegality

The parallels between Justin Bieber and 21 Savage are striking. Two musicians whose legions of fans regularly fill arenas. Two hard-working performers who have reached the pinnacle of an industry that spits out talent. Two men vaulted into fame as teenagers. Two celebrities whose failures are captured on camera and whose life travails are the stuff of gossip columns. Two emblems of U.S. pop culture born abroad.

It's their differences, though, that are more important. While Bieber has pleaded guilty to multiple crimes in Canada and the United States, 21 Savage's sole conviction was erased, meaning as far as criminal law is concerned, he has never been convicted of anything. While Bieber enjoys his homes in both countries, 21 Savage had to fight to get out of an ICE prison.

While Bieber flies and in and out of the United States, 21 Savage can't leave the country. While Bieber is white, 21 Savage is Black.

These are two lives, but they represent many others. Across the United States, migrants of color are frequently tarred and punished more harshly than are white migrants. When thousands of Ukrainians fleeing violence arrived at the border with Mexico, for example, the Biden administration quickly launched an initiative to welcome them, Uniting for Ukraine. Within a year, more than 125,000 Ukrainians had found safety in the United States. But when Venezuelans and Nicaraguans arrived a few months later, fleeing repressive governments, Biden administration officials tapped a Trump-era policy to quickly expel them even if they hoped to request asylum. As a result, Ukrainians made their way into homes throughout the United States. Venezuelans and Nicaraguans found themselves in shelters in Mexico City and living in makeshift refugee camps along the Río Grande.

After a lot of pressure from activists who pointed out the blatantly different treatment that these groups were receiving, the administration shifted course. Using Uniting for Ukraine as its model, the administration announced that it would allow into the United States as many as 360,000 Cubans, Haitians, Nicaraguans, and Venezuelans annually. Even as it created a legal path into the United States, the Biden administration made things harder than it had for Ukrainians. It would only allow Cubans, Haitians, Nicaraguans, and Venezuelans into the United States under this policy if the Mexican government agreed to accept as many as 360,000 citizens of those countries if the United States chose to deport them. The Biden administration's insistence that Mexico accept citizens of other countries is extraordinary. Governments aren't often interested in taking in deported people who aren't their own citizens, and certainly not on a scale like this. There's nothing similar in Uniting for Ukraine or any other policy. Adding to the differences from the program for Ukrainians, DHS announced that anyone who didn't follow the rules would be deported and, if they came back, would face criminal prosecution for illegal reentry.[22] While the policy was in its early days, a Mexican immigration prison in Ciudad Juárez, across the border from El Paso, caught fire, leaving forty migrants dead. Most were from countries that don't qualify for the new program.

Meanwhile, the stain of criminality adds to the consequences for migrants of color. "It's all about race," Kuck told me. "I dare you to try to detect his British accent." What he meant was that his client, 21 Savage, was facing ICE's wrath more harshly because he's not white. In this sense, 21 Savage is a lot like most African Americans who end up on ICE's radar. He was raised in Atlanta's dynamic African American community, and his British citizenship is masked by his look as just another young Black man from urban Atlanta. Having encountered the criminal legal system, 21 Savage was facing immigration problems even without a conviction. Three out of every four Black migrants deported in 2013 suffered that end because of some interaction with the criminal legal system, much higher than the overall rate of 45 percent.[23] Had he not been immediately recognizable to the prison guards as a celebrity, he might've wound up in solitary confinement as is more likely for Black migrants in ICE detention.

What immigration officials gain in policing prowess, immigration law loses in legitimacy. Relying on criminal law to determine who can live in the United States requires ignoring or accepting the biases that are part of criminal legal processes. Over and over again, we see examples of troubling policing practices that impact communities of color and poor people most heavily. Born and raised in a Texas border community where the Border Patrol was a constant presence on the streets, I was used to a heavy law enforcement presence from the very beginning. In high school, I volunteered for a program in which local cops asked students to snitch on each other. My task was to decide how much reward money to hand out to anonymous tipsters.

Growing up in this environment, seeing the police around wasn't uncommon. But it wasn't until I got to college that I got used to crime. I'd never seen as much illegality as I did as an undergrad. In that picturesque New England college campus, there was drug use and violence, underaged drinking, theft and fraud. Brown wasn't unusual. I've spent most of my adult life at universities. At all of them, police would see crime all around if only they'd bother to look. Eighteen years old when I arrived on Brown's campus, I quickly realized that the cops seemed to work harder to not see crime than to see it in dorm rooms, hear it at parties, or smell it in the marijuana wafting out of open windows. Wealth and whiteness are powerful indeed.

From Trayvon Martin's murder to the agonizing scene

of George Floyd's last minutes, it is impossible to ignore the racial undertone of anti-crime policing in the United States. Today, the criminal legal system in the United States reflects the racism that we've never left behind. The Jim Crow era of explicitly racist laws and social practices is dead. Laws no longer allow explicit discrimination, and cultural norms no longer permit open-faced racism. Instead, as the influential critic of incarceration Michelle Alexander memorably put it, we live in an era of "the new Jim Crow." Politicians criminalize the ills that affect communities of color and prosecutors aim criminal law's harshest weapons against people of color. Police target people of color and prisons fill with Black and brown men.

On top of this, police, prosecutors, and judges routinely treat migrants worse than citizens. Reviewing 7.8 million arrests in California and Texas from 2006 to 2018—every time a police officer in those states arrested an adult who they suspected of having committed a felony—researchers found that migrants were significantly more likely to be convicted and imprisoned than U.S. citizens arrested for the same crime and with similar criminal histories. That might not be surprising coming from Texas, where Republican politicians target migrants through laws like S.B. 4. But in California, where Democrats run state government, there's a well-organized and immense activist community that pushes for migrant-friendly policies and regularly wins. The criminal legal system is harsher on migrants in Texas than it is in California, but, even there, migrants can expect to get 13 percent longer sentences than citizens.[24]

Adding immigration consequences to the outcome of criminal proceedings at best requires that we stick our heads in the sand to ignore underlying biases. At worst, it means accepting the racial and citizenship fault lines of criminal legal proceedings. Tacking immigration imprisonment and deportation to the back end only augments the problem. Worse, casting immigration law consequences as the necessary byproduct of sound legal processes makes invisible the troubled dimensions of criminal law.

Policymakers in Washington almost never deal with this. Instead, they trot out the usual claim that targeting migrants who have been touched by the criminal legal system in some way makes the United States safer.

6

WEAPONIZING FAMILY TIES

The last time Colorado-born Neda Samimi-Gómez saw her father, in the summer of 2017, was for lunch at a Chick-fil-A in suburban Denver. Neda and her sister wanted to treat him to lunch, so they picked him up one afternoon and let him choose the destination. Her father, Kamyar Samimi, an Iranian citizen, said he wanted to go to some "Chick place," which Neda and her sister realized was Chick-fil-A. "This is the best chicken sandwich," she remembers Kamyar telling the restaurant employees. "He was so excited about this Chick-fil-A," she says. Remembering that lunch five years later, Neda laughs. It was just a normal Chick-fil-A sandwich, she says. There wasn't anything special about it. "That was just the passion he carried," she explained. To her father, anything could become extraordinary.

Neda didn't realize then that soon all she would have of her father were memories like this. After four decades in the United States, Immigration and Customs Enforcement agents would stop by Kamyar's house in November 2017 and take him to a private immigration prison outside of Denver. He was a lawful permanent resident so he had the government's permission to live and work in the United States, but a twelve-year-old drug possession conviction was enough to make him a target for ICE. Thanks to a law President Clinton signed in 1996, Kamyar's conviction made him detainable and potentially deportable.

It was just a couple weeks after Neda's twenty-fourth birthday when her father's friend and roommate called to tell her family that he'd been picked up by immigration agents. Neda knew next to nothing about immigration at the time. She hoped he'd be released soon but didn't know whether that was an option. It was. Immigration law treats convictions like the one her father had as relatively minor. It's not an aggravated felony. Instead, it's what lawyers call a controlled substance offense.

This is an important distinction. Anyone convicted of an aggravated felony is pretty much out of luck when it comes to getting out of immigration prison and escaping deportation. It's a twenty-one-part phrase that sounds sinister, but that, in addition to serious crimes like murder, includes offenses like forging a passport and failing to show up for court dates. Sprawling though the definition is, ICE is required to detain anyone convicted of an aggravated felony. Once in the immigration detention and deportation pipeline, most legal options for avoiding removal from the United States are off-limits.

It's a different story when it comes to drug crimes that immigration law defines as controlled substance offenses. Sometimes people with these crimes on their records aren't deportable at all. The rest of the time they are deportable, but immigration judges can grant a pardon called cancellation of removal. Just like it sounds, Congress gave immigration judges the power to cancel a migrant's removal from the United States. With that comes the power to release them from immigration prison.

The same day that ICE arrested Kamyar, the agency also filed papers with the local immigration court to begin a deportation case against him. Legally, he would've been able to go before an immigration judge and argue that he wasn't deportable or that he deserved to have his removal canceled. He's exactly the kind of person who's most likely to push back against ICE's claims, and most likely to win. Sixty-four years old by the time ICE arrested him, he'd spent two-thirds of his life in the United States with the government's permission. His children were here, as was a sister. There was nothing meaningful for him back in his native Iran.

What the law says is one thing. What's possible is another. In ICE's hands, Kamyar didn't survive long enough to wage the fight that immigration law says he could have. Arrested on November 17, he died in ICE's custody on December 2, fifteen days later. At the time, ICE issued a press release saying he died the same day he got sick. An internal investigation report that the agency released only after Neda sued tells a different story.[1] Kamyar entered the immigration prison fine. He told a prison nurse about drug problems he'd had in the past and explained that he took methadone every day to help control his addiction. Within hours of arriving, he began telling prison staff that he felt horrible.

From there things just got worse. Over the next five days, a nurse would note that he was shaking uncontrollably and having difficulty walking. The prison doctor spoke to nurses, but never stopped by to see Kamyar. By the end of his first week at the immigration prison he was crying out in pain. Unable to eat or drink normally, he was getting by on ice chips until the moment when he collapsed onto the floor of his cell unconscious. A nurse was able to get him back, but the nurse hadn't left his side when he lost consciousness a second time.

Again, the nurse brought him back to consciousness, then talked to him about the importance of drinking fluids and wrote in his medical file that he was "possibly drug-seeking." The nurse isn't even sure anyone called the doctor. He was hard to get a hold of by phone, the nurse told investigators.

A couple days later, Kamyar was still sick. Now he was having trouble speaking. Eleven days into his incarceration, he collapsed onto the hallway floor. Later that day he tried to kill himself. Guards and nurses stopped him before he could get far and put him on suicide watch. Two days after that, he asked for ice water and a nurse told him to drink from the sink.

On December 1, two weeks into his ordeal, a nurse saw him try to drink water out of the toilet. Still the prison doctor didn't see him. That night a guard noted that Kamyar appeared to be spitting up blood.

The morning of December 2, the day Kamyar finally died, he appeared in such bad shape that a guard took to checking to see if he was still breathing. Finally, a nurse decided to tell the doctor that Kamyar should go to the hospital. The doctor wasn't at the prison, so the nurse left messages on the doctor's cell phone and home phone. The doctor says he never got the messages.

A few minutes later, a supervisory guard looked into Kamyar's cell and saw him lying colorless, breathing heavily, and wet from his own urine. It was obvious he was in crisis, the guard recalled. He asked the nurse to call an ambulance, but when the nurse didn't, he issued the order himself.

Kamyar couldn't talk and couldn't sit. By then, guards wondered whether he was even breathing, but to ICE he was still a potential threat. They couldn't let him leave the prison without an armed escort. As a couple of ICE officers readied weapons to accompany Kamyar to the hospital, the ambulance EMTs arrived to find him without a pulse. His heartbeat had flat-lined. Kamyar was dying. Seventeen minutes after arriving at a nearby emergency room, Kamyar was pronounced dead.[2]

It took ICE two days to get in touch with Neda to give her the news. When I asked her whether she realized her father could be deported after ICE arrested him, she said she did. When I asked her if she thought he might die, her shoulders dropped like I'd just let out her spirit. "Why would that happen?" she asks me.

The news she got from ICE was matter-of-fact and logistical. The ICE officer wanted her address so they could send her Kamyar's belongings. "I don't remember the next four days. It was like I blacked out," she tells me. Five years later, when I spoke with her, Neda was still grieving her father.

ICE's press release lists Kamyar's crimes, but it didn't mention Neda, her sister, or her brother. It says he's an Iranian citizen, but it didn't mention Neda's aunt, Kamyar's sister, who also lives in Colorado. That's how it usually is. Political conversations about immigration policies routinely mention the targeted migrant only, and their sins—the criminal alien that politicians love to hate.

This is shortsighted. Like Kamyar Samimi, migrants form part of vibrant communities. Many migrants are married, have children, work, or go to school. Some have developed meaningful friendships in the United States. Others live alongside relatives. Whatever the specific circumstances, immigration policies that pluck migrants from their lives create a gap in social life. Children are left without a parent, spouses without a partner.

"He brought a lot of happiness and laughter to my life," Neda says. It's clear he still does. She hasn't forgotten his flaws. She's simply chosen to emphasize his ordinariness. "I honor my father by drinking a Pepsi because it was his favorite thing to drink," she says smiling.

In the first memory Neda has of her father she was three years old and dealing with one of those stomach viruses that every kid gets. Kamyar sat with her on the family's couch watching TV. "I barfed all over him," she told me, apologizing for the story's grossness. "He was so sweet, gentle, understanding, and helpful."

Harming Migrants

Speaking with Neda, I was struck by how open she was about Kamyar's flaws. Yet seeing him as the imperfect person he was doesn't stop her from seeing him as the only loving father she will ever have. Too often, politicians ignore the complicated web of relationships that migrants are part of when there's a criminal record to point to.

Efraín Romero de la Rosa had been in the United States since 2000 piling up a string of crimes. Struggling with acute schizophrenia, he bounced through Virginia's jails and prisons for many years, at one point even being declared mentally incompetent to help his own lawyers. Most of his crimes were low level, but a couple of carjackings in 2004 stand out. He was sentenced to fifteen and twenty years for those crimes, though he didn't serve the entire term. For several years he fell from police's radar. One day in 2018, he was picked up for larceny in Raleigh, North Carolina. After that, things went downhill. The judge sentenced him to the twenty-eight days he'd already spent in the Wake County jail waiting for the criminal case to end. Thanks to a 287(g) agreement, de la Rosa never left custody. He went from the county jail straight to the Stewart Detention Center. He predicted he would die there, telling mental health providers that he would be dead within three days and describing himself as the anti-Christ. It actually took four months from the time he arrived at Stewart, but de la Rosa indeed died. He'd been on suicide watch in the early part of his time at Stewart. At one point, facility staff even sent him to an outside center for inpatient treatment. When he returned, they sent him back to solitary confinement where it was easier to control his outbursts and keep track of his movements.[3]

We know that de la Rosa died on July 10, 2018, but we don't know the time. After ICE investigated the lead-up to de la Rosa's death, the agency realized that the security officer on duty signed a clipboard outside de la Rosa's cell three times claiming to have checked in on him. He hadn't. By the time the shift changed and the next security officer looked into the cell, the schizophrenic who had survived years of going in and out of state and county prisons and jails was hanging from socks wrapped around his neck.[4]

It happens this way too often. People spend years in the United States. A few weeks or months in ICE's custody, though, and they're dead. Like Kamyar, Efraín de la Rosa had relatives whom he left behind. "When they gave me the news, all of a sudden, the entire world collapsed," de la Rosa's brother Isaí Romero said.[5]

Political conversations about migrants who commit crimes paint a picture of a world that often doesn't exist: innocent victims tormented by maladjusted wrongdoers who don't have meaningful ties to the people left behind. Kamyar Samimi, Efraín de la Rosa, and the family members who loved them shatter that myth. Even pinning the dreaded moniker of "criminal alien" on a migrant doesn't erase their genuine ties to other people. Had they been deported, as was ICE's goal, the harm of their crimes wouldn't have been erased. Upon their deaths, the harm of their transgressions was augmented by the harm of ICE's involvement. Afterward, relatives were left to deal with the trauma of government negligence masquerading as legitimate law enforcement.

Terrorizing Families

Death is the extreme consequence of immigration policies, but imprisonment and forced removal are also hard on migrants' families and communities. Children in Iowa know this all too well. In rural Postville, hidden in the state's northeast corner, the Agriprocessors meatpacking plant once dominated the town's economy. In a town of two thousand, it employed around nine hundred people.[6] Owned by the Rubashkin family, Hasidic Jews who arrived in Postville in 1987 from Brooklyn, Agriprocessors was the largest kosher slaughterhouse in the United States in the early aughts. A region where Scandinavians had once dominated the workforce was, by the early twenty-first century, led by Jews who ran a butcher line staffed mostly by Mexicans and Guatemalans.

Around ten o'clock on the morning of May 12, 2008, almost nine hundred law enforcement agents, led by ICE, converged on the plant. From one side, they entered town in a long line of black SUVs. From the other side, they entered in buses promising "Homeland Security."[7] Decked out in black fatigues, carrying rifles, and wearing bulletproof vests, agents stormed the slaughterhouse while a Black Hawk helicopter circled overhead. Within minutes, 390 men, women, and teens—the unlucky morning shift—were arrested in the largest workplace immigration raid in recent memory, perhaps ever.[8]

Trained to kill cows, the slaughterhouse workers were instead rounded up like cattle. They would end up handcuffed and shackled by ICE agents. As armed officers poured into the plant, frantic parents and spouses called home and children hid under beds. "I started to cry because I was fifteen years old," Joel Rucal said about the moment when he got a call from his mom. She had already been arrested. Now it was up to Joel, who also worked at the plant but was home when the raid happened, to take care of his little sister.

Schools emptied out, sometimes quickly as frightened parents rushed to get their kids and sometimes slowly as parents who had been arrested wondered what would happen next from inside the National Cattle Congress, an enormous barn-like structure in Waterloo, seventy-five miles away, that had been turned into a makeshift jail and court. There they waited to be criminally prosecuted, all for crimes related to their immigration status. Most wouldn't wait long. Three days after the raid, federal prosecutors announced that 297 people arrested at the meatpacking plant had already pleaded guilty. Of those, 253 were convicted of using a false ID to get their job. Another thirty-two were convicted of using a fake social security number. The last dozen were convicted of illegal reentry.[9] When classes started up again in Postville, classrooms failed to fill.[10]

In an instant, Postville changed forever. To people in other parts of the United States, the town became a symbol of immigration policing overreach. But to Latines in Iowa, the raid was more personal, more direct, more impactful. After the shock came the trauma. In a detailed study comparing all children born in Iowa in the thirty-seven weeks before the raid to children born in the state in the thirty-seven weeks after the raid, a team of researchers from the University of Michigan found alarming signs. While Latinas who gave birth before the raid were just as likely to experience low birth weight and pre-term birth as white mothers, that changed almost immediately. After the raid, low-birth-weight rates continued to improve for white women, but for Latinas, things got worse, and it didn't matter whether they were born in the United States or not. Targeting Latin American migrants is tough on Latinas even if they're U.S. citizens, it turns out.[11]

Trauma doesn't understand citizenship. By targeting the Agriprocessors meatpacking plant, ICE didn't turn loose the violence of an armed raid in which parents are swept into waiting buses and children left to fend for themselves on just the people violating immigration law. Everyone in town felt it, but for Latinas and their babies it turned into a health risk. Immigration law can say that U.S. citizens are immune from ICE's tactics, but in the aftermath of the Postville raid it became clear that Latina U.S. citizens in Iowa weren't so sure.

Separating Families

Immigration policing would become a source of terror for families again in the summer of 2018 when Trump's family separation policy erupted onto a global stage. Early that summer, Efrén Olivares, a civil rights lawyer in the Río Grande Valley of South Texas, began to hear about adults showing up in federal court claiming that U.S. officials had taken their kids away. Officers in green uniforms told them they would see their kids again after returning from court, Olivares was hearing repeatedly. When the parents returned from being prosecuted for illegal entry or reentry, the kids were nowhere to be found. Some of the people he spoke with didn't know who the people in green were, but Olivares did: Border Patrol. "The agents had led virtually all the parents to believe that they had been separated because their children couldn't come to court, and that once their court appearance was over, they would be reunited," Olivares recalled in a memoir.[12]

Through Facebook feeds dispatched from shaky cell phones outside the federal courthouse, Olivares and his colleagues alerted the world about the trauma they were seeing. In the name of prosecuting immigration crime, Trump administration officials were taking kids from their parents. Antonio Bol Paau, from Guatemala, told Olivares he had been ushered into a jail cell while his son was kept outside. By the time he left the cell, his son was gone, and agents were only willing to tell him they'd see each other tomorrow.[13] Over and over again, tomorrow came, but his son did not. Sometimes agents just lied. It was easier that way.

Things could get ugly if migrants figured out what was happening. Marco Antonio Muñoz figured it out. With his wife Orlanda, Muñoz had spent several years in North Carolina, where the couple married and their oldest son was born. Eventually, though, they returned to Honduras to be closer to family. For a time, things appear to have been fine. Their younger son—known in court papers only as D.M.A.—was born during the family's time there. But by 2018, six years after returning to Honduras, they no longer felt safe. Early that year, Orlanda's brother was murdered. In an interview she gave police officers in Texas months later, she blamed a drug gang linked to the town mayor and said that men in masks began following Marco. Whatever the details, it was enough to scare Marco and Orlanda. They didn't want to be next. They didn't want their boys to be next.

The couple left Honduras again, this time with their kids. From Reynosa, just across the border from McAllen, Texas, they put their oldest son on a plane to North Carolina. It was safer this way. More important, as a U.S. citizen, it was possible. Neither Marco, Orlanda, nor their youngest son, just three years old at the time, could go with him. To outsiders, this kind of family separation is just the unavoidable consequence of immigration law doing what it does. To migrant families, though, it's a routine form of brutality.

Instead of flying with their oldest son, just outside of Reynosa, Marco, Orlanda, and their youngest waded across the Río Grande into Texas. They didn't have a choice. If they'd walked across the bridge, even to request asylum, CBP officers would've turned them back immediately. Instead, like many Central American families crossing into South Texas over the last decade, they soon found Border Patrol agents.

Despite having a history in North Carolina, a U.S. citizen son there, and a legitimate fear of death if sent back to Honduras, Border Patrol agents—trained to see everything through the lens of crime-fighting—turned to the power of criminal law. Agents at the Border Patrol station in McAllen separated Marco from his family and, following the Trump administration's policy in the spring and summer of 2018, they told him that he would be prosecuted for illegal entry. Marco would only see his wife and son twice more: once for fingerprinting and another time because he pleaded with agents. He couldn't hug the three-year-old because his hands were handcuffed to the back of a chair, so Orlanda held the child on Marco's lap, she later told police investigators.

Perhaps sensing what the rest of us would soon learn was happening as a matter of official policy, after Border Patrol agents released the handcuffs, Marco did not go quietly. When agents tried to take the boy, the father held on as if his life depended on it. Maybe it did. "The guy lost his shit," a Border Patrol agent said. Agents ripped the boy out of the arms of his visibly distraught father, then dragged Marco away from Orlanda and D.M.A., the family later claimed in a lawsuit. The agent agreed. "They had to use physical force to take the child out of his hands." [14]

After that, Marco fell apart. Seeing that he was not well, agents decided to transfer him to the Starr County Jail, forty miles away in Río Grande City. McAllen isn't in Starr County—it's in neighboring Hidalgo County, which has two of the region's major population centers and its own jail—but that's where they sent him anyway. To get there, agents had to take the single highway that connects McAllen to Río Grande City. This is a stretch of road that I know well. From the Border Patrol station, it's not far to South Texas Health System or Río Grande Regional Hospital, two hospitals that stare at each other from across a street. Both can deal with trauma. Doctors and nurses at both helped my father many times more than a decade ago when his health was worsening. The agents transporting Marco didn't stop there. Along the way, they had to pass the Mission Regional Medical Center, whose emergency department also boasts a trauma center. They didn't bother to stop there either.

That was never their plan. Instead, on May 12, 2018, one day after Marco and his family reached Texas, where they'd hoped to find safety, Border Patrol agents left him at the Starr County Jail. Sheriff's deputies there put Marco inside a padded cell equipped with a surveillance camera, but they didn't seek psychiatric care. The next day, Marco was dead, having strangled himself with a sweater.[15] According to the jail guard that found him, no one bothered to give Marco first aid. "If Muñoz appears to be dead, then don't move him," the deputy who found him told state police investigators he was instructed.[16] Dead within a day of coming into contact with Border Patrol agents, Marco was never even charged by prosecutors with the crime that immigration officials used to justify taking him away from his family.

Throughout the spring and early summer of 2018, as Border Patrol agents were putting Marco and Orlanda through misery, the federal government couldn't even agree on what was happening. Just days before Marco's death, Trump's attorney general at the time, the longtime immigration hardliner Jeff Sessions, declared, "If you cross this border unlawfully, then we will prosecute you. It's that simple." More ominously, he added, "If you are smuggling a child, then we will prosecute you and that child will be separated from you."[17] Meanwhile, his counterpart at DHS, Secretary of Homeland Security Kirstjen Nielsen, was busy claiming nothing unusual was happening. As late as mid-June, six weeks after Sessions laid out the administration's policy in the clearest of terms and more than five weeks after Marco had his three-year-old son ripped out of his arms, Nielsen took to Twitter, writing,

"We do not have a policy of separating families at the border. Period." The journalists, lawyers, and members of Congress pointing to what everyone could see weren't just wrong. They were "irresponsible and unproductive," she added.[18]

Soon even Nielsen had to bend to reality. Every day, more parents were being hauled into federal courtrooms in McAllen asking about their children. Over 2,700 immigration prosecutions in one week alone nationwide, a senior DHS official boasted in late May.[19] In that corner of the United States, usually far from the attention of anyone who doesn't have ties to the region, the federal government's family-separation policy was a real-life horror film that took 3,925 kids away from their parents before it was all over.[20] It was a policy meant to exploit the family ties that bring the most meaning to many of us and twist them into vulnerabilities that push pain deep into the bones. We all have families. Most of us can imagine that being separated from our families would rip apart our hearts and terrorize our minds, snatching from us "all that makes life worth living," as the Supreme Court Justice Louis Brandeis wrote about the stakes of immigration enforcement in 1922 and that his colleagues have been quoting ever since.[21]

Clearly Marco suffered a level of pain that I can't imagine and that I pray I never will. But the pain didn't end with him. His wife, Orlanda, and their son felt it too. Accompanied by the local consul for Honduras, Orlanda and the three-year-old saw Marco for the last time at a funeral home. They stood beside the casket, crying. Afterward, with an electronic bracelet wrapped around Orlanda's ankle, they headed north to reunite with the couple's U.S. citizen son.[22]

Trump's policy of separating families is in the past, but the trauma that Orlanda and her children suffered remains in the present. The ordeal of being separated, even from one parent, leaves kids to suffer academically and emotionally for years, maybe forever. "Highly stressful experiences, like family separation, can cause irreparable harm, disrupting a child's brain architecture and affecting his or her short- and long-term health," the president of the American Academy of Pediatrics said.[23] The reasons are different, but, for Marco's children, losing a parent in the government's zeal to police immigration is like losing a parent to criminal incarceration, a context in which the effects of family separation are well known. "Why punish the children?" a landmark study about incarcerated mothers and their children asked in 1978.[24]

The family's ordeal was made more tragic by the fact that it was so easily avoidable. There was no need to separate Marco from his wife and son. This was a family returning to a place they had once called home. If Border Patrol agents had asked if they feared for their lives in Honduras, they might have learned about Orlanda's brother and his death at the hands of drug traffickers. Instead, agents said that Orlanda would stay with the couple's three-year-old while Marco was sent away for prosecution. In the eyes of U.S. immigration law, he was a criminal, the agents announced, and it was the policy of the federal government to send every single person caught entering the United States without the federal government's permission to federal prosecutors "without exception," as Jeff Sessions promised in 2017.[25]

Fueling Instability

Conversations about immigration law frequently imagine that deportation is the end: the final step in a legitimate legal process. The reality is more complicated. For people removed from the United States, deportation is only one punishment among many. It's common for their citizenship to be overpowered by their deportation from the United States. In Haiti, for example, deported migrants were for many years taken from the airport to a police station and from there to prison. Sometimes they were released within hours or days. Other times they were left to fend for themselves in crowded, decrepit cells, either because authorities had decided they were dangerous or because they didn't have anyone to take them in.[26] In the Dominican Republic, police officers met deported migrants at the airport, then transported them to police headquarters for questioning. Most people would be released after a night. Despite that short stay, they would remain on the police's radar, and police admitted to viewing them suspiciously. "Whenever there is a crime in an area where we have deportees, we begin interrogating them," the director of the country's Department for Deportees once explained.[27]

Even when the local police don't treat returned migrants so harshly, it's often still hard to build a stable life. Some people tap their English skills and cultural fluency to find work in tourism or answering customer-service calls from the United States. A man with a wife and three kids in Manhattan who had been deported to the Dominican Republic told researchers that he hustled to do errands for English-speaking tourists.

On a good day he could make as much as $20.[28] In Mexico, call centers recruit people who speak English natively and understand U.S. cultural norms. Most people who fit this description have lived in the United States for many years. Many would still be there had they not been deported. Instead, they turn to office jobs that at $60 to $300 per week make it hard to rebuild a life.[29] Under these circumstances, deportation simply plants migrants in fertile ground for launching a return journey to the United States. Having already been deported, they will have to come back without the government's permission, committing the crime of illegal reentry the second they step across the border.

Attending a Mexico City conference in 2023 about Mexican citizens deported from the United States, an audience member who acknowledged going in and out of U.S. prisons before being deported turned to listing the many family members he left behind in California. His mother, a sister, children, and more. "Obviously I had to return," he said in the distinctive English of L.A. Chicanos.

Cross-border ties tainted by U.S. immigration policies have taken a particularly deadly turn in parts of Central America. In their intimate biography of powerhouse transnational gang Mara Salvatrucha 13, journalist brothers Óscar Martínez and Juan José Martínez follow the group's birth and development across cities whose names today reflect their centuries of intertwined history. From Los Angeles to San Salvador and all points in-between, MS-13's growth is the story of U.S. involvement in El Salvador's civil war, urban chaos in California, and the War on Drugs euphoria that saw in every problem policing as the best solution. In the late 1980s and 1990s, around the time Wynnie Goodwin moved to California, young people fleeing wartime violence in El Salvador began organizing themselves into small groups in L.A.: *clicas* they're called in Spanish. In search of comfort and security, some eventually formed the MS-13 and got involved with the booming drug trade. Led by the Reagan administration, deportation became policymakers' chosen remedy for migrants caught up in this deadly mix.

A short-sighted embrace of policing planted the seeds of instability and another round of migration decades later. "The gang's rise was a misfire by U.S. officials that thought that deportation could solve their problems. They thought that they were spitting out, but really, they were spitting into the air above them," the Martínez brothers write.[30] Deported to El Salvador while it was still struggling to rebuild after years of fighting, these youths had little to fall on except each other and little to do except tell stories of California. There was Mauricio Solano, dubbed Ozi in honor of heavy metal celebrity Ozzy Osbourne, who joined a *clica* based near L.A.'s famous MacArthur Park. After his deportation in 1991, he became one of MS-13's first leaders.[31] José Antonio Terán was a member of the U.S.-backed National Police in El Salvador who fled the war in which he fought. He joined MS-13 in California's San Fernando Valley. After his deportation, he started the Hollywood Locos Salvatrucha clica.[32] And there's El Diablito—the Little Devil—who was born in San Salvador as Borromeo Henríquez Solórzano but raised in Los Angeles. There he joined the Hollywood Locos clica. Also deported in the 1990s, he rose through the gang's ranks, becoming such a key figure that in 2013 the U.S. Treasury froze his assets. Rooted in California and exported to El Salvador, the transnational violence that they experienced as young people in war-weary El Salvador, then in gang-torn California, helped launch a transnational menace.

Despite those clear ties between the social fault lines of California a few decades ago and the violence that constantly rattles Central America today, politicians in the United States insist on more of the same. "Central American gangs, such as Mara Salvatrucha and the 18th Street Gang, largely serve as cross-border couriers, smuggling drugs and people" into the United States, Biden's secretary of homeland security, Alejandro Mayorkas, told Congress.[33] In his trademark viciousness, Trump described gang members as animals.[34] Obama took a softer tone, but he also emphasized their crimes while ignoring their humanity. As sound bites, these are powerful tactics. But as policy, continuing to deport gang members just as we have done in the past means that the future of immigration policy is likely to look a lot like the present. "The MS-13 is the product of those who chose deportation without knowing that history does not stop when someone is no longer in their country," the Martínez brothers wrote.[35]

In recent years, the gang that Ozi, El Diablito, and others built after their deportation from the United States has become motivation, at least in part, for many Central Americans to uproot. If they can't find safety or a future for their children in Guatemala, El Salvador, or Honduras, they are willing to head north with the hope that there they might breathe a bit more easily. In these new migrants, U.S. immigration policies of the past repeat themselves. The violence of 1980s drug policing becomes the violence of 1990s gang-member deportations, which then becomes the twenty-first-century violence of MS-13 attacks and forced displacement.

At the U.S. border and in communities throughout the United States, this new group of Central American migrants are met by the enormous policing apparatus that led to the earlier round of deportations. It's a cyclical pattern documented by academics and journalists, but that policymakers seem allergic to. Instead, they continue to cling to the possibility—a myth, really—that illegality says something about a person's soul, and to the fantasy that deporting migrants who commit crime removes a problem without creating a new one. It doesn't now, and it never has.

7

ALTERNATIVE FUTURES

Five days before Marco Antonio Muñoz died in the Starr County Jail, Jeff Sessions stood in front of a crowd of Border Patrol agents within sight of Tijuana and declared, "We are not going to let this country be overwhelmed." With the steel pillars of the border wall behind him, the top Justice Department official at the time continued, "We need legality and integrity in the system."[1]

Five years later, Biden's secretary of homeland security, Alejandro Mayorkas, announced that DHS would bring illegal reentry cases against people who hoped to request asylum in the United States if they didn't start the application process from abroad, putting in place a narrow interpretation of federal law that Trump imagined doing but never got off the ground. "We are a nation of immigrants. We are also a nation of laws," Mayorkas said.[2]

Sessions and Mayorkas are correct that the United States needs legality and integrity. But the trauma of separating families for the sake of prosecuting parents doesn't magically create legality and integrity. The legal system can bulldoze over people searching for safety, but when it does it creates a mountain of rubble out of the very credibility it relies on. Sessions and his collaborators in the Trump administration seem to have forgotten that. Or maybe they never cared to begin with. Perhaps to them, immigration law enforcement is just a hammer wielded by the strongest person standing. Mayorkas and his colleagues in the Biden administration put a nicer sheen on their approach, but even they seem to forget that when the law clashes with the complicated realities that spur people to migrate, it's the law that should change, not the people.

Boosting Legitimacy

Political conversations about immigration law often rest on an unstated assumption that migrants will violate the law if given the chance. That's why we need to spend billions of dollars every year staffing Immigration and Customs Enforcement and the Border Patrol, equipping them with fancy computers, arming them with powerful guns, and paying for jails and prisons where they can send the targets of their attention. But the premise isn't true. Most people try to comply with the law most of the time. All of us fail to do so some of the time. Some of us own up to it. Most of us don't.

People generally decide to comply with a law when the process the government uses to enact and enforce the law seems just. Academics steeped in a field called law and society refer to this as procedural justice. Basically, it means that people decide whether to comply with a law by gauging whether the process seems just. That's probably why the most thorough and influential study about procedural justice has a straightforward title: *Why People Obey the Law*. Its author, Tom Tyler, interviewed almost 1,600 people in Chicago in the mid-1980s, then followed up with about half of them. He wanted to figure out whether people's interactions with legal authorities altered their decision to obey or disobey the law. As the book's title suggests, it does. In Tyler's words, "People obey the law because they believe that it is proper to do so, they react to their experiences by evaluating their justice or injustice, and in evaluating the justice of their experiences they consider factors unrelated to outcome, such as whether they have had a chance to state their case and been treated with dignity and respect."[3]

Tyler's findings show that people engage in normative judgments when interacting with the law and legal authorities. If they believe that the law is just and legal authorities act fairly, most people, most of the time, will simply comply with the law without the need for enforcement. They'll do what's expected without having to be watched.

This holds true across a range of contexts. Tyler's study asked Chicagoans about a narrow set of crimes: speeding, parking violations, excessive noise, littering, shoplifting, and drunk driving. Since then, other studies have tested Tyler's findings in other contexts and found pretty much the same thing. People are more likely to pay their taxes if they can tell IRS officials their side of the story and if the IRS officials seem to care about them and their concerns.[4] Perhaps more surprising, men accused of domestic violence were less likely to have police called on them again if the first time around the police treated them fairly. Fair treatment is at least as important as how long they're detained, researcher Raymond Paternoster and his colleagues found. In the somewhat surprised tone of their academic article, "it would appear that being treated fairly does indeed matter."[5]

Thanks to legal scholar and sociologist Emily Ryo, we know that fairness also matters in immigration. The law might say they're aliens, but, when it comes to following the law, it turns out that migrants act a lot like other humans. They make normative judgments about fairness. To try to figure out why people might head to the United States without authorization—that is, why they might choose to commit the crime of illegal entry—Ryo asked a group of Mexicans about their thoughts on U.S. border policing and the morality of violating immigration law. In part, her work tests the frequent claim made by politicians that migrants undergo a cost–benefit analysis. The risk of getting caught crossing the border weighed against the possibility of higher earnings, safety, or a life with relatives already in the United States if they make it through. Raising the cost of migration was one of the reasons Secretary of Labor James Davis rallied behind Blease's proposal back in 1929, and it's the centerpiece of the Border Patrol's Consequence Delivery System more recently. It's still attractive to politicians. For decades, Republicans and Democrats have pushed hard to increase the cost of unauthorized crossing by paying for more Border Patrol agents, walls, prosecutions, and detention beds. Their goal is to raise the cost of crossing.

Ryo's research shows that people don't take such a simple approach to deciding whether they will uproot themselves by becoming migrants. It's not that migrants don't care about the costs of migration. They do consider the emotional cost of leaving relatives behind, the financial cost of paying for a coyote to smuggle them across the border, and the potential safety cost that comes with a trek that can involve physical violence, even death. Doña Francis knew that the journey would be difficult for her and her young daughter, my friend Pati, and her voice still breaks when talking about it. Like for Doña Francis, for many of the Mexicans Ryo spoke with these aren't hypothetical considerations. They know people who have gone before them, so they realize that it's a dangerous journey, but it's not out of reach.[6] Doña Francis, for example, knew she could count on her friend's brother to help them reach the life she dreamed of.

Alongside the costs of migration, though, Ryo found that Mexicans also consider the morality of heading to the United States. These are "moral agents," she writes, who think about U.S. immigration law in much the same way as Chicagoans do about the criminal laws Tyler asked about. Fairness matters. Mexicans who believe that U.S. immigration agents treat Mexicans fairly are more likely to say that the United States can legitimately limit immigration and substantially less likely to believe that it's okay for Mexicans to violate U.S. immigration law. On the flip side, Mexicans who think that U.S. immigration agents treat dark-skinned migrants worse than light-skinned migrants are almost twice as likely to say that Mexicans have a right to be in the United States in violation of U.S. immigration law. What doesn't seem to affect Mexicans' thoughts about violating U.S. immigration law is how likely they are to get caught or what will happen to them if they are.[7]

Putting it differently, the way that U.S. immigration agents treat Mexicans affects how Mexicans view the legitimacy of U.S. immigration laws. Treat people well and they're more likely to comply. Treat them poorly and they will ignore your wishes. Toss all your balls into the immigration-policing bucket, featuring police agents, criminal prosecutions, prisons, and deportation, and you're certain to spend a lot of money, but you're probably not going to do much to keep people from coming to the United States.

Politicians can try to criminalize and deport their way to controlling migrants by ratcheting up the pain of violating immigration law, but this is nothing more than a fantasy. In an earlier study, Ryo mined government records from 1882 to 1943 during the era of Chinese exclusion and came to much the same conclusion. Many Chinese viewed U.S. laws barring their entry as repugnant and offensive. Today, we would say that they viewed these laws as racist. Because many Chinese saw these laws as immoral, they didn't have qualms violating them. Chinese political powerbrokers in the United States criticized the laws. Diplomats representing the Chinese government complained through formal channels. Ordinary Chinese migrants weren't especially keen on the laws either. Despite the registration requirement being well known in Chinese communities, the majority of Chinese failed to heed this command.

When they were caught violating the exclusion laws, many fought back in court. They didn't so much deny that they crossed the border. Instead, they sometimes claimed to be U.S. citizens or challenged the fairness of the immigration process; for example, by demanding access to lawyers. Other times they asked to be sent back to Mexico or Canada, from which they had entered the United States, presumably because they knew that it wouldn't take much to return, irritating people like Albert Johnson, who lived near the Canadian border in Washington State and would later team up with Coleman Blease in Congress.[8] Like with Mexicans a century later, Chinese during these decades thought that it was perfectly fine to make use of the options available to evade the immoral treatment they would almost certainly receive at the hands of U.S. immigration authorities. And so they did.

Treating people poorly isn't the only way to destroy the legitimacy of a set of laws. It's also possible to do that by sending mixed signals about what the law is supposed to accomplish. Take theft as an example. Everyone agrees that theft is a crime. But what about deportation that follows a conviction for theft? Is that punishment? The courts say it's not. Going back more than a century, courts claim that deportation is just about ensuring that people are on the side of the border where they belong. In 1893, when Fong Yue Ting challenged the Chinese registration requirement imposed by the exclusion laws, the Supreme Court declared that deportation removes people from the United States "without any punishment being imposed or contemplated."[9]

Under this view, which remains the law today, deportation isn't legally a question of morality. ICE and Customs and Border Protection aren't authorized to deport people because

Congress has decided it's right to punish them for violating immigration law. Instead, legally, removal is a question of organizing people on the face of a planet almost entirely divided into distinct countries. People have to be somewhere, and U.S. immigration law just reflects who Congress thinks should be in the United States and who should not. When immigration agents force people out of the United States, they are simply moving people around the map, like pieces on a chessboard. This isn't right or wrong, courts would have us think. It's just the way the game of life is played in the modern world.

Migrants understandably disagree. If a conviction leads to deportation, it's hard not to feel that the inability to live in the place you call home, see the people you love, and continue working at the job you've been doing isn't punishment. That's exactly what migrants and their families say repeatedly, no matter how much the courts say otherwise. By blurring the divide between criminal law and civil administrative law, the current reliance on criminal activity to trigger immigration law consequences damages the legal system's credibility. In the words of scholars Paul Robinson and John Darley, blurring the boundary between criminal law and civil law is nothing short of "foolish." [10] It's illogical. "Every one knows that to be forcibly taken away from home and family and friends and business and property, and sent across the ocean to a distant land, is punishment, and that oftentimes most severe and cruel," Supreme Court Justice David Brewer wrote in his dissenting opinion in Fong Yue Ting's case. [11]

For a migrant convicted of theft, it's not the jail sentence or fine that's hardest to swallow. Often, it's the deportation that follows. Judge Learned Hand understood this. Thirteen years before Louis Loftus Repouille killed his son, the judge weighed in on the case of Walter Klonis. Born in Poland, Klonis arrived in the United States at ten years old. Eventually, he learned English and spent some time working as a carpenter. He also seems to have busied himself with thievery. Twice he was convicted of burglary. After his second conviction, immigration agents caught up with him and started the deportation process. Learned Hand would have none of it.

It's bad enough to deport someone who spent the bulk of their life in the United States, the judge wrote on behalf of his colleagues on the federal appellate court in New York. But it's worse to deport someone with a criminal record. No matter the migrant's background, "deportation is to him exile, a dreadful punishment," Learned Hand explained. "Such, indeed, it would be to any one, but to one already proved to be incapable of honest living, a helpless waif in a strange land, it will be utter destruction." [12]

Wynnie Goodwin felt this way. When prosecutors in Orange County charged her with attempted murder, she wasn't happy about pleading guilty. Her lawyer told her it was a lot better than the alternative, life in prison, and she agreed. Even after the judge sentenced her to twelve years in prison, Wynnie was willing to accept how things had turned out. She knew prison time was likely, so she didn't complain. Imprisonment is an accepted form of punishment. It signals to the person locked up that they can't be trusted and to others that this person is dangerous. It says that what the prisoner did was so wrong that they have to be removed from social life.

There are a lot of criticisms to be lodged against punishment through imprisonment, and legal scholars, geographers, sociologists, criminologists, and more make them regularly. My bookshelves are lined with examples, some of which I've made too. We don't buy the reasoning, but we all agree that criminal punishment is a common justification for incarceration.

None of this is what got to Wynnie. What really upset her, and what she came to fear most, was the deportation she faced. Had she known that pleading guilty meant possibly never living with her family again, Wynnie would've gone to trial. Had she known that admitting she'd tried to kill those two girls might mean she'd be sent to a country she'd left long before she learned to walk, she wouldn't have signed the plea deal. At least then she would've forced the prosecutor to prove the case against her and maybe lucked out with a skeptical jury.

To Wynnie, deportation wasn't just any punishment that she didn't have to like but was willing to accept after being convicted of two crimes. It was the worst of all possible outcomes. It was certainly a far worse punishment than the incarceration that the judge sentenced her to. Insisting that deportation to Vietnam, a country she can't be said to have ever known, was just sending her where she rightfully belongs is ludicrous. Blocking immigration agents' attempt to deport Walter Klonis, Learned Hand wrote, "He knows no other language, no other people, no other habits, than ours." For that reason, "deportation is to him exile, a dreadful punishment."[13] Surely Wynnie would agree.

When I asked Wynnie what would've happened if she'd

been deported like an immigration judge said she should be, she paused. "A lot of things could've gone wrong," she answered, before adding, "I would've found a way to survive." It was a more positive answer than I expected. It would've been hard, but she's convinced she would've made it. Maybe she's right. She did, after all, put together a successful career and build a happy family in the United States, even after years in prison. But it's a roll of the dice that I'm sure she's glad she didn't have to make.

So long as courts continue to insist that immigration law doesn't punish, they send the message that what matters is the law as it's written not the law as it's lived. This is a myth embedded into immigration law that has harsh consequences for migrants and harsh consequences for the legitimacy of the legal system. Unhinged from reality, the entire set of laws that enforce immigration law's claim that the punishment ended the day a migrant walked out of jail loses credibility. And laws that rely on myths are laws that aren't defensible.

Burying Blease

To create a set of immigration laws that match the world that exists we need to begin disentangling criminal law and immigration law. Instead of hammering hard on people when they mess up, we can imagine an immigration law framework that tries to keep people from violating immigration law in the first place. That begins with the easy options. People don't commit illegal entry because they want to. My friend Pati didn't walk across the mountains near Tijuana for fun. I've never met a client who swam across the Río Grande to avoid standing in the hot sun waiting their turn to speak to a CBP agent at an official crossing. "They want to do things right, but they're not allowed," a journalist wrote in the spring of 2023 about Venezuelans trying to navigate a smartphone app that CBP demands they use.[14]

Migrants violate immigration law by sneaking into the United States clandestinely because there isn't a better alternative. The international boundary between Mexico and the United States is so dangerous to cross that the superstar band Los Tigres del Norte describe it as "la tumba del mojado," the unauthorized migrant's tomb. The band's members, some of whom violated immigration law at one time or another, know this. Ordinary migrants do too. People are willing to run the risk because staying put isn't really an option. In 2021, as the Biden administration flew airplanes into Port-au-Prince full of people recently caught trying to enter the United States, the head of Haiti's migration office described their future in the simplest way. "For these people, Haiti is hell," Jean Negot Bonheur Delva said.[15]

Congress should begin transforming immigration law by putting Coleman Blease to rest. The only way to do that is by erasing his legacy from immigration law: illegal entry and illegal reentry. If Congress repealed those laws and did nothing more, DHS would continue to have at its disposal the convoluted set of laws that dictate who can come to the United States and under what conditions they can be deported. Violating immigration law could still lead to deportation, but at least Blease and his racist law would finally rest in the dustbin of history in which it belongs.

Once Blease's handiwork is pushed firmly into the past, Congress can turn toward more recent additions to immigration law. To avoid police forces becoming adjuncts of federal immigration authorities, as Texas chiefs of police feared when the state legislature was debating S.B. 4, Congress should delete from the Immigration and Nationality Act another key provision: section 287(g), which regularly funnels people from ordinary interactions with local police into life-altering problems with ICE. By eliminating the legislative authorization for state and local law enforcement to work hand-in-hand with federal immigration agencies, Congress would put a stop to situations in which mundane infractions become years-long ordeals that affect migrants, traumatize their families, and leave communities struggling to fill gaps created from one day to the next.

It's also up to Congress to remove the many tentacles of immigration law that make deportation upon conviction for many crimes "virtually inevitable," as the Supreme Court explained in José Padilla's case.[16] All of the laws that Congress enacted in the 1980s and 1990s made it easy to fall into the immigration prison and deportation pipeline and hard to get out. It doesn't make much sense to argue that the reason to deport migrants who commit a crime is to make the United States safer. That's what the police, prosecutors, and criminal courts are supposed to do. If the enormous, well-financed criminal legal system treats someone like Sandra Castañeda or Wynnie Goodwin as capable of living in the community, modern immigration law should too. Let's let Sandra focus on rebuilding her life, and let's let Wynnie focus on her flourishing career.

Congress certainly has an important role to play, but so do the executive branch agencies that create most of immigration policy: DHS and the Justice Department. As ICE and CBP's parent agency, stripping away criminal policing's influence on immigration policy will only come courtesy of significant changes at Homeland Security. DHS's law enforcement network is massive. Through CBP it reaches across the southwestern border and through ICE into cities throughout the nation's interior. Through its partnerships with private data brokers, it touches every other aspect of ordinary life—from driver's license records to home utility payments. As long as Congress continues to shower DHS with lavish funding, the agency is certain to continue expanding its policing practices.

The moment Congress begins to cut back the department's funding, though, it will have to scale back. Tech companies don't work for free. Palantir and Amazon aren't interested in partnering with DHS out of a commitment to the public good. These aren't social ventures. These are business deals. They are interested in making money. Lots and lots of money. Cut the amount of money DHS has available to share with these profit-hungry businesses, and suddenly the department will find itself with fewer friends. Without generous congressional support, the "immigration industrial complex," as the sociologist Tanya Golash-Boza describes the network of government agencies and private companies that collaborate to identify and deport migrants, would collapse.[17]

Whatever the specific initiative, ICE continues to rely heavily on local police to feed it the names, addresses, and bodies of people who might be removable from the United States. Making a pitch for more cooperation with ICE, Biden's secretary of homeland security, Alejandro Mayorkas, painted ICE as a reformed agency. He didn't mention Trump, but he didn't have to. "ICE, the agency of today and what it is focused upon, and what it is doing, is not the agency of the past," Mayorkas told a gathering of city mayors in January 2021, one year into the Biden presidency. "We are not engaged in indiscriminate enforcement, but we are focused on making our communities safe," he assured the city leaders. As proof, Mayorkas pointed to a memo he released on September 30, 2021, instructing ICE and CBP to target people "who present a current public safety threat, a threat to national security, or a threat to our border security." We can imagine that Sandra Castañeda, Wynnie Goodwin, José Padilla, and Kamyar Samimi might all have committed the crimes that Mayorkas's memo placed in DHS's sights. Marco Antonio Muñoz certainly fits the border security threat that the memo lists. No one else, Mayorkas claimed, would be the focus of DHS's attention.[18]

What Mayorkas failed to mention was that his memo was already mired in litigation. Republican-led Texas and Louisiana claimed that the memo's enforcement focus violated immigration law. They wanted DHS to target anyone convicted of a much broader range of crimes. "The core of the dispute is whether the Executive Branch may require its officials to act in a manner that conflicts with a statutory mandate imposed by Congress," Trump appointee Judge Drew Tipton wrote in his opinion's first paragraph. Clearly DHS can't force its staff to violate federal laws, so after starting like this no one should've been surprised about the judge's answer: "It may not." [19] Almost two years after Mayorkas released it, the memo was still on hold. It would take a Supreme Court decision in June 2023 before DHS could put Mayorkas's memo into effect. [20]

Just as Judge Tipton delayed the Biden administration from reorienting its immigration prosecutorial priorities for almost two years, the courts have an important role to play in taking criminality out of immigration matters. During the worst days of the pandemic, courts repeatedly caught ICE and its lawyers in the Justice Department lying about the need to imprison migrants in the name of public safety. Since then, the Justice Department has insisted that Blease's law isn't permanently stained by his racism and the hatred of Mexicans that motivated many of his colleagues in Congress.

Advocates have started challenging the constitutionality of illegal entry and reentry, claiming that they discriminate illegally. So far, they have run into an unsurprising roadblock: judges blind to the real-world consequences of immigration law. Congress revamped all of immigration law in 1952. By then, Blease was dead and almost everyone who had voted on his bill was gone. New representatives and senators filled their seats. The newer law wasn't "tainted" by the earlier one simply because the 1952 Congress didn't distance itself from its 1929 version, the U.S. Court of Appeals for the Ninth Circuit concluded in May 2023. Though the text of Blease's law has changed slightly over the decades, it has never mentioned race explicitly, so proving that it is unconstitutionally racist requires more than showing that it was enacted by members of Congress who regularly used racist language, who denigrated Mexicans, and who even overrode President Truman's veto of a different law that he described as racist. Congress is owed a "presumption of legislative good faith," the court added, so Blease's bill will fall only if the last time that Congress revisited it legislators kept it on the books for the purpose of discriminating.[21]

The court's reasoning misreads how members of Congress operate. Why would they bother to add a racist endorsement of a law that already exists? Instead of shielding the legal vestiges of our nation's richly racist past under the cloak of a presumption of good faith, courts should look closely at the goals those policymakers talked about repeatedly and explicitly, skeptically analyzing the impact those laws have on the criminalization of migrants of color now.

And finally, it's long past time for the Supreme Court to revisit the laughably false claim that deportation isn't punishment. Anyone who has ever talked with a migrant ripped from their home, separated from their family, and denied access to their job knows that it is. When they deny what everyone can see, judges and DHS officials look like they live in a fantasyland, and a legal system made of fantasies is a legal system that can only be defended by the thumping of boots and the slamming of prison doors. Policing immigration law through violence has never been good at boosting compliance. All that it does is weaken the legitimacy of the laws one strong-armed police operation at a time.

Difficult as it may seem, it is possible to disentangle

immigration law from criminal law. I know it is, because almost everything I'm suggesting has been done. Before Blease's law was enacted in 1929, there were no prosecutions for illegal entry or reentry because it wasn't a crime to enter the United States without the government's permission. From then until the end of George W. Bush's presidency, the former INS mostly ignored immigration law violations or put people through the immigration court system rather than flag them for criminal prosecution. In 1961, for example, federal prosecutors charged 2,459 people with a federal immigration crime.[22] Prosecutors brought almost as many cases every single month from early 2008 to early 2020.[23] Bush's time in the White House might seem like a few lifetimes ago, but in reality we're talking about 2008. Even my students, who look shockingly younger every year, were already well into elementary school by then.

Other tactics that DHS relies on to tie the criminal legal system to the immigration law system are also new. Until 1988, there was no such thing as an aggravated felony. Before Bill Clinton signed the Illegal Immigration Reform and Immigrant Responsibility Act in 1996, there was no section 287(g). DHS and its two immigration-focused units, ICE and CBP, didn't exist until 2003. In the history of U.S. law, these are specks on the timeline.

Separating criminal and immigration law isn't a solution to all problems. Democrats aren't going to trust Republicans more. The cultural divisions that exist between the country's diverse urban centers, where immigrant populations find relative welcome, and its rural areas, where support for anti-migrant policies is common, aren't going to close. But taking evidence of criminal activity out of decisions about who gets to live in the United States will strengthen communities now and increase the legitimacy of the legal system.

There's nothing anyone can do to erase the harm that Wynnie Goodwin and her friends caused in 1993. Had immigration law's blind reliance on criminal convictions been allowed to move forward unchecked, and had she not been very lucky, Wynnie wouldn't have built the stable, loving family she now has. Her children wouldn't have their mother with them, her parents couldn't count on her support in their old age, and she couldn't have built a successful professional career. Wynnie is able to contribute to life in California only because a decades-long political stalemate between the United States and Vietnam meant she couldn't be deported when an immigration judge said she should be. For that reason alone, she was still here, managing a team of human resources professionals, when California gave her a lifeline by letting her erase her convictions. Released from prison, returned to her family, and allowed to go to school and get a job, she has done what most people convicted of a crime do as they get older: move on.

Reconstructing Immigration Law Again

Getting rid of the alphabet soup of programs that tie local police to ICE would be a start to ending the heavy-handed immigration policing that currently exists, but even that wouldn't be enough. It's necessary to build a strong alternative to today's network of immigration law agencies that fetishize policing. The towering intellectual Angela Davis describes the effort to build new institutions and practices alongside the end of destructive practices as abolition democracy. Writing specifically about abolishing prisons, Davis explains that it's necessary to "propose the creation of an array of social institutions that would begin to solve the social problems that set people on the track to prison, thereby helping to render the prison obsolete."[24] Davis herself acknowledges that she's borrowing the concept of abolition democracy from W.E.B. DuBois, who applied it to the original mass movement for abolition in the United States—the anti-slavery struggles that preceded the Civil War and the laws and policies that developed across the country after the war.

In *Black Reconstruction in America*, his classic take-down of the nation's post–Civil War lost opportunity, DuBois wrote of an unholy alliance of Southern white planters and poor white people who "drove the Negro back toward slavery." By the closing decades of the nineteenth century, Jim Crow brought the possibility of abolition democracy to a rapid, deadly end. Together with Northern industrialists, they "murdered democracy" by rejecting the possibility of building a nation of equals on top of slavery's ashes.[25] Instead of land on which to live, tools with which to work, schools in which to learn, and votes with which to change the political landscape, Black people across the United States got systematic racial violence. "Lawlessness and terror filled the land, and terror stalked abroad by day, and it burned and murdered by night," writes DuBois.[26]

Reading DuBois today it's easy to miss his book's

significance. Written in the 1930s, his 750-page tome went against the narrative that had won the intellectual battle of history. At the time, the South was commonly painted as a martyr and the poverty of Black masses described as the necessary result of their own inherent inferiority and self-degradation. "Fortified by long study of the facts, I stand at the end of this writing, literally aghast at what American historians have done to this field," he wrote in the book's closing pages. Out of "loyalty to a lost cause," the policy possibilities and political drama that followed the Civil War were transmogrified "under the leadership of those who would compromise with truth in the past in order to make peace in the present and guide policy in the future," he bemoaned.[27]

As a scholar grounded in the political struggles of his era, DuBois wrote a history that today, in our own era, models an analytical framework for understanding the future. *Black Reconstruction in America* makes clear that in the late 1800s, abolition needed to involve more than deconstruction. Just as it was important to topple the legal system that protected slavery and the enforcement mechanisms that breathed hell's flames onto Black bodies, it was important to build the legal and practical means for "real democracy" in the post–Civil War United States.[28]

The same is true today. To survive, democracy requires more political participation, not less. The United States could have done that after the Civil War, but we didn't. Black people suffered, and the democratic experiment did too. Instead of turning the aspiration of democracy into reality, the United States stepped away from the precipice of equality. White supremacy ruled the day with legal complicity and extra-legal violence as its weapons.

Using the abolition democracy framework that DuBois pioneered and Davis popularized, it's possible to begin the long march toward an immigration legal process that bolsters justice and legality while reducing harm. "There is no road map for justice," the leading abolitionist activist today Mariame Kaba writes.[29] From where we stand now it's impossible to know all the answers. We can't even know all the right questions to ask.

To be sure, none of what I'm proposing is politically possible right now. That's the point. To trot out what Kaba describes as an "incomplete" vision when the political moment is right is to be late to the game. The time to imagine a reconstructed form of immigration law isn't in the days leading to Congress debating a bill that might garner the votes needed to land on the president's desk. That time is now, well before anyone can see when in the far-off future today's ideas might become tomorrow's laws and policies.

Louis Loftus Repouille's experience is a reminder that for most of the history of the United States, migrants didn't suffer a second round of punishment no matter their deeds. Instead of measuring him by his worst moment, immigration law saw Louis as the whole, complicated, contradictory person he was. He was arrested, convicted, and punished as the judge thought was appropriate just as any U.S. citizen would have been. Like for Louis, most of the time that was the end of the story.

And yet the United States didn't come tumbling down.

The nation didn't cease to be sovereign. Its borders didn't cease to exist. The nation's enemies didn't send troops. The law wasn't affected one bit. Courts opened, juries reached verdicts, judges issued sentences, and the criminal legal system operated with all its imperfections. If "the 20th century is the American century," as Henry Luce famously wrote in *Life* magazine almost eighty years ago, then we have to acknowledge that the United States steered the world's course not despite the diverse set of migrants that reached its borders, but because of them.[30] Few were anything but ordinary people.

When Repouille was alive and most migrants coming to the United States were white, immigration law also took the position that migrants were just ordinary human beings. Now it expects extraordinariness. To get into the United States, they should have strong family relationships, as if the United States is the picture of close families. Lacking that, a Ph.D. will usually do, as if terminal degrees are the norm. To stay in the United States, migrants should remain free of crime, as if the population of the United States isn't full of people with criminal histories. From Davy Crockett to Lex Luthor, villains fill our myths. From James Dean to Justin Bieber, rebels enliven our culture, their crimes searing their images in our collective memories. From Richard Nixon to Donald Trump, crime spews out of our seats of political power. As we have done in the past, perhaps one day in the future we will again come to see migrants, in culture and in law, as the ordinary people who they are, flaws and all.

8

REIMAGINING CITIZENS

Ravi Ragbir doesn't hide from his past—not even the legal problems that have shaped much of his life. In the 1990s, about a decade after arriving in the United States from his native Trinidad and Tobago, he made some questionable decisions. At the time, he was working as a mortgage processor, acting as a relay between people who wanted a loan and the company that issued the loans. He was supposed to check that the information people gave him was correct, but, as he told police after they arrested him, he didn't. Instead, he worked with someone named Robert Taylor to get loans for homeowners who needed cash. "I would get the loans through for him," he told police. "It was good for me also because I was making commission on it and was receiving recognition from my co-workers and management."[1]

In the years before the housing market collapsed, loans like this were common and easy to come by. Partnering with Taylor was helping Ravi build a solid reputation with his supervisors and co-workers. Plus, the money he was bringing in for himself and the company all pointed to the good work he was doing, he told me years later.

Eventually the good times ended. In 2000, a jury convicted Ravi of six counts of wire fraud. For that he spent three years under house arrest and another three in prison. At that moment, Ravi became the criminal alien that politicians warn about. The worst kind, in fact: an aggravated felon, according to Immigration and Customs Enforcement and an immigration judge.[2]

Until then, Ravi's immigration status in the United States had been clear. He had come to the United States in 1991 on a short-term visa, which he had later converted into a green card. As long as he stayed out of trouble, Ravi could live and work here for as long as he wanted. Now that he had a criminal record, everything was up in the air. It took ICE six years, but eventually immigration officials started a deportation case against Ravi, claiming that wire fraud is an aggravated felony, the harshest type of crime that can make a migrant removable.

Ravi fought back. His daughter was young at the time, and he wanted to make sure to see her grow. For two years he held out inside ICE's prisons challenging the government's attempt to deport him. Finally, even ICE agreed that he wasn't dangerous and was likely to show up to court dates, so they released him while his legal case made its way through the courts.

That's when Ravi's life took another turn. In 2008, he started volunteering with Families for Freedom, a young organization that created networks of support and education about the impacts of deportation. Soon he would be named chair of the organization's board of directors. With a budding commitment to activism, in 2010 Ravi turned his energy to a different organization, the New Sanctuary Coalition, dedicating himself fully to migrants' rights activism as a community organizer. Quickly he built the group into a powerhouse. In the process, Ravi became the group's executive director and a stalwart of New York City's activist community.

Under Ravi's leadership, New Sanctuary Coalition volunteers accompanied migrants to hearings in immigration court and meetings with ICE agents. They held prayer vigils outside New York's immigration courts and organized clergy to walk alongside migrants who faced the risk of deportation. Time and again, Ravi spoke loudly and harshly about ICE's tactics. On the streets, in front of legislators, or with journalists, for years he could be counted on to lob fierce criticisms at ICE and defend migrants. For longtime immigration lawyer Amy Gottlieb, he could also be counted on for friendship and love. Their work in the migrants' rights movement brought them together, but companionship—eventually leading to marriage—kept them together.

ICE hasn't made that easy. From ICE's perspective, Ravi was a convicted federal offender who now doubled as an enormous annoyance. Unprompted, one of the top officials in ICE's New York office once complained to a minister, "Everybody knows this case."[3] A few days later, during one of his regular mandatory check-ins at the local ICE office, immigration agents arrested Ravi. The same ICE official who had complained about how everyone knew about Ravi also decided that he wasn't likely to win his remaining legal challenges. This was reasonable, Justice Department lawyers would later tell a federal court, because the Trump administration's immigration policies prioritized migrants with a criminal history.[4]

It's hard to blame ICE agents for believing that everyone knew about Ravi's situation. "I have a tendency to argue with authority," he told me, with a grin of obvious pride on his face. I already knew that. I'd flown to New York to meet with Ravi precisely because he'd long been willing to argue with ICE.

In one sense, it was our first time meeting. We'd never shaken hands or sat in the same room. But Ravi is hard to miss in the activist world, so over the years I'd Zoomed into multiple panels alongside him. Fitting for the Covid era, we knew each other digitally, but I'd never been close enough to see the way his mustache bends when he recalls how he's prone to making life annoying for ICE agents. Sitting at a Thai restaurant in downtown Brooklyn on a frigid December afternoon, I could see that the criminal alien across the table got a kick out of being a political pest.

ICE had threatened to arrest him before, but on the day that they strapped handcuffs on his wrists, January 11, 2018, Ravi didn't think they would go through with it. They told his lawyer they weren't going to. He hadn't even bothered to pack a bag, he told me. Being an organizer requires being a bit of a romantic—able to see possibility when everyone else sees despair. But romantic doesn't mean foolish. By the time Ravi walked through the doors of ICE's Manhattan office that morning, he had organized his supporters for whatever might happen. Good thing he had. "They kidnapped me," he said. He had fainted and, almost as soon as he knew what was going on again, he was being escorted into an ambulance and out of ICE's office.

Outside, a crowd was waiting for word on his meeting with ICE. Handcuffed and on the way to an airport wasn't what they had been hoping for, but it was certainly something they were prepared for. "We had steps that while we were there people would be doing," he explained. Like the experienced activists that they were, Ravi's supporters quickly moved past hope and into action trying to stop his deportation. "As the ambulance inched its way out of 26 Federal Plaza in Manhattan, I caught glimpses of the chaos outside. Faces of friends swam in and out of view," Gottlieb, his wife, later wrote.[5] The speaker of the New York City Council said ICE agents shoved him. Another City Council member said agents used a chokehold on him. A photographer caught the moment when an NYPD officer pushed Councilor Jumaane Williams's face onto the hood of a car while handcuffing him behind his back.[6]

With Ravi locked inside an ambulance, ICE agents skipped passing through the agency's processing center on Manhattan's Varick Street, as would have been normal, because Ravi's supporters were already there. Instead, with help from New York police officers, ICE agents reached the Newark, New Jersey, airport, where they planned to stick Ravi on a flight to Florida. Surrounded by ICE officers, they moved him through the busy airport and onto the plane. He would spend two weeks imprisoned at an ICE facility near Miami as federal officials tried to deport him and his lawyers tried to get him back to Brooklyn.

Eventually the lawyers succeeded. In its quest to rid the United States of Ravi, ICE broke the law, a federal court concluded. Immigration law gives ICE the right to deport Ravi, but the Constitution requires that they use a process that avoids "unnecessary cruelty," the judge explained. ICE should've told Ravi that the time had come to get his affairs in order, pack his bags, and say final goodbyes to the city and the friends to which he'd given so much. "That is the process required after a life lived among us," the judge wrote.[7]

Arresting Ravi ripped a hole in the community. Upon hearing that he wouldn't walk out with his family and reunite with his friends, Ravi fainted. After helping revive him, then being split from him, Gottlieb experienced the kind of personal nightmare that she had long become used to seeing in her clients' lives. "It hurts more than I ever thought it would. I come home to an empty apartment, and everything screams Ravi's absence," she wrote.[8]

Nightmares aren't unusual in immigration law enforcement. What makes Ravi's situation special is that he had so much support. Years of activism had helped him build the network of friends who were willing to put themselves in front of a vehicle to stop his deportation and to drag along the journalists who would capture every second of their efforts and pester ICE over each step in Ravi's ordeal. A team of lawyers mobilized just as quickly. They claimed agents targeted him specifically because he was such an outspoken critic. "If we can take Ravi with all of these people, the community is going to get distressed," Ravi told me he imagined ICE officials saying to each other.

About fifteen months after arresting Ravi and flying him to Florida, once he was back in New York, a different federal court from the one that had ordered his release from the Florida immigration prison agreed that ICE had gone after Ravi to quiet him down. Deporting Ravi wouldn't just get him out of their way. It would also send a message to other migrants: open your mouths to criticize immigration policies and ICE will come knocking. "His criticism, and its prominence, played a significant role in the recent attempts to remove him," the court wrote. That was an "outrageous" violation of Ravi's First Amendment right to free speech.[9] In the name of improving public safety by arresting and attempting to deport Ravi, ICE again proved itself willing to violate the law.

Anchored in the Past

For four decades, immigration law has imagined that there is no place in the citizenry for people like Ravi. That his crime means he's undeserving. That instead of living here, he should be sent there. For Ravi, there is Trinidad, a place he hasn't lived in for decades. Were that to happen, ICE agents around New York would be delighted.

Through his tireless activism, Ravi is proving that immigration law is built on a fantasy. Ravi didn't just make a life for himself in New York. He's built a community there, one that isn't confused about his past or his present. When ICE came for him, the community fought back, and the meal I shared with Ravi was proof that almost seventeen years after he was supposed to leave the United States, the community was winning.

Instead of the demonization that characterizes immigration politics and the policing fetish that fuels immigration law and policy, we should reimagine citizenship to reflect the people who breathe life into communities around the country. In a period in which the world is almost entirely carved into different countries, citizenship is indispensable.

It's also dangerous. To be a citizen means to be different from someone who is not a citizen. In the language of U.S. immigration law, there are citizens and there are "aliens." People can move from one category to the other, but, legally, there is no one in-between. In practice, citizenship means having access to a special claim to belonging that everyone else doesn't have. When it comes to immigration law, that's the difference between getting to live in the United States and facing the threat of immigration imprisonment and forcible removal.

The problem with U.S. citizenship, though, is that the difference between those of us who can rightfully claim it and those who can't usually has nothing to do with us. Instead, our parents matter more. U.S. citizen parents can convey their citizenship to their kids even if the children are born abroad. Academics call this *jus sanguinis* citizenship, a Latin phrase that means that citizenship transfers through biological relationships. In the United States, there are a bunch of laws on the books that fall into the jus sanguinis citizenship category. All of them are complicated. Most of them are odd. Some of them are patently repulsive. Take, for example, the provision that applies only to some people "born before noon (Eastern Standard Time) May 24, 1934"—the day before

President Franklin Roosevelt signed a bill letting women of all nationalities hold citizenship independent of their husbands.

Far more common is the *jus soli* form of citizenship, another Latin phrase, but one that focuses on the soil. You're a citizen of the territory in which you're born. In the United States, the very first sentence of the Fourteenth Amendment captures jus soli citizenship: "All persons born or naturalized in the United States, and subject to the jurisdiction thereof, are citizens of the United States and of the State wherein they reside." Twenty-eight words that are the source of citizenship for most U.S. citizens, including me. I am a U.S. citizen because my mother was in Texas when I was born, all of seven miles north of the border. Had she been seven miles south, where my parents and siblings had lived until just a few years earlier, I might not be able to call myself a U.S. citizen. I might have made my life in Mexico, the country in which I sit as I write these words. But there she was so here I am: a U.S. citizen armed with a U.S. passport.

I'm not opposed to either form of citizenship. Rather, the problem with citizenship laws is that they are too limited. Neither blood nor birthplace say anything about a person's commitment to the experiment in democracy that is the United States. To tie the freedom to live in the United States to citizenship is to tie it to the past—either a parent's citizenship or the place where a person's mother happened to be at just the right moment. This is a form of protection from the coercive power of immigration imprisonment and deportation that is anchored in time.

For me, protection from the Border Patrol agent's probing

questions—Where do you live? What were you doing abroad? What are you carrying?—is grounded in January 1980 when my mother had the foresight to be in Texas. She could've chosen to be in Mexico then, perhaps so that her mother or older sister could be nearby when she went into labor with me, but she didn't. She could've been visiting friends in Reynosa, the Mexican border city where she lived for several years and gotten stuck in the traffic back-ups that were notorious at the port-of-entry even then, but she wasn't. My mother made the decisions necessary to ensure that I was born in the United States so that I could be a U.S. citizen. And so, I am.

My mom is also the reason I'm a Mexican citizen. Like the United States, Mexican law lets children claim citizenship based on their bloodline. My mom was born in the Mexican state of Querétaro, meaning she's a Mexican citizen. As her son, I am too. The irony is that I didn't know this until I moved to Mexico City while writing this book. Reading an article in a popular magazine, I spotted a description of people a lot like me: children born and raised in the United States with at least one parent born in Mexico. I consulted with a Mexican immigration lawyer and, sure enough, Mexican law says I have been entitled to citizenship from the day I was born.

Suddenly, I'd transformed from a U.S. citizen to someone busy gathering the documents necessary to prove that I am a Mexican citizen too. Indeed, I've been one for exactly as long as I've been a U.S. citizen—every day of my life. Thanks to the coincidence of reading a magazine article and a bit of help from a high-priced lawyer, my citizenship purse has gotten heavier. Nothing else about me has changed. In every other way, I'm the same person.

More than four decades after I was born, what continues to matter most is my mom: where she was when I was born as far as the United States is concerned and where she was when she was born as far as Mexico cares. Neither makes me any better than someone whose mother made different choices or was born in a different place. It doesn't make me more fit for U.S. or Mexican citizenship than someone whose mother didn't have the option of choosing to be in one country or the other. Forty-four years later, my mother's choices continue to protect me, but they show absolutely nothing about my commitment to any core values of life in the United States or Mexico.

Leaving the Past Behind

Instead of focusing on the past, we could instead focus on the present. Rather than hinging a rightful claim to belonging in the United States on who my parents are or what decisions they made, U.S. law could instead prioritize a migrants' willingness to embrace the best features of this experiment in democratic self-governance. A leading philosopher of migration, Joseph Carens, argues, "As irregular migrants become more and more settled, their membership in society grows in moral importance, and the fact that they settled without authorization becomes correspondingly less relevant." Scholars who specialize in citizenship call a version of this the membership theory of citizenship. All that means is that citizenship should focus on a person's participation in key parts of community life. The political theorist Sarah Song argues that "political membership is valuable because it provides an indispensable scheme of social and economic cooperation and because it enables collective self-determination." [10]

I'm sympathetic to this view. Belonging should be about a commitment to some of what helps a group gel, and about a willingness to participate in the group's life. I don't call myself Catholic because my parents did. I call myself Catholic because I share a lot of the Catholic Church's core beliefs: the adoration of saints, reverence for the Holy Trinity, and an affinity for the Church's remarkable pageantry. I've hung an image of San Pacracio, patron saint of work, in three offices at two universities, forever grateful for the blessing of having the best job I know of: university professor. But if I'm being honest, even I can't claim to participate in the life of the Church. I don't go to Mass very often. Unless I'm with my mom, I'm more likely to be inside a church as a tourist than as a worshipper. I believe, but I don't participate, giving me just one half of the membership requirement. Both matter.

Where standard membership theory falls short when it comes to migration is in its typical refusal to embrace the unsavory aspects of community life—especially crime. Even Carens argues that "it makes sense to focus on the really dangerous violators." [11] He thinks it's morally correct to deport them. But Carens doesn't explain why it's okay to punish migrants twice: once through the criminal law process that declares a person dangerous and again through the immigration law process that declares them fit for deportation.

In the modern United States, it makes little sense to tar twice what the criminal legal system is charged with doing once. The very reason that we have criminal laws, police forces responsible for preventing and investigating criminal activity, prosecutors charged with accumulating evidence of guilt, and courts obligated to mete out a penalty is to discourage people from committing crime and punish whoever does.

Clearly that doesn't work. In part because so much is criminalized, there is no shortage of criminal activity in the United States—and no shortage of criminals. Many of us manage not to get caught, and more of us manage to avoid prosecution. Only about two out of three murders lead to an arrest, as do one out of three rapes. Far fewer burglary and theft crimes do.[12] Just because a lot of people get away with crime doesn't change the fact that the United States is a country where crime is commonplace and criminals come in every form. Carens says it's appropriate to target people who drive "so recklessly as to endanger lives," but how many of us haven't at one time gotten behind the wheel of a car when we shouldn't have? Maybe we didn't have a real alternative. Mass transit doesn't exist in most of the United States. Where it does, it's usually so inconvenient as to be off the table for those of us with private cars.

That's just one example of crime's deep-seated role in the United States, but there are many more I could point to. Brett Kavanaugh was elevated to the Supreme Court despite Christine Blasey Ford's highly publicized claims that he sexually assaulted her while drunk at a high school party. On the campaign trail, a video surfaced of Donald Trump boasting about his sexual assault of women. "When you're a star they let you do it. You can do anything," the future president told *Access*

Hollywood reporter Billy Bush in 2005.[13] More than fifteen years later, as president, Trump sat in the White House as his supporters stormed the U.S. Capitol in Washington, DC. They broke windows, tore through doors, attacked police officers, and chanted fantasies of hanging Speaker of the House Nancy Pelosi. In response, Trump recorded a video telling the crowd that he loved them.

Laws That Forgive

Crime isn't just common and commonly overlooked. In the United States, the law makes room for criminals, overlooking or forgiving past transgressions so that people, especially wealthy, white citizens, can continue life as part of the community. While most people in the United States pay federal income tax, every year there are still hundreds of billions of dollars owed to the U.S. Treasury that it never gets. Before we start pointing to low-wage house cleaners and babysitters, we should instead look to where the big amounts are hidden. According to a 2021 study, the top 1 percent of income earners owed 36 percent of unpaid taxes in 2019. Had they paid every cent, the federal government would've had another $173 billion in revenue that year. That is about 10 percent of the amount of taxes that the IRS collected in 2019.[14] Despite the fact that tax evasion by some of the wealthiest people in the United States is a widescale problem involving eye-catching amounts, the IRS tends to avoid bringing down the hammer of criminal prosecution. Instead, its primary goal is to collect tax revenue, so the agency is often open to a tax payment plan. This is so common that the IRS calls it a "compromise in offer." There's even a form for this that comes with an explanatory thirty-two-page booklet and convenient tool available on the agency's website that tells you whether you pre-qualify.

Another example comes from the bankruptcy courts that regularly forgive corporate debts, allowing businesses that fall into financial problems an escape. When makeup giant Revlon filed for bankruptcy in June 2022, for example, it owed $3.5 billion.[15] It was the most indebted company to request bankruptcy assistance that month, but it wasn't the only one. Another thirty-eight big businesses filed for bankruptcy in that month alone.[16]

Neither tax evasion nor racking up unpaid debts involves physical violence, but both certainly involve harm. Wealthy tax scofflaws aren't just illegal freeloaders who shun their responsibility onto those of us who try to pay the taxes we owe. The billions of dollars that they deny the U.S. Treasury also punch all of us who rely on the government's revenue to pay for valuable services. Similarly, forgiving corporate debt often means the company's least powerful vendors don't get paid. Revlon, for example, got court approval to prioritize payments to private equity funds and hedge funds despite objections by other creditors that they wouldn't be able to recoup any of their loans. Three months after its bankruptcy filing, a judge approved $36 million in bonuses to the company's executives, while debts continued to sit unpaid.[17]

The area of U.S. law that probably pops into most people's minds when they think about the legal system, criminal law, also makes room for forgiveness. Statutes of limitation, for example, bar the government from convicting someone after a certain number of years even if the evidence of their guilt is overwhelming. Just how long it takes to trigger a statute of limitation differs depending on the state and the crime, but in every state and for most crimes there is a period after which Trump's claim that "you can do anything" becomes true as a matter of legal doctrine.

In other situations, criminal law forgives because the legal system prefers the crime to whatever else was going on. There's no better example than self-defense. Every state lets people protect themselves from injury. The details differ, but the basic idea is that it's better to hurt someone than let them hurt you. The easiest way to justify self-defense is to think of violence between intimate partners. It took a long time, but now criminal law sometimes accepts that the survivor of years of domestic violence will take matters into their own hands to protect themselves.

Much less justifiable is self-defense raised to protect racial violence. When George Zimmerman was prosecuted for killing Trayvon Martin, he pointed to Florida's self-defense law. The seventeen-year-old was walking around suburban Florida with nothing more dangerous than a bag of Skittles and a hoodie. Zimmerman thought that was enough to shoot and kill. A Florida jury thought that was enough to show that Zimmerman acted to prevent imminent death or a forcible felony, the two reasons state law permits.

A few years later, teenager Kyle Rittenhouse left his home carrying a long gun. His destination was a Black Lives Matter rally in Kenosha, Wisconsin. Displeased by the unwelcome reception he received, he ran through the rally. Shooting into the crowd, he killed two people. His lawyers also turned to self-defense. Hard as it is to believe, his lawyers claimed that he had to use his gun because one of the people he killed, Joseph Rosenbaum, was trying to take it from him. The twisted logic goes like this: If Rosenbaum, who didn't have a gun, took the gun from Rittenhouse, who showed up with the gun, the guy without the gun might kill the guy with the gun. And so, Rittenhouse pulled the trigger. Harder still to believe it worked. A jury acquitted Rittenhouse.

Justified or not, self-defense law always begins with the idea that sometimes it is okay to commit a violent crime. The law doesn't pretend that violence didn't occur. It merely justifies the violence that did occur. These aren't situations where the prosecutor failed to show that the defendant did what the government says they did, as happened in the murder prosecution of José García Zarate when prosecutors failed to convince the jury that he even knew he was holding a gun. These are situations in which the defendant says, "Yes I did hurt someone, because that was the lesser of two evils." By giving people a right to commit violence to protect themselves, the law of self-defense forgives them for the harm that they caused.

Criminal law also puts the power to forgive directly in the hands of prosecutors. Armed with the power to decide whether a prosecution is even merited, prosecutors have almost unreviewable, unilateral power to forgive. If a prosecutor chooses not to file charges, that's the end of the story. Good reason, bad reason, or no reason, it doesn't matter why the prosecutor decides not to move forward. If the evidence doesn't hold up, the suspect's parents are friends with the district attorney, or there just aren't enough prosecutors to go around, the courts take the same position: "the decision whether or not to prosecute, and what charge to file or bring before a grand jury, generally rests entirely in his discretion," the U.S. Supreme Court declared in 1978, giving full-throated embrace to prosecutorial discretion.[18]

When a prosecutor moves forward with a criminal case, juries can also choose forgiveness. Judges tell jurors that they are supposed to decide whether the prosecution has met its burden of proving, beyond a reasonable doubt, that the defendant committed the crime charged. But a little-known vestige of the English legal system embedded within our own laws lets juries ignore that instruction. If they think that it would be unjust to convict, jurors can simply declare a person not guilty. Facts be damned. Evidence ignored. In the hands of a jury, the government can lose, and the little guy win out, all entirely legally. It's supposed to be that way. The men who debated and wrote the U.S. Constitution were deeply afraid of government power. They had just waged a bloody war to secede from an overbearing sovereign, and they hadn't forgotten their complaints. Even if the powerful could tap prosecutors to bring criminal charges against ordinary people, the founders made sure that, through the jury, the little guy always stood a chance. Jury nullification is part of that evening of the playing field.

Few people know about jury nullification today, but it hasn't always been that way. In the mid-1800s, juries often nullified prosecutors' best efforts in one specific type of case:

violations of the Fugitive Slave Act. Enacted by Congress in 1793 and made harsher in 1850, the law targeted abolitionists. Today there are monuments celebrating the Underground Railroad, but back then anyone who helped a Black person escape slavery could be sent to prison. By ignoring the evidence, nullification let jurors turn their ideological commitment to freedom and an enslaved person's right to move across state borders into practice. "This was jury nullification's finest hour," writes legal scholar Paul Butler.[19]

Even after a conviction, judges can also forgive criminal behavior when they get around to sentencing. Prosecutors wield more discretion when it comes to deciding to launch a criminal case, but judges have a lot of wiggle room when it comes to sentencing. Often, judges can choose between issuing sentences that run concurrently or that run consecutively. They can pick a period of imprisonment at the high end of the legal range or at the low end. Or they can simply choose to postpone a sentence. The judge who oversaw Louis Loftus Repouille's trial, for example, sentenced him to five to ten years imprisonment, but immediately suspended all of it. With the stroke of a pen, Louis was allowed to go home in time to celebrate Christmas of 1941 with his wife and the kids he hadn't killed.[20]

In addition to forgiveness, sometimes criminal law formally forgets criminal activity. Every state lets judges hide the details of a conviction—even the fact of conviction. Called "sealing," this puts the details of a criminal legal process off-limits to almost everyone. Without knowing the outcome of a case, it's impossible to know whether the defendant was convicted or not. Without knowing the crime charged, it's hard to know what to make of a prosecution.

It's also possible for people who have been convicted to erase a conviction. They can rewind the legal system's clock by vacating an old conviction. In effect, they can be unconvicted. When Charles Kuck says that his client, 21 Savage, didn't have a conviction on his record when ICE arrested him, that's what he means. Sandra Castañeda, Wynnie Goodwin, and 21 Savage can all say that they don't have a conviction, because their old convictions have been vacated. No one ever said that the logic of the law was straightforward.

Whether by forgiving or forgetting, these are all examples of criminal law's redemptive quality. Criminal law doctrine makes room for the fact that people are imperfect. We mess up. Just like parents forgive children and children forgive parents, the law forgives so that the people whom we value as members of our communities can return to the fold. "Forgiving involves ceasing to let the wrongdoing count in one's feelings toward the wrongdoer, even while maintaining recognition of the wrong," the legal scholar Martha Minow writes. By forgiving or forgetting past crimes, criminal law shows mercy. More than a century ago, the Supreme Court explained that the law sometimes treats forgiveness as "more expedient for the public welfare than prosecution and punishment."[21]

If today it is hard to believe that criminal law can forgive or forget, that's because we have strayed so far from mercy. But these tendencies have always been part of criminal law in the United States, and their core remains even if poorly known and little used.

Recognizing that we are each fallible lets me remember that there isn't anything altruistic about embracing criminal law's merciful qualities. I'm in it for myself at least as much as I'm in it for others. I don't have any interest in running through my list of possible or probable crimes, but I would be lying if I claimed to have lived four-and-a-half decades without getting closer to criminal behavior than I would have liked.

Unequal Citizenship

Citizenship is undeniably important, but it's equally hard to deny that its history reveals the unholy consequence of ideas about who was fit for full participation in civic life that, today, are disturbing. Beginning with the first naturalization law that made citizenship available to white people only, citizenship had a racial restriction until the middle of the twentieth century. In its earliest days, the United States killed off Indigenous people thought unworthy of life. Embroiled in ridding the growing country of people deemed racially undesirable, citizenship didn't even enter the conversation. In the throes of white supremacy, the United States enslaved Black people thought fit to be property and servants, but nothing more. After the Civil War, the Fourteenth Amendment guaranteed that African Americans were citizens. It would take another eighty years, until 1943, when the United States was wooing China as an ally in World War II, for the Chinese to be able to naturalize. After that, it wouldn't be until 1952 that Congress eliminated racial restrictions on naturalization once and for all.[22]

The racism that these laws reflected may have been simple,

but putting it into practice wasn't. When states around the United States regularly barred "negros" from citizenship, they ran into the problem of not knowing who fit that description. Perhaps sensing the effect of racial categorizations, Oregon kept the bar high. To be a negro in Oregon, a person had to have more than one Black grandparent.

It was the opposite in Louisiana. There even one out of thirty-two Black ancestors was enough. That meant that one Black great-great-great grandparent was enough to disqualify a Louisianian from citizenship. Susie Phipps, who was born in 1934, came from a long line of white people. "My children are white. My grandchildren are white. Mother and Daddy were buried white. My Social Security card says I'm white. My driver's license says I'm white. There are no blacks out where I live, except the hired hands." But sometime around 1760 there was a white plantation owner in Alabama who'd had a child with a Black woman. After that there were a few other distant, distant relatives who had Black blood, leading a genealogist hired by the state to conclude that Susie exceeded the limit: she was three-thirty-seconds Black.[23] Living in the late twentieth century, Susie suffered the embarrassment of learning she was not quite who she thought she was. She refused to tell her husband, passing up a trip to South America that would've required a passport that she could have received only by obtaining a copy of the birth certificate that described her as "colored." In the 1980s, she lobbied to change Louisiana's racial standard—in secret at first. Had she been born a century earlier, Susie could have avoided the embarrassment of not getting a passport by focusing on the consequences of not being a citizen.

For much of the same period, U.S. citizenship was also limited by gender. Until the early twentieth century, married women didn't possess citizenship on their own. Citizenship was tied to their husbands. Since the mid-1800s, marrying a U.S. citizen automatically made a U.S. citizen out of a woman.[24] The opposite was also true. Marrying a man who wasn't a U.S. citizen meant losing citizenship. A law passed in 1907 put the legal consequences clearly: "Any American woman who marries a foreigner shall take the nationality of her husband." That had been the law for many years by then, and it would stay that way until 1922 when Congress passed another law saying that a U.S. citizen woman wouldn't lose her citizenship upon marriage to a foreigner unless she married someone who was "ineligible to citizenship."[25] Who was ineligible to become a U.S. citizen in 1922? Asians.

The law's logic was as simple in its misogyny as in its racism. According to a federal court in Detroit, "the husband, as the head of the family, is to be considered its political representative, at least for the purposes of citizenship."[26] Whatever citizenship the husband held, so too did the wife and children.

Nellie Grant learned this the hard way. Just a teenager when her famous father, the war hero Ulysses S. Grant, was elected president, Nellie's 1874 wedding captured the recovering nation's attention. That summer the soldier credited with keeping the United States intact was tasked with walking his only daughter, twenty years old at the time, into the East Room of the White House. Dressed in white satin, with a six-foot-long train on her dress, the popular young daughter of the beloved family must have stunned the crowd. In the East Room, Nellie's fiancé, Algernon Sartoris, was waiting. Within hours, the party over and the couple off to their honeymoon, President Grant lost the nerve he was celebrated for and fell onto his daughter's empty bed, sobbing. Nellie wasn't just away for a post-wedding vacation. She was off to start her life in the United Kingdom, her new husband's native land.

Nellie Grant had married a British citizen. As a result, she was no longer a U.S. citizen. Her life as a British citizen was tolerable until Algernon's drinking got out of control. With his parents' support, the couple divorced, and Nellie returned to the United States with their children. Returning to her native country, where her father was still celebrated and she was still remembered as the beautiful young White House bride, was the easy part. Nellie had lost her U.S. citizenship the moment she married Algernon, but getting it back wasn't nearly as simple as ending her marriage. It would take an act of Congress to get it back. Fortunately, her family's name still carried weight around Washington, so Nellie eventually resumed life in the United States as the U.S. citizen she had once been.[27]

Citizenship's Evolution

Today, these examples of citizenship's formal limits appear like historical relics. Each has ended, maybe even been forgotten. When I teach my students about citizenship, everyone knows that enslaved people were excluded, but few are aware of the struggles women waged to grab hold of their own citizenship. My students can all point to the Civil War, but almost no one knows about the debates that followed the Fourteenth Amendment's enactment: did it really grant citizenship to people of any race born in the United States?

At every turn, citizenship's borders have been contested. People who have wanted to make citizenship available to more people have faced off against those who have wanted to keep citizenship static—hold it in place for fear that expanding its reach would weaken its value. Would adding Black people destroy democracy? Could the Chinese disavow the emperor in favor of the United States? Could women be trusted to think for themselves? These are specific questions that mask existential crises. People who were described as unfit to participate in democratic self-governance, incapable of reasoning, immature in their self-control, prone to violence, susceptible to coercion, immoral, or untrustworthy demanding their place at democracy's table. The undesirable demanded access to the temple of civic life.

At every turn, they won. Slowly, painfully, and at times bloodily, but always in the direction of allowing more people to claim the banner of U.S. citizenship. The Fourteenth Amendment tore down racial restrictions on citizenship, first for freed slaves and their descendants, then for the children of Chinese migrants. Decades later Congress would clarify that even native peoples born in the United States were citizens from birth. Women too would come to possess their own citizenship.

Citizenship's constant evolution shows that there is nothing sacred about the most important legal status tying the person to the political community. Declaring one person a citizen and another a foreigner is simply the product of politics. Sadly, the ugly politics of the moment frequently inject into citizenship law the biases of the era. Who is a citizen says more about the character of the lawmakers than it does the character of the people divided into citizen and foreigner. "Your foreignness has nothing to do with your habits, education, religion, or linguistic skills—it is a purely legal category," the citizenship scholar Dimitry Kochenov writes.[28]

True to its political nature, citizenship is full of permutations, limitations, and contradictions.

Even today, citizenship isn't the same for everyone. Different people feel its effects differently. Immigration scholar Ming Hsu Chen argues that there isn't a simple division between citizens and everyone else. Instead, Chen describes citizenship as a spectrum. Even people whose claims to formal U.S. citizenship are not in doubt can struggle to make "informal claims to social belonging." She's getting at the idea that formal citizenship is needed to fully participate in civic life—from voting to avoiding deportation. But even some of us who have formal citizenship still have our belonging and participation questioned or thwarted because our membership is doubted—perhaps because of the way we look, how we talk, who our parents are, or whether we have a criminal record.[29]

Citizenship, it turns out, isn't the equalizing force it's sold as. It isn't experienced the same way for all people who legally possess it, nor is it experienced the same way under all circumstances. On the contrary, it's meant to divide people into legal categories, and it does that quite effectively. It holds out the promise of privileges to the few over the many—citizens versus aliens—through "a cocktail of punishing randomness and hypocrisy," in Kochenov's words.[30] Even those of us promised the good stuff don't always get it.

Expanding Citizenship

We could toss aside the entire concept, bashing citizenship as the discriminatory legal status that it is, wrapping politicians' biases in the sanitizing sheath of a made-up tie between the nation and the person. The problem with moving away from citizenship like this is that history offers a frightening example of life, and death, when citizenship's role is reduced. To best imagine the consequences of a modern world without citizenship, we have to turn to the worst moments of twentieth-century human history. After rising to power, Nazis rewrote German citizenship laws to exclude Jews from citizenship. Stripped of their citizenship, all that remained was the alien. To the alien, the German state owed nothing, not even legal rights. As a result, German officials did what they wanted with the aliens in their midst.

But it wasn't just the German government that treated newly stateless Europeans poorly. Other countries did too. Standing on Europe's edge in the French port city of Marseilles, a man known simply as Weidel watched Europe's refugees try, often in vain, to leave the continent. Marseilles was full of "Mothers who had lost their children, children who had lost their mothers," Weidel observed, as if he was talking about James Davis's family in New York decades earlier or Central American mothers in South Texas during the Trump years. These were the "human hordes who had been chased from all the countries of the earth," hopeful that on a ship or on dry land anywhere but there they might do nothing more romantic than live.[31]

Weidel was not a real person. He was the narrator in *Transit*, a novel by Anna Seghers. Through that fictional citizen turned alien, Seghers relived what she saw. As a Jewish Communist intellectual, Seghers could not survive the Nazi takeover of Germany, so she fled. Soon Europe proved too dangerous. Eventually she found safety in Mexico City. Having survived, she wrote about the ordinariness of all those who didn't. Having obtained the prized documents needed to breathe, to live, to think, to dream, to write, she reflected on those who had not. "What harm would it do to a giant nation if a few of these saved souls, worthy, half-worthy, or unworthy, were to join them in their country—how could it possibly harm such a big country?" her narrator Weidel asked as death approached.[32]

Having been pushed outside of citizenship, Europe's displaced peoples were suddenly left clinging to nothing more than the rights inherent in humans. Put to the test, human rights failed miserably. The German Marxist philosopher Walter Benjamin fled to Spain, where he could find no comfort under Franco's regime, ultimately taking his own life. Two hundred fifty of the people who stood on the *St. Louis* in 1939 watching Miami's lights twinkle in the distance as they waited for permission to enter the United States, permission that never came, didn't survive their forced return to Europe.[33] The Jewish philosopher Hannah Arendt fled to

Paris, and then, courtesy of forged travel documents, to New York.[34] Having survived, like Seghers she too asked why the world had let so many die. "The world found nothing sacred in the abstract nakedness of being human," she wrote.[35]

I always think of Arendt's words when I think about citizenship's unsavoriness. I take her assessment of the past as a warning about the future. As the foundational legal tie between a person and the state, citizenship is the soil on which all other obligations grow. It is the source, as Arendt famously put it, of the "right to have rights." Without citizenship, there is no right to be heard. Once the law refuses to recognize a right to be heard, there can't be said to be a right to speak. After all, what does it matter if I can speak if no one listens? Without a right to speak, to complain, to demand that government officials treat them with dignity, the right to being treated as human means whatever government officials want it to be. The Europe that Arendt and Seghers fled forever reminds us that that is a frightening possibility from which we should stay away.

Rather than shuck citizenship altogether, we should reimagine it. Let's honor the imaginative activists and blood-stained history of citizenship in this country by demanding that it finally reflect the motley crew of people who actually constitute the United States. Instead of a version of "we the people" that includes only free white men, as it did for generations, or that reflects some romanticized version of the past in which most U.S. citizens were up-by-the-bootstraps, morally righteous lovers of liberty, I imagine a version that includes the colorful characters, flawed personalities, and the ordinary lot of the rest of us whose days are mostly mundane and lives are mostly boring. We are the people who constitute the United States. We are the people who have always breathed life into the political union. Crime is no more a stranger to this version of the people than is art, music, manufacturing, or inventing. Some of us get caught up in one or another thing, but all of us reveal some good and some bad. The righteous is always tied up with the reprehensible, with the distinction between the two often blurred by perspective: Louis Repouille the good father, Louis Repouille the child killer; Ravi Ragbir the fraudster and pest, Ravi Ragbir the courageous activist.

Just as criminal law is willing to accept people back into the fold of the community, citizenship law should admit that we already accept people who have committed crime into the citizenry. And then immigration law should stop repelling people who want to make their own imperfect lives here. As Judge Learned Hand explained in Walter Klonis's case, adding deportation to the back end of criminal proceedings would be "a cruel and barbarous result" worthy of "national reproach." [36]

The law won't tumble at the sight of mercy. On the contrary, it requires redemption to prosper. "A people confident in its laws and institutions should not be ashamed of mercy," the late Supreme Court Justice Anthony Kennedy told a group of lawyers in 2003.[37] Laws aren't meant to bludgeon people into submission. They are meant to help us become better versions of ourselves. The U.S. Constitution's famous opening passage, "We the people of the United States, in order to form a more perfect Union," has never been accurate because ours has never been a perfect political community merely aspiring to greater perfection. It would've been more accurate when it was written, and it certainly is now, to say that we should constantly be attempting to form a less imperfect union. Instead of searching endlessly for perfection, we would do well to learn from the past so as to avoid repeating history's mistakes well into the future.

Despite the country's many attempts to improve itself by barring various people from citizenship, there isn't a single moment in the nation's history in which the United States did so. Imposing racial and gender bars to citizenship were common for decades, but they only hurt the nation's democratic experiment, revealing it to be, on its best days, a farce. Today, I hope, these reminders from the past are flag posts of the worst moments in the nation's legal history.

Meanwhile, white men have repeatedly been forgiven even when they violently disowned U.S. citizenship and threatened the nation's very existence. The Fourteenth Amendment, added to the U.S. Constitution in response to the Civil War, bans insurrectionists from holding public office, but it says nothing about banning them from citizenship. On the battlefield, the terms of surrender that Union General Ulysses S. Grant proposed to his secessionist counterpart Robert E. Lee at Appomattox Court House included a wartime amnesty provision. Confederate troops under Lee's command could return home "not to be disturbed by the United States authority," Grant promised.[38]

That would be only the first of several forms of mercy shown the troops and officers who tore the nation in two.

About five weeks after Lee's surrender, in May 1865, Andrew
Johnson, who became president after Lincoln's assassination,
issued a blanket "amnesty and pardon" to Confederate troops
and officials except a few high-level officials. As Johnson put
it, forgiveness toward these battlefield enemies was necessary
so "that the authority of the government of the United States
may be restored, and that peace, order, and freedom may be
established." Secessionists were required to sign a simple written oath to support the U.S. Constitution and the very "union
of the States" that they had just tried to destroy. There was
no irony intended in their claims of allegiance to the country they vowed to end. But if they did pledge allegiance, they
could escape any threat of criminal liability for their wartime
efforts to kill and plunder in defense of white supremacy.[39] All
would be forgiven if only they would ask. Some didn't bother.

Only a few who held high posts in the secessionist government or military could not be redeemed. That was a limitation on mercy imposed by law, so it could be altered by law.
Extending his merciful view, on Christmas Day in 1868,
President Johnson issued a sweeping "pardon and amnesty
for the offense of treason against the United States" to anyone who supported the Confederacy. In Johnson's view,
even tearing the United States in two, ravaging the country,
participating in a war that killed three-quarters of a million
people, and pushing the country to the brink of destruction
wasn't too much to keep redemption off the table. This was
an astonishing turn for a president who had previously advo-
cated harsh treatment of the secessionists. Johnson, who was
no friend to Black people, had stuck with the United States

even after Tennessee, which he had led as governor and represented in Congress, sided with the Confederacy. While Lincoln was president, Johnson had little appetite for his fellow
white southerners who were willing to kill people and destroy
the country. Once in charge, he quickly concluded that "con-
fidence and fraternal feeling among the whole people" could
only come after "universal amnesty and pardon."[40]

Clearly, Johnson cared little of what the nation's newest citizens thought. In the war's aftermath, the Fourteenth
Amendment granted citizenship to former slaves and Black
people who had never been enslaved. But, as today, the gap
between formal citizenship and real belonging was wide. "We
must never forget that victory to the rebellion meant death
to the republic," Frederick Douglass said at Arlington National Cemetery in 1871 as he honored soldiers whose lives
and names had been lost in the war. The very people who, in
Douglass's words, "came forth with broad blades and bloody
hands to destroy the very foundation of American society,"
were, to Johnson, worthy of redemption.[41] What Douglass
saw as an existential threat to the nation, Johnson saw as an
unfortunate consequence of impassioned loyalty.

Despite multiple amnesties that eventually included almost everyone who sided with the South, there was one major
exception lingering: Confederate General Robert E. Lee. In-
dicted for treason, he was fortunate to avoid prosecution for
any wartime crimes.[42] After famously surrendering to Grant
in 1865, Lee sought forgiveness. In June of 1865, about two
months after laying down arms, Lee sent President Johnson
a written pardon request. A few months later, Lee signed an

"amnesty oath" pledging allegiance to the country he'd tried to destroy and the Constitution he so violently ignored.[43]

Johnson did not sign off. It appears he may never have even received Lee's plea. In 1970, a State Department archivist found Lee's amnesty request in some old files.

One hundred and five years after Lee's death in 1870, President Gerald Ford erased the last legal disability on the secessionist leader's life.[44] On the House floor, Virginia congressman Caldwell Butler asked, "If Robert E. Lee is not worthy to be a U.S. citizen, then who is"?[45]

Ravi Ragbir. Wynnie Goodwin. José Padilla. Sandra Castañeda. Kamyar Samimi. Marco Antonio Muñoz. 21 Savage. Even Justin Bieber.

CONCLUSION

For too long, immigration law and policy have been cloaked in myth. We glorify history's white migrants without seeing in those brave newcomers their petty crimes and violent deeds. We sing praises to the penniless adventurers, without revealing their theft and graft. We build monuments to their achievements, while ignoring their failures. We romanticize their greatness, while overlooking their ordinariness.

In *Black Reconstruction in America*, W.E.B. DuBois wrote that "Negroes were ordinary human beings," a position he recognized would "seriously curtail my audience."[1] Likewise, *Welcome the Wretched* takes the position that migrants are ordinary human beings. The formal language of immigration law might call them aliens and political rhetoric might suggest they're especially dangerous, but these are just myths.

Myths aren't real, but myths matter. "Give me your tired, your poor, Your huddled masses yearning to breathe free, The wretched refuse of your teeming shore. Send these, the homeless, tempest-tost to me," Emma Lazarus wrote in the famous passage mounted onto the Statue of Liberty. In a testy exchange with a CNN reporter in 2017, Trump's immigration advisor Stephen Miller dismissed Lazarus's words, explaining that the poem wasn't always part of the monument. "The poem that you're referring to was added later and is not actually part of the original Statue of Liberty," Miller told CNN's Jim Acosta.[2] Democrats criticized him, suggesting he had ejected a time-honored tradition.

While in the White House, Miller was as single-minded as he was sinister. With all his energy focused on immigration law and policy, he proved remarkably capable of seeing in any situation an opportunity to bring more heartache to migrants. But perhaps there was some truth to Miller's claim. Had he just pointed the White House press corps to the laws that Congress has already passed, and that DHS enforces, he could have made his point with specific examples.

Under immigration law as it currently stands, the tired, the poor, the huddled masses, and wretched refuse are expected to steer clear of common failings. Whatever storm brought you to these shores, an updated and honest version of Lazarus's famous poem might add, be sure to hide the effects of its trauma. If poverty weighs on your shoulders, immigration law's present-day emphasis on interactions with the criminal legal system suggests, you should be sure to reserve your precious dollars for private space in which to live your weakest moments away from the eyes and ears of the police.

Life in the United States has never been as romantic as the Lazarus poem makes it out to be. Instead, like all good fiction, the real history of the United States has been a complicated mess of contradictions. The United States is a radical experiment in self-governance, brimming with idealism and marked by moments of greatness. It is also a country founded by violent rebels who chose war when politics reached its limits. It was shaped by the uncouth who saw in their Christianity a divine right to enslave Africans and kill Indigenous people— and created a host of laws to justify both. It was enriched by misfits who poured into their music, literature, poetry, and politics a toxic but creative mix of drugs and philandering, egomaniacal self-destruction and genocidal profit.

We in the United States like to imagine ourselves as extraordinary. When it comes to migrants, immigration law demands of them the exceptionalism U.S. citizens imagine in ourselves. If migrants were indeed aliens, as the formal language of immigration law says, then demanding extraordinariness would be the least we could ask. *Alien* is the right word to describe Superman, that mysterious extraterrestrial who migrated aerially to the plains of rural Kansas with a love of coiffed duplicity and a penchant for violence. But for everyone else, *alien* is a poor fit. Wynnie Goodwin is a California business leader whose roots in the United States stretch her entire life minus one month. José Padilla fought for the United States in Vietnam then became a long-haul truck driver. Ravi Ragbir is a father, husband, and key player in the messiness of New York City's small-d democratic politics.

All three are also longtime green-card holders with criminal records. Their entrepreneurialism and activism, like their violence, marijuana possession, and financial fraud, fit neatly into the complicated affairs of ordinary life in the United States. They are far from the first to get caught up with guns, drugs, and white-collar crime. That imperfection doesn't set them apart from U.S. citizens. On the contrary, that

imperfection ties them firmly to the long tradition of suc-
cesses and failures, victories and struggles that dot the lives of
all U.S. citizens—at least those of us who reflect honestly on
the memories that we regret.

No matter the moment, the history of the United States
is peppered by migrants who fell short of moral ideals. And
yet the country has continued on, simultaneously struggling
and thriving in search of the "more perfect union" that the
nation's Constitution imagines.

Just as the ranks of heroes and celebrities are full of sin-
ners big and small, complicated contradictions are not new to
the U.S. legal tradition. Redemption and rehabilitation have
always been aspirations, regrettably relegated more often to
myth than given life as reality. The imposing bronze doors
of the U.S. Supreme Court building feature the hero Achilles, the legendary Greek warrior whose anger toward King
Agamemnon split the Greek forces. In Homer's account,
Achilles's anger turns to payback, first against Agamemnon
by refusing to fight against the Trojans, then, after the Trojans kill his friend, by slaughtering them. In the Supreme
Court's doors, angry violence becomes a glorious symbolic
decoration for the most important site in the U.S. judicial
system. Through the artisan's careful touch, Achilles has been
rehabilitated.

Like for the ancients, immigration law in the United States
has at times welcomed people despite their flaws. Louis Loftus Repouille was arrested, prosecuted, and convicted. But
the outcome of the legal process wasn't the end of the story.
Weighing his future against his past, the judge released him in

time to celebrate Christmas at home. His ability to stay in the United States and his near-miss attempt to become a U.S. citizen, successful the second time around, are a reminder that immigration law used to take a different, more understanding approach to migrants.

Not anymore. To John Ashcroft, writing in 2002 when he was head of the Justice Department, a person convicted of the same crime as Louis is a "dangerous or violent felon" who doesn't deserve asylum.[3] More than two decades later, Ashcroft's view remains the law of the land. These days removal is almost assured for committing a wide variety of crimes, and citizenship is just a foolish hope.

Insisting that life in the United States is rightly available only to people who steer clear of criminality ignores the basic reality that crime is a feature of life in the United States. Migrants don't bring crime here. It's already here. It always has been and always will be. It's in our families, on our campuses, in our homes, and on our streets. We watch it in our movies, see it in our leaders, and learn about it in our schools. At every turn, it's lamentable, but at every turn there it is. Deporting migrants for doing what so many of us who carry the banner of U.S. citizen also do imposes a second layer of punishment onto some people simply because they were found to be just like most of us are: imperfect, fallible, and sometimes criminal.

Standing in the political moment in which we find ourselves, it's hard—perhaps impossible—to imagine a radical reconstruction of immigration law. But a radical reconstruction is what gave us immigration law's current fascination with criminal activity. In the harsh politics of the 1980s and 1990s, with its excessive attention to drug activity, and the post–September 11 fear of terrorism, migrants were easy targets. It was easy to blame them for all that we didn't like. It was easy to demand that they be the versions of ourselves we wished we were.

This fantasy is not reason enough to keep moving along the same path, tinkering at the edges. The psychiatrist turned political theorist Frantz Fanon understood well the importance of wholesale alterations. In his anti-colonial tour de force celebrating the people who would be cast off as wretched, Fanon reminds us that a social order built upon white supremacy is a social order built upon violence. In the United States, immigration law's reliance on criminal law masks the violence of the racism that is at work in determining what is criminalized and why, who is criminalized and why.

Rather than allow immigration law to protect violence until the legal system spirals into illegitimacy, a new legal reality is necessary. But imagining a new reality doesn't happen in the moment. Wholesale political realignments don't happen without a vision for a future different from the present we know. If the United States is going to cut the criminal legal system out of immigration law decision making, it's only going to be because we thought about how to make that happen long before the politics of the moment made it feasible to bring a bill to a vote. The time for radical reimagining is now.

ACKNOWLEDGMENTS

I started working on this book in the scary days of 2020 when many of us were locked indoors and death ripped through the air with the sound of cities turned eerily silent. Across the street from the Denver house where I was holed up for safety, construction workers pounded nails into walls. Even in the worst days of the pandemic, they never stopped. Almost all of them were Mexican migrants. As I watched them from across the street, I appreciated their labor and enjoyed their music. I also worried about the future, concerned that the pandemic could unleash whatever restraints still existed on the Trump administration's immigration policies. Canvassing the possibilities, I began to think about the migrants who were easiest to demonize: people who had committed crimes. It would take a few years before words began appearing on a page, but in the spring and summer of 2020, I embraced the challenge of unapologetically defending migrants, blemishes and all.

Writing this book was an exercise in asking for favors and being lucky enough to receive them from friends, colleagues, and strangers alike. None are more important than the people who opened their life stories to me and allowed me to share their struggles and losses with readers: Sandra

Castañeda, Wynnie Goodwin, Pati and her mother, Doña Francis, Ravi Ragbir, and Neda Samimi. Attorneys Charles Kuck, Sara Neel, Stacy Tolchin, and Jenny Zhao either spoke to me about their clients or put me in touch with them. For that I am thankful. Hopefully I have done well by the difficult stories they shared.

At Ohio State University, the College of Law provided me with the material support needed to write the manuscript. I wrote most of the book while living in Mexico City, only possible thanks to course release that Dean Lincoln Davies extended. Just as valuable, the college allowed me to tap librarian Natasha Landon, whose brilliant assistance tracking down obscure sources was a godsend. I could not have done the research for this book without her. I am also grateful to Lauren Hamlett for performing the unpleasant task of reviewing citations.

In South Carolina, the staff at the state's Department of Archives and History was wonderfully gracious, allowing me to review Coleman Blease's records. Flipping through old letters with the guidance of the department's kind staff, I was reminded of the public good that archives serve. Without them, it would be next to impossible to safeguard memories of forgotten figures and enrichen our understanding of the past.

Various chapters benefited from careful consideration by colleagues and students. Kelly Lytle Hernández, Ming Hsu Chen, Joy Milligan, and Bertrall Ross, students in Joy and Bertrall's Law and Inequality Colloquium at the University of Virginia, and the participants at the 2023 Criminal Justice Roundtable, especially Daniel Harawa, provided critical feedback on individual chapters. I am indebted to Ben Woodward at The New Press and Rebecca Shapiro for their thoughtful edits.

Through their curiosity, Z and X pushed me to clarify my thoughts. Through their steadfast commitment to principles, they kept me from hiding behind my own biases.

As always, Margaret Kwoka gave me the support I needed to sit with a project for years. She listened to its permutations and my complaints with the encouragement that only love makes possible. Through a delicate mix of questioning and prodding, she kept the project moving forward until the last sentence was written, edited, and proofread. Gracias.

NOTES

Introduction

1. Louis Sahagun & Emily Alpert Reyes, *Fatal Shooting in San Francisco Ignites Immigration Policy Debate*, Los Angeles Times (July 4, 2015).

2. Evan Sernoffsky, et al., *S.F. Drug Warrant Helped Accused Killer Stay in U.S.*, SFGate (July 7, 2015).

3. Valerie Richardson, *Dianne Feinstein Blames San Francisco Sheriff's Department in Kathryn Steinle Death*, Washington Times (July 7, 2015).

4. *CNN Exclusive: Hillary Clinton's First National Interview of 2016 Race*, CNN (July 7, 2015).

5. Doug Stanglin, *Trump: San Francisco Shooting Case for Securing Border*, USA Today (July 4, 2015).

6. Araceli Cruz, *Trump Blasts San Francisco Court Over Verdict in Kate Steinle Case*, TeenVogue (Dec. 1, 2017).

7. ABC News, *Donald Trump's 2016 Republican National Convention Speech*, ABC News (July 21, 2016).

8. Thomas Peele, *Kate Steinle Killing: Ballistics Expert Calls Fatal Shot Accident*, The Mercury News (August 27, 2015).

9. Associated Press, *San Francisco Jury Acquits Immigrant of Murder Charge, and Trump Flips Out*, CNBC (Nov. 30, 2017); Press Release, U.S. Dep't of Justice, U.S. Att'y's Off., N. Dist. of Cal., *Jose Inez Garcia-Zarate Remains Under Federal Firearm Charges in the Northern District of California* (Sept. 3, 2019), https://www.justice.gov/usao-ndca/pr/jose-inez-garcia-zarate -remains-under-federal-firearm-charges-northern-district.

10. *Jose Inez Garcia Zarate Gets Time Served in 2015 Kate Steinle Shooting Death*, CBS News Bay Area (June 6, 2022); Matt Gonzalez & Francisco

Ugarte, *An Open Letter to the Biden Administration: It's Time to Drop Charges Against José Ines García Zarate*, The Davis Vanguard (Sept. 14, 2021).

11. Judgment, United States v. García-Zarate, No. 17-cr-00609 (N.D. Cal. June 11, 2022).

12. *See* Docket for USA v. Dominguez-De La Parra, No. 2:09-cr-01278 (W.D. Tex. Oct. 14, 2009); Petition for Warrant or Summons for Offender Under Supervision, USA v. Dominguez-De La Parra, No. 2:09-cr-01278 (W.D. Tex. July 14, 2015); Order Revoking Supervised Release and Re-Sentencing Defendant, USA v. Dominguez-De La Parra, No. 2:09-cr-01278 (W.D. Tex. Oct. 18, 2022).

13. National Alliance to End Homelessness, *The State of Homelessness in America*, tbl. 1.1 at 7 (2016).

14. U.S. Dep't of Housing and Urban Development, *HUD 2020 Continuum of Care Homeless Assistance Programs Homeless Populations and Subpopulations*, 1-2 (Dec. 15, 2020), https://files.hudexchange.info/reports /published/CoC_PopSub_NatlTerrDC_2020.pdf.

15. Devon W. Carbado, Unreasonable: Black Lives, Police Power, and the Fourth Amendment 11 (The New Press, 2022).

16. Memorandum from Alejandro N. Mayorkas, Secretary of Homeland Security to Tae D. Johnson, Acting Dir., Immigr. and Customs Enf't, Guidelines for the Enf't of Civ. Immigr. L. (Sept. 30, 2021).

1. Celebrating Criminals

1. 8 U.S.C. §§ 1324a(a)(1), (a)(3), (e)(4).

2. Daniel Kanstroom, Deportation Nation: Outsiders in American History 27 (Harv. Univ. Press, 2007); Abbot Emerson Smith, Colonists in Bondage: White Servitude and Convict Labor in America, 1607–1776, at 92 (Univ. of North Carolina Press, 1947).

3. The Transportation Act, 4 Geo. I, c. 11 (1717).

4. Abbot Emerson Smith, Colonists in Bondage: White Servitude and Convict Labor in America, 1607–1776, at 90–91 (Univ. of North Carolina Press, 1947).

5. Abbot Emerson Smith, Colonists in Bondage: White Servitude and Convict Labor in America, 1607–1776, at 104 (Univ. of North Carolina Press, 1947).

6. Daniel Kanstroom, Deportation Nation: Outsiders in American History 41 (Harv. Univ. Press, 2007).

7. Daniel Kanstroom, Deportation Nation: Outsiders in American History 42 (Harv. Univ. Press, 2007).

8. Adam Goodman, The Deportation Machine: America's Long History of Expelling Immigrants 11 (Princeton Univ. Press, 2020).

9. Adam Goodman, The Deportation Machine: America's Long History of Expelling Immigrants 12 (Princeton Univ. Press, 2020).

10. Mae Ngai, The Chinese Question: The Gold Rushes and Global Politics 144 (W.W. Norton Co., 2021).

11. Ronald Takaki, Strangers from a Different Shore: A History of Asian Americans 101 (Little Brown & Co., 1989).

12. Erika Lee, At America's Gates: Chinese Immigration During the Exclusion Era, 1882–1943, 23, 29 (Univ. of North Carolina Press, 2003).

13. Ulysses S. Grant, Sixth Annual Message to Congress, The American Presidency Project (December 7, 1874), https://www.presidency.ucsb.edu/documents/sixth-annual-message-3.

14. Page Act of 1875, 18 Stat. 477, §§ 1–3 (March 3, 1875).

15. Chinese Exclusion Act, 22 Stat. 58, ch. 126, §§ 1, 4, 14 (May 6, 1882).

16. Scott Act, 25 Stat. 504, ch. 1064 (Oct. 1, 1888).

17. Geary Act, 27 Stat. 25, ch. 60, §§ 2, 6 (May 5, 1892).

18. Fong Yue Ting v. United States, 149 U.S. 698, 711 (1893).

19. Magna Carta, cl. 41 (1215).

20. Emmerich de Vattel, The Law of Nations, at Book I, chapter 19, § 230; Book II, chapter 9, §§ 120–122 (T & J.W. Johnson ed. 1856) (1758).

21. Fong Yue Ting v. United States, 149 U.S. 698, 706, 717 (1893) (quoting Ping v. United States, 130 U.S. 581, 606 (1889)).

22. Fong Yue Ting v. United States, 149 U.S. 698, 729 (1893).

23. Adam Goodman, The Deportation Machine: America's Long History of Expelling Immigrants 15–16 (Princeton Univ. Press, 2020); *The Fire, Lucky Truckee, Chinatown Holocausted*, Truckee Republican, May 29, 1875, at 3; Jean Pfaelzer, Driven Out: The Forgotten War Against Chinese Americans 171 (Univ. of California Press, 2007).

24. Beth Lew-Williams, The Chinese Must Go: Violence, Exclusion, and the Making of the Alien in America 247–250 appx. A (Harv. Univ. Press, 2018).

25. Julian Samora, et al., Gunpowder Justice: A Reassessment of the Texas Rangers 26 (Univ. of Notre Dame Press, 1979).

26. William D. Carrigan & Clive Webb, Forgotten Dead: Mob Violence Against Mexicans in the United States, 1848–1928, 100 (Oxford Univ. Press, 2013).

27. Walter Prescott Webb, The Texas Rangers: A Century of Frontier Defense 478 (Univ. of Texas Press, 1935) (1965).

28. Julian Samora, et al., Gunpowder Justice: A Reassessment of the Texas Rangers 28, 29, 37 (Univ. of Notre Dame Press, 1979).

29. Monica Muñoz Martinez, The Injustice Never Leaves You: Anti-Mexican Violence in Texas 294 (Harv. Univ. Press, 2018).

30. Brief for Appellants, Wong Wing v. United States, 163 U.S. 228, 8 (1895).

31. Judgment, Wong Wing v. United States, 163 U.S. 228 (July 20, 1892), *reprinted in* Record, Case No. 15236, U.S. Supreme Court, at 4.

32. Paul W. Keve, *Building a Better Prison: The First Three Decades of the Detroit House of Correction*, 25 Michigan Historical Review 1, 3, 5 (1999).

33. Brief for Appellants, Wong Wing v. United States, 163 U.S. 228, 2–3, 8–9 (1895).

34. *Jacob M. Dickinson Dies in 78th Year*, New York Times, Dec. 14, 1928, at 29.

35. Brief for the United States, Wong Wing v. United States, 163 U.S. 228, 9 (1895).

36. Brief for the United States, Wong Wing v. United States, 163 U.S. 228, 19 (1895).

37. Brief for the United States, Wong Wing v. United States, 163 U.S. 228, 19 (1895).

38. Wong Wing v. United States, 163 U.S. 228, 235–238 (1896).

2. Making Criminals

1. Cole L. Blease, Governor of S.C., Annual Address to the General Assembly of S.C. 42 (Jan. 12, 1915).

2. Francis Butler Simkins, Pitchfork Ben Tillman: South Carolinian 486 (Univ. of S.C. Press, 1944).

3. Francis Butler Simkins, Pitchfork Ben Tillman: South Carolinian 486 (Univ. of S.C. Press, 1944) (criticizing an opposing candidate and a newspaper editor); Cole L. Blease, Governor of S.C., Annual Address to the General Assembly of S.C. 10 (Jan. 12, 1915) (criticizing Clemson College).

4. W.J. Cash, The Mind of the South 253 (Knopf, 1941).

5. A.J. McKelway, *The Governor's Conference*, The Survey: A Journal of Constructive Philanthropy, vol. XXIX, No. 12, at 347 (Dec. 21, 1912).

6. Reports and Resolutions of the General Assembly of the State of South Carolina, vol. 3, at 305 (Jan. 13, 1914).

7. Amy Louise Wood, *Cole Blease's Pardoning Pen: State Power and Penal Reform in South Carolina, in* Crime & Punishment in the Jim Crow South 147, 147 (Univ. of Ill. Press, 2019).

8. Ronald Dantan Burnside, The Governorship of Coleman Livingston Blease of South Carolina, 1911–1915, at 91 (1963) (Ph.D. dissertation, University of Vanderbilt).

9. *Little Enthusiasm at Yorkville*, The (Charleston) News and Courier (July 2, 1910), at 1.

10. Ronald Dantan Burnside, The Governorship of Coleman Livingston Blease of South Carolina, 1911–1915, at 153 (1963) (Ph.D. dissertation, Indiana University).

11. Cole L. Blease, Governor of S.C., Annual Address to the General Assembly of S.C. 34 (Jan. 12, 1915).

12. Francis Butler Simkins, Pitchfork Ben Tillman: South Carolinian 490 (Univ. of S.C. Press, 1944).

13. Ronald Dantan Burnside, The Governorship of Coleman Livingston Blease of South Carolina, 1911–1915, at 39 (1963) (Ph.D. dissertation, Indiana University).

14. Selden K. Smith, *Smith, Ellison Durant*, South Carolina Encyclopedia (Aug. 1, 2016), https://www.scencyclopedia.org/sce/entries/smith-ellison-durant/.

15. Kelly Lytle Hernández, City of Inmates: Conquest, Rebellion, and the Rise of Human Caging in Los Angeles, 1771–1965, at 137 (Univ. of N.C. Press, 2017).

16. *Lancaster Folk More Emphatic*, The (Columbia) State (July 2, 1914), at 1.

17. Ronald Dantan Burnside, The Governorship of Coleman Livingston Blease of South Carolina, 1911–1915, at 289 (1963) (Ph.D. dissertation, Indiana University).

18. Letter from Coleman Blease to Clarence J. Owens, Managing Director, The Southern Commercial Congress (Nov. 26, 1914) (located in South Carolina Archives, Group S532005, location 239M03-240A04, Box 42).

19. W. Anthony Gengarelly, *Secretary of Labor William B. Wilson and the Red Scare, 1919–1920*, 47 Penn. History 311, 314–316 (1980).

20. William B. Wilson, *Deportation of Aliens*, 20 The American City 318, 319 (Apr. 1919).

21. Cong. Rec. H5349, 5352 (June 19, 1884) (Statement of Rep. Martin Foran).

22. Terence V. Powderly, Annual Address of the General Master Workman, Record of the Proceedings of the Eighth Regular Session of the General Assembly of the Knights of Labor 569, 576–577 (September 1884) (quoting a letter he published in the Scranton Truth in June 1884).

23. Cole L. Blease, Governor of S.C., Annual Address to the General Assembly of S.C. 34 (Jan. 12, 1915).

24. President's Veto Message, H.R. 10384, 64th Cong., 2nd Sess. (Jan. 29, 1917).

25. Regulation of Immigration—Veto Message, Cong. Rec. 2616, 2629, 64th Cong., 2nd Sess. (Feb. 5, 1917).

26. Immigration Act of 1924, 43 Stat. 153, 159, § 11(a)-(c) (May 26, 1924); Select Commission on Immigration and Refugee Policy, U.S. Immigration Policy and the National Interest Staff Report 195–196 (1981).

27. David A. Reed, *America of the Melting Pot Comes to End*, New York Times, April 27, 1924, at 3.

28. Immigration Act of 1924, 43 Stat. 153, 155, § 4(c) (May 26, 1924).

29. Kelly Lytle Hernández, Migra! History of the U.S. Border Patrol 28 (Univ. of Cal. Press, 2010).

30. Immigration Bill, Vol. 65, pt. 6, Cong. Rec. H. 5640, 5657 (April 5, 1924).

31. Eric S. Fish, *Race, History, and Immigration Crimes*, 107 Iowa Law Review 1051, 1073–1074 (2022).

32. S. 5094, 70th Congress, 2nd Sess., U.S. Senate (Dec. 22, 1928).

33. Cong. Rec. S2092 (Jan. 23, 1929).

34. Kelly Lytle Hernández, City of Inmates: Conquest, Rebellion, and the Rise of Human Caging in Los Angeles 1771–1965, at 137 (Univ. of N.C. Press, 2017).

35. Kelly Lytle Hernández, City of Inmates: Conquest, Rebellion, and the Rise of Human Caging in Los Angeles 1771–1965, at 138 n. 20 (Univ. of N.C. Press, 2017).

36. James J. Davis, The Iron Puddler: My Life in the Rolling Mills and What Came of It 42, 45–46 (Bobbs-Merrill Co., 1922).

37. James J. Davis, The Iron Puddler: My Life in the Rolling Mills and What Came of It 51–52 (Bobbs-Merrill Co., 1922).

38. Page Act, 18 Stat. 477, Chap. 141 (1875).

39. 22 Stat. 214, 214, § 2 (Aug. 3, 1882).

40. Aileen Elizabeth Kennedy, The Ohio Poor Law and Its Administration 12 (Univ. of Chicago Press, 1934).

41. An Act for the Relief of the Poor, Ohio Gen. Assembly, 62nd Sess., Vol. 73, page 233 § 35 (April 12, 1876); Ohio Gen. Assembly, 56th Sess., Vol. 62, page 18, § 40 (Feb. 23, 1865).

42. Ohio Gen. Assembly, 56th Sess., Vol. 62, page 18, § 9 (Feb. 23, 1865).

43. James J. Davis, The Iron Puddler: My Life in the Rolling Mills and What Came of It 61 (Bobbs-Merrill Co., 1922).

44. James J. Davis, Selective Immigration 25, 36, 173 (Scott-Mitchell Publishing Co., 1925).

45. James J. Davis, Selective Immigration 207–208 (Scott-Mitchell Publishing Co., 1925).

46. U.S. Dep't of Justice, Immigration & Naturalization Service, 1999 Statistical Yearbook of the Immigration and Naturalization Service, 15 chart A & 16 chart B (2002).

47. Alfred J. Hillier, Albert Johnson, Congressman, 36 Pacific Northwest Quarterly 193, 198 (1945).

48. Rep. Albert Johnson, Appendix to the Cong. Rec. 260–261 (August 13, 1913).

49. Resolutions of Allied Patriotic Societies on Various Pending Bills, Hearings Before the Committee on Immigration and Naturalization, House of Representatives, 69th Congress, 1st Sess., Hearing No. 69.1.11, at 149 (1926).

50. Kristofer Allerfeldt, "And We Got Here First": Albert Johnson, National Origins and Self-Interest in the Immigration Debate of the 1920s, 45 J. Contemporary History 7, 19 (2010).

51. Comments by the Age Editors on the Sayings of Other Editors, New York Age, March 16, 1929, at 4; Raymond Arsenault, Blease, Coleman Livingston, American National Biography (Feb. 2000).

52. *Editorial Paragraphs*, The Nation, Feb. 13, 1929, at 175.

53. Clarence N. Stone, *Bleaseism and the 1912 Election in South Carolina*, 40 N.C. Historical Review 54, 58 (1963); *The Cabinet: Moose Member*, Time, Sept. 3, 1928, at 7.

54. Kelly Lytle Hernández, City of Inmates: Conquest, Rebellion, and the Rise of Human Caging in Los Angeles, 1771–1965, at 138 (Univ. of N.C. Press, 2017).

55. Letter from James J. Davis, Sec'y of Labor, to Hon. Hiram W. Johnson, U.S. Senator (Jan. 2, 1929).

56. Memorandum from U.S. Dep't of Labor, Senate Report No. 1456, S. 5094 (Jan. 17, 1929).

57. Kelly Lytle Hernández, City of Inmates: Conquest, Rebellion, and the Rise of Human Caging in Los Angeles, 1771–1965, at 138 (Univ. of N.C. Press, 2017).

58. Letter from James J. Davis, Sec'y of Labor, to Hon. Hiram W. Johnson, U.S. Senator (Jan. 2, 1929).

59. Jonathan Peter Spiro, Defending the Master Race: Conservation, Eugenics, and the Legacy of Madison Grant 357 (Univ. of Vt. Press, 2009).

60. *Letter from Hon. Madison Grant*, Hearings Before the Committee on Immigration and Naturalization, House of Representatives, 69th Congress, 1st Sess., Hearing No. 69.1.11, at 179 (1926).

61. Desmond S. King, Making Americans: Immigration, Race, and the Origins of the Diverse Democracy 173–174 (Harv. Univ. Press, 2002).

62. *Statement of Dr. Harry H. Laughlin*, The Eugenical Aspects of Deportation, Hearings Before the Committee on Immigration and Naturalization, House of Representatives, 70th Congress, 1st Sess., Hearing No. 70.1.4, at 3 (1928).

63. S. 5094, 70th Congress, 2nd Sess., U.S. House of Representatives, Union Calendar No. 752 (Feb. 5, 1929).

64. Memorandum from the American Civil Liberties Union to the House Committee on Immigration and Naturalization, On the Deportation

of Certain Aliens and For the Punishment of the Unlawful Entry of Certain Aliens (February 1929), *included in* Hearings Before the House Comm. on Immigration and Naturalization (Feb. 20, 1929), at 2–3.

65. Cong. Rec. H3766, vol. 70 (Feb. 19, 1929).

66. House Conf. Report, S. 5094 (March 1, 1929).

67. *Presidential Approvals*, Cong. Rec. S5224, 5225 (March 2, 1929).

68. *See* Act of March 4, 1929, ch. 690, §§ 1(a), 2, 45 Stat. 1551, 1551.

69. *See* INA §§ 275(c), 276(b).

70. Mark Motivans, *Immigration Offenders in the Federal Justice System, 2010*, 22 tbl.6, 29 tbl.9 (July 2012, rev. Oct. 2013).

71. United States v. Diaz-Ramirez, 646 F.3d 653, 655 n.2 (9th Cir. 2011).

72. Admin. Conf. of the U.S. Courts, *U.S. District Courts—Judicial Business 2019*, https://www.uscourts.gov/statistics-reports/us-district-courts -judicial-business-2019.

73. Admin. Conf. of the U.S. Courts, *U.S. Magistrate Judges—Judicial Business 2019*, https://www.uscourts.gov/statistics-reports/us-magistrate -judges-judicial-business-2019.

74. Human Rts. Watch, Turning Migrants into Criminals: The Harmful Impact of U.S. Border Prosecutions 35 (Human Rts. Watch, 2013).

3. Imagining Aliens

1. Proclamation No. 5797 (Apr. 18, 1988), https://www.reaganlibrary .gov/archives/speech/proclamation-5797-crime-victims-week-1988.

2. Tali Mendelberg, The Race Card: Campaign Strategy, Implicit Messages, and the Norm of Equality 143, 150 (Princeton Univ. Press, 2017).

3. Robert Reinhold, *Gang Violence Shocks Los Angeles*, New York Times, Feb. 8, 1988, at A10.

4. William Overend & Bob Baker, *Total Murders Down Despite Record High in Gang Killings*, Los Angeles Times, Jan. 10, 1989.

5. William J. Clinton, *Address Accepting the Presidential Nomination at the Democratic National Convention in New York*, The American Presidency

Project (July 16, 1992), https://www.presidency.ucsb.edu/documents/address
-accepting-the-presidential-nomination-the-democratic-national-convention
-new-york.

6. C-Span, Joe Biden in 1993 Speech Warned of "Predators on Our
Streets," CNN, (Nov. 18, 1993).

7. Jana K. Lipman, *A Refugee Camp in America: Fort Chaffee and Vietnamese and Cuban Refugees, 1975–1982*, 33 Journal of American Ethnic History 57, 58 (2014).

8. Jill H. Wilson, *"Recalcitrant" Countries and the Use of Visa Sanctions
to Encourage Cooperation with Alien Removals*, Cong. Res. Service (July 10,
2020).

9. Trinh v. Homan, 333 F. Supp. 3d 984, 993 (C.D. Cal. 2018).

10. Kelly Lytle Hernández, Migra! A History of the U.S. Border Patrol
206 (Univ. of Cal. Press, 2010).

11. Gillian Brockell, *She Was Stigmatized as the "Welfare Queen." The
Truth Was More Disturbing, A New Book Says*, Washington Post (May 21,
2019); Noel A. Cazenave, The Urban Racial State: Managing Race Relations
in American Cities 136 (Rowman & Littlefield Publishers, 2011).

12. *Haitians Who Fled to U.S. Suing for Asylum as Political Refugees*,
New York Times, Oct. 17, 1975, at 56.

13. Statement of Sen. Paula Hawkins, in U.S. Cong., S. Comm. on the
Judiciary, Subcomm. on Immigration and Refugee Policy, *United States as a
Country of Mass First Asylum: Hearing Before the Subcomm. on Immigration
and Refugee Policy*, U.S. S., 97th Cong., 1st Sess. 37 (July 31, 1981).

14. White House Statement, June 7, 1980, *included in* U.S. Dep't of
State Bull. 75 (August 1980).

15. *Exodus from Cuba*, 80 U.S. State Dep't Bull. 80, 81 (July 1980).

16. Carl Lindskoog, Detain and Punish: Haitian Refugees and the
Rise of the World's Largest Immigration Detention System 17, 27, 34–35, 43
(Univ. of Fla. Press, 2018).

17. William K. Stevens, *Arkansas Fort Receives First of Thousands of Cubans*, New York Times, May 10, 1980, at 11.

18. Paul Heath Hoeffel, *Fort Chaffee's Unwanted Cubans*, New York Times, Dec. 21, 1980, at 31.

19. Jo Thomas, *Refugees at Ft. Chaffee Wait in Boredom and Uncertainty*, New York Times, June 6, 1980, at 34.

20. Paul Heath Hoeffel, *Fort Chaffee's Unwanted Cubans*, New York Times, Dec. 21, 1980, at 31.

21. *Better Security for Camp Asked as Refugees Flee*, New York Times, May 28, 1980, at 14.

22. Mark S. Hamm, The Abandoned Ones: The Imprisonment and Uprising of the Mariel Boat People 55–56 (Ne. Univ. Press, 1995).

23. Jo Thomas, *Troops Are Ordered to Arkansas Camp After Refugee Riot*, New York Times, June 3, 1980, at 1.

24. Brian Stanford Miller, Car Tags and Cubans: Bill Clinton, Frank White and Arkansas' Return to Conservativism 125 (Univ. of Miss., 2006).

25. Bill Clinton, My Life 282–287 (Vintage Books, 2005).

26. Katherine Beckett, Making Crime Pay: Law and Order in Contemporary American Politics 55–57 (Oxford Univ. Press, 1997); Susan Schmidt & Tom Kenworthy, *Cocaine Caused Bias' Death, Autopsy Reveals*, L.A. Times, June 25, 1986.   .

27. Anti-Drug Abuse Act of 1986, Pub. L. No. 99-570, § 1152, 100 Stat. 3207-047.

28. Anti-Drug Abuse Act of 1986, Pub. L. No. 99-570, § 1002, 100 Stat. 3207-047.

29. Erik Eckholm, *Congress Moves to Narrow Cocaine Sentencing Disparities*, New York Times, July 29, 2010, at A16.

30. Anti-Drug Abuse Act of 1988, Pub. L. No. 100-690, 102 Stat. 4181.

31. *Final Report of the Grand Jury*, Fla. Cir. Ct., 11th Jud. Dist., Fall Term 1981, at 1–3 (May 11, 1982).

32. *See* César Cuauhtémoc García Hernández, Migrating to Prison: America's Obsession with Locking Up Immigrants 61–63 (The New Press, 2019).

33. Memorandum from Ron Klain, White House Chief of Staff, to the Att'y Gen. and Carol Rasco, Dir. Pol'y Council of the U.S. (Nov. 22, 1994), https://www.documentcloud.org/documents/2820704-RonKlain-November1994.html.

34. Violent Crime Control and Law Enf't Act, Pub. L. 103-322, 108 Stat. 1796, 2023, § 130001(b) (amending 8 U.S.C. § 1326(b)).

35. U.S. H.R., Comm. on the Judiciary, Int'l Terrorism: Threats and Responses (April 6, 1995) (Statement of Rep. Schumer), https://archive.org/details/internationalter1996unit/page/6/mode/2up.

36. Anti-Terrorism and Effective Death Penalty Act, Pub. L. 104-132, 110 Stat. 1214, 1278, § 440(g) (amending 8 U.S.C. § 1252a) (relating to deportation procedure) (April 24, 1996); *id.* at § 440(e) (amending 8 U.S.C. § 1101(a)(43)) (relating to aggravated felony definition).

37. Immigration Act of 1917, Pub. L. 301, 39 Stat. 874, 875–877, § 3 (Feb. 5, 1917).

38. Matter of Silva, 16 I&N Dec. 26, 30 (BIA 1976).

39. INS v. St. Cyr, 533 U.S. 289, 294–297 (2001).

40. U.S. Senate, Comm. on the Judiciary, Subcomm. on Immigr., Hearing on Activities of the Immigration and Naturalization Service, Serial No. J-104-24, at 5, 8, 46 (May 11, 1995).

41. Benjamin Gonzalez O'Brien, Handcuffs and Chain Link: Criminalizing the Undocumented in America 99–101 (Univ. of Virginia Press, 2018).

42. U.S. House of Rep., Comm. on Judiciary, Subcomm. on Immigr. & Claims, Serial No. 103, at 37, 40 (Sept. 5, 1996).

43. William J. Clinton, Statement on Signing the Omnibus Consolidated Appropriations Act, 1997, at 1935, 1937 (Sept. 30, 1996).

44. Demore v. Kim, 538 U.S. 510, 521 (2003) (quoting Mathews v. Diaz, 426 U.S. 67, 79–80 (1976)).

45. IIRIRA, 110 Stat. 3009-597, § 304(b).

46. Padilla v. Kentucky, 559 U.S. 356, 364 (2010).

47. Att'y Gen. John Ashcroft, *Prepared Remarks for the US Mayors Conference* (October 25, 2001), https://www.justice.gov/archive/ag/speeches/2001/agcrisisremarks10_25.htm.

48. Press Release, Homeland Security Presidential Directive-2, Combating Terrorism Through Immigration Policies (Oct. 29, 2001), https://georgewbush-whitehouse.archives.gov/news/releases/2001/10/20011030-2.html.

49. Cristina Rodríguez et al., *A Program in Flux: New Priorities and Implementation Challenges for 287(g)*, at 6 fig. 1 (2010).

50. *Delegation of Immigration Authority Section 287(g) Immigr. and Nationality Act*, Dep't of Immigr. and Customs Enforcement, https://www.ice.gov/identify-and-arrest/287g.

51. Santos v. Frederick County Board of Commissioners, 725 F.3d 451, 465–466, 469 (4th Cir. 2013).

52. I.N.S. v. Lopez-Mendoza, 468 U.S. 1032, 1040 (quoting *In re Lopez-Mendoza*, No. A22452208 (BIA 1979)).

53. Complaint, Medrano v. Jenkins, No. 19-cv-02038 (D. Md. July 11, 2019).

54. Illegal Immigration Reform and Immigrant Responsibility Act of 1996, Pub. L. No. 104-208, § 110, 110 Stat. 3009, 3009-571.

55. USA PATRIOT Act, Pub. L. No. 107-56, 115 Stat. 272, § 414(a) (Oct. 26, 2001); Brown v. Board of Education, 349 U.S. 294, 301 (1955).

56. American-Arab Anti-Discrimination Committee, NSEERS: The Consequences of America's Efforts to Secure Its Borders 9 (Penn State's Dickinson School of L., 2009).

57. American-Arab Anti-Discrimination Committee, NSEERS: The Consequences of America's Efforts to Secure Its Borders 17–18 (Penn State's Dickinson School of L., 2009).

58. Sahar Aziz, The Racial Muslim: When Racism Quashes Religious Freedom 175 (Univ. Cal. Press, 2022).

59. Homeland Sec. Act of 2002, Pub. L. 107-296, 116 Stat. 2135, 2142, § 101(b), codified at 6 U.S.C. § 111 (Nov. 25, 2002).

60. Dep't of Just., Office of the Inspector Gen., *The Immigration and Naturalization Service's Contacts with Two September 11 Terrorists* 19 (May 20, 2022).

61. President George W. Bush, The Dep't of Homeland Sec. 2 (June 2002).

62. President George W. Bush, The Dep't of Homeland Sec. 12, 16 (June 2002).

63. U.S. Immigr. and Customs Enf't, https://www.ice.gov/; *About CBP*, U.S. Customs and Border Prot., https://www.cbp.gov/about.

64. U.S. Immigration Commission, Immigration and Crime 1 (Univ. of Penn., 1911).

65. Katherine Benton-Cohen, Inventing the Immigration Problem: The Dillingham Commission and Its Legacy 124 (Harv. Univ. Press, 2018).

66. Michael Tonry, *Race, Ethnicity, Crime, and Immigration, in* The Oxford Handbook of Ethnicity, Crime, and Immigration 10 (Sandra M. Bucerius & Michael Tonry, eds., 2014).

4. Policing Without Boundaries

1. Fong Yue Ting v. United States, 149 U.S. 698, 730 (1893).

2. Defendant's Opposition to Plaintiff's Motion for Preliminary Injunction, Castaneda v. Garland, No. 21-cv-01418, at *20 (C.D. Cal. Sept. 10, 2021).

3. Padilla v. Kentucky, 559 U.S. 356, 364 (2010).

4. Sam Levin, *Her Murder Conviction Was Overturned. US Immigration Still Wants to Deport Her*, The Guardian (May 2, 2022).

5. U.S. Immigr. and Customs Enf't, *Directive Number 11072.1: Civil Immigration Enforcement Actions Inside Courthouses* (Jan. 10, 2018).

6. Letter from William J. Barr, Att'y Gen., and Chad F. Wolf, Acting Sec'y of Homeland Sec., to Chief Justice Walters and Chief Justice Fairhurst (Nov. 21, 2019).

7. Letter from Jefferson B. Sessions, III, Att'y Gen., and John F. Kelly, Sec'y of Homeland Sec., to Chief Justice Tani G. Cantil-Sakauye (March 29, 2017).

8. Dep't of Justice, *Attorney General Jeff Sessions Delivers Remarks Announcing the Department of Justice's Renewed Commitment to Criminal Immigration Enforcement* (April 11, 2017), https://www.justice.gov/opa/speech/attorney-general-jeff-sessions-delivers-remarks-announcing-department-justice-s-renewed.

9. Budget-in-Brief: Fiscal Year 2006, Dep't of Homeland Sec., at 15 (May 24, 2022).

10. Budget-in-Brief: Fiscal Year 2022, Dep't of Homeland Sec., 23–32 (Sept. 11, 2021).

11. Memorandum from John Morton, Dir., Immigr. and Customs Enf't, to All ICE Emp.'s, *Civil Immigration Enforcement: Priorities for the Apprehension, Detention, and Removal of Aliens* (March 2, 2011).

12. Arizona v. United States, 567 U.S. 387, 396 (2012).

13. David Pughes & Art Acevedo, *Texas Police Chiefs: Do Not Burden Local Law Enforcement Officers with Federal Immigration Enforcement*, Dallas Morning News, April 28, 2017.

14. City of El Cenizo v. Texas, 885 F.3d 332 (5th Cir. 2018), *superseded by* 890 F.3d 164 (5th Cir. 2018).

15. Human Impact Partners, *The Effects of Forced Family Separation in the Rio Grande Valley: A Family Unity, Family Health Research Update* 12 (2018).

16. Arthur C. Clarke, Profiles of the Future: An Inquiry into the Limits of the Possible 21 (Harper & Row, 1973 edition).

17. Geo. L. Ctr. on Priv. & Tech., *American Dragnet: Data-Driven Deportation in the 21st Century*, American Dragnet, Figure 1: Estimated ICE Surveillance Spending (2008–2021), https://www.americandragnet.org/finding1 (May 10, 2022).

18. Dep't of Homeland Sec., Immigr. and Customs Enf't, *Total Searches and Reports* (2021); Sam Biddle, *ICE Searched LexisNexis Database Over 1 Million Times in Just Seven Months*, The Intercept, June 9, 2022 (Information about the NCATC relies on government records obtained by *The Intercept* and described by journalist Sam Biddle).

19. Dep't of Homeland Sec., *Immigration and Customs Enforcement Budget Overview, Fiscal Year 2022 Congressional Justification*, at ICE—O&S—131.

20. Dep't of Homeland Sec., Immigration and Customs Enforcement, Searches and Reports by ICE Component (2021).

21. Dep't of Homeland Sec., Privacy Impact Statement for the Data Analysis System, DHS/ICE DAS/PIA-048, 2, 6–7 (Sept. 29, 2017).

22. Dep't of Homeland Sec., *Office of Immigration Statistics, 2020 Yearbook of Immigration Statistics*, 52 tbl. 20 (April 2022).

23. Seth Freed Wessler, *Is Denaturalization the Next Front in the Trump Administration's War on Immigration?*, New York Times Magazine, Dec. 19, 2018.

24. United States v. Olivas-Perea, 297 F. Supp. 3d 1191, 1195–1197 (D. N.M. 2017).

25. United States v. Valadez-Muñoz, 2018 U.S. Dist. Lexis 241389 (C.D. Calif. April 25, 2018) (unpublished).

26. Criminal Complaint, United States v. Valadez-Muñoz, No. 17-cr-00702-RGK (C.D. Calif. Oct. 10, 2017).

27. J.R.R. Tolkien, The Silmarillion 290 (Christopher Tolkien, ed. 1977).

28. Michael Steinberger, *Does Palantir See Too Much?*, New York Times Magazine, Oct. 21, 2020.

29. SEC, *Palantir Technologies Form S-1 Registration Statement* (2020), https://www.sec.gov/Archives/edgar/data/1321655/000119312520230013/d904406ds1.htm.

30. Geo. L. Ctr. on Priv. & Tech., *American Dragnet: Data-Driven Deportation in the 21st Century*, American Dragnet (May 10, 2022), https://www.americandragnet.org/finding1.

31. Mike Allen, *Palantir CEO Hits Silicon Valley "Monoculture," May Leave California*, Axios (May 26, 2020).

32. David Runciman, *Competition Is for Losers*, London Review of Books (Sept. 23, 2021).

33. U.S. Immigr. and Customs Enf't, *Homeland Security Investigations (HSI)—An Introduction*, YouTube, (Feb. 4, 2011), https://youtu.be /rUDGdK29SIE; *ICE, Who We Are*, U.S. Immigr. and Customs Enf't (April 12, 2023), https://www.ice.gov/about-ice/homeland-security-investi gations.

34. Dep't of Homeland Sec., *Privacy Impact Assessment Update for the FALCON Search & Analysis System*, DHS/ICE/PIA-032(b) FALCON-SA, at 4, 33, 35 (Jan. 22, 2021).

35. New York Civil Liberties Union, Stuck with Suspicion: How Vague Gang Allegations Impact Relief & Bond for Immigrant New Yorkers 14–15 & n.56 (2019).

36. Geo. L. Ctr. on Priv. & Tech., *American Dragnet: Data-Driven Deportation in the 21st Century*, American Dragnet (May 10, 2022), https:// www.americandragnet.org/finding1.

37. Mijente, Sabotaging Sanctuary: How Data Brokers Give ICE Backdoor Access to Colorado's Data and Jails 3 (2022).

38. Cust. & Border Prot., Border Enf't Contracting Div.: Order for Supplies or Servs. (U.S. Border Patrol San Diego Sector—ARJIS and eSun Accessed July 1, 2023) (on file with author).

39. Mark Noferi & Robert Koulish, *The Immigration Detention Risk Assessment*, 29 Geo. Immigr. L.J. 45, 50 (2015).

40. Kate Evans & Robert Koulish, *Manipulating Risk: Immigration Detention Through Automation*, 24 Lewis & Clark L. Rev. 789, 794 (2020).

41. FOX and Friends, *FOX News July 6, 2020 3:00am–6:00am*, Internet Archive (July 6, 2020), https://archive.org/details/FOXNEWSW _20200706_100000_FOX_and_Friends; César Cuauhtémoc García Hernández, *It's Still Time to Abolish ICE*, The Nation, Feb. 26, 2021.

42. Order Granting Motion for Preliminary Injunction, Zepeda Rivas v. Jennings, No. 20-cv-02731 (N.D. Cal. June 9, 2020).

43. Modified Preliminary Injunction and Additional Findings of Fact, Hernandez Roman v. Wolf, No. 20-cv-00768 (C.D. Cal. Sept. 29, 2020).

44. Emily Green, *Trump's Asylum Policies Sent Him Back to Mexico. He Was Kidnapped 5 Hours Later by a Cartel*, Vice (Sept. 16, 2019).

45. Caitlin Dickerson & Michael D. Shear, *Before Covid-19, Trump Aide Sought to Use Disease to Close Borders*, New York Times, May 3, 2020.

46. *Two Years of Suffering: Biden Administration Continues Use of Discredited Title 42 Order to Flout Refugee Law*, Human Rights First (March 2022), https://humanrightsfirst.org/wp-content/uploads/2022/06/TwoYears ofSuffering.pdf.

47. *CBP Enforcement Statistics Fiscal Year 2023: U.S. Border Patrol Recidivism Rates*, Customs and Border Prot. (2023), https://www.cbp.gov /newsroom/stats/cbp-enforcement-statistics

48. Off. of Inspector Gen., *Streamline: Measuring Its Effect on Illegal Border Crossing*, OIG-15-95, Dep't Homeland Sec. (May 2015); *Border Patrol: Actions Needed to Improve Oversight of Post-Apprehension Consequences*, U.S. Gov't Accountability Off., 14 (Jan. 12, 2017); *CBP Enforcement Statistics Fiscal Year 2023*, Customs and Border Prot., https://www.cbp.gov/news room/stats/cbp-enforcement-statistics.

49. *Most Border Patrol Apprehensions Are for Repeat Crossers, But Agency Data Doesn't Yet Provide the Full Picture*, TRAC (Sept. 9, 2022), https://trac .syr.edu/reports/694/.

5. Illegal Isn't Illegal

1. *Despairing Father Kills Imbecile Boy*, New York Times, Oct. 13, 1939, at 25; Robert A. Burt, Death Is That Man Taking Names 33 (Univ. of Cal. Press, 2004).

2. Repouille v. United States, 165 F.2d 152 (2nd Cir. 1947).

3. *Fiscal Year 2019 Entry/Exit Overstay Report*, Dep't of Homeland Sec. 14–15 tbl. 2 and 30 tbl. 6 (March 30, 2020).

4. *Immigration Enforcement Actions: 2019 Annual Flow Report*, Dep't of Homeland Sec., 10 tbl. 5 (Sept. 2020).

5. Maria Elena Fernandez, *No Drugs Found in Search of Justin Bieber's Plane in N.J.*, NBC News, Jan. 31, 2014.

6. *Justin Bieber: Judge Orders Arrest in Argentinian Assault Case*, TMZ, https://www.tmz.com/2015/04/10/justin-bieber-arrest-ordered-argentina-assault/.

7. CNN Staff, *Justin Bieber Found Guilty of Assault, Careless Driving in Canada*, CNN, June 5, 2015.

8. Alan Duke, *Justin Bieber Charged with Assault After ATV Crash in Canada*, CNN, Sept. 4, 2014.

9. CNN Staff, *Justin Bieber Found Guilty of Assault, Careless Driving in Canada*, CNN, June 5, 2015.

10. Zach Baron, *Amazing Grace*, GQ, 37, 41 (May 2021).

11. Jordan v. DeGeorge, 341 U.S. 223, 238 (1951) (Jackson, J., dissenting).

12. Repouille v. United States, 165 F.2d 152 (2d Cir. 1947).

13. Brian Hood, *21 Savage Addressed Immigration During "Tonight Show" Performance*, Page Six, Feb. 4, 2019.

14. Jacqueline Stevens, *America's Secret ICE Castles*, The Nation (Dec. 16, 2009).

15. *21 Savage: Rapper "Will Fight" Against Deportation from US*, BBC, Feb. 4, 2019; @SincerelyAde, Twitter (Feb. 4, 2019, 4:03 p.m.), https://twitter.com/SincerelyAde/status/1092528991502782465?s=20&t=QwyNpm10Okm_3ZvuFv3VZg; Francisco Navas, *21 Savage: Why Was the Rapper Arrested and What Happens Next?*, The Guardian, Feb. 7, 2019.

16. Memorandum from S. Poverty L. Ctr. et al. to Homeland Sec. Advisory Council, *Conditions of Confinement and Due Process Violations at Privatized Immigration Detention Facilities in the South*, at 4 (Oct. 14, 2016).

17. ICE Response to FOIA Request, Final Locked Redacted-FOIA 2019-31276 ADP By Month (on file with the author).

18. Letter from Project South to Joseph V. Cuffari, Inspector General, Dep't of Homeland Sec. et al., *Lack of Medical Care, Unsafe Work Practices, and Absence of Adequate Protection Against COVID-19 for Detained Immigrants and Employees Alike at the Irwin County Detention Center* 19 (Sept. 14, 2020).

19. Dep't of Homeland Sec., Office of Inspector General, *Medical Processes and Communication Protocols Need Improvement at Irwin County Detention Center,* OIG-22-14, at 7 (Jan. 3, 2022).

20. Press Release, Immigr. and Customs Enf't, ICE to Close Two Detention Centers (May 20, 2021), https://www.dhs.gov/news/2021/05/20/ice-close-two-detention-centers.

21. *21 Savage: Immigration Status Still Up in the Air . . . Criminal Case Causing Delay,* TMZ, April 7, 2022.

22. Dep't of Homeland Security, Press Release, *DHS Continues to Prepare for End of Title 42; Announces New Border Enforcement Measures and Additional Safe and Orderly Processes* (Jan. 5, 2023), https://www.dhs.gov/news/2023/01/05/dhs-continues-prepare-end-title-42-announces-new-border-enforcement-measures-and.

23. Black Alliance for Just Immigration, Part II of *The State of Black Immigrants,* at 21 tbl. 1.

24. Michael T. Light et al., *Noncitizen Justice: The Criminal Case Processing of Non-US Citizens in Texas and California,* 129 Am. J. of Sociology 162, 198, 204 (2023).

6. Weaponizing Family Ties

1. *Denver-Area ICE Detainee Passes Away at Local Hospital,* U.S. Immigr. and Customs Enf't, Dec. 4, 2017, https://www.ice.gov/news/releases/denver-area-ice-detainee-passes-away-local-hospital; Brittany Freeman, *ICE Review of Immigration Detainee's Death Finds Medical Care Deficiencies at Aurora Facility,* Public Broadcasting Service, April 13, 2020, https://www.rmpbs.org/blogs/news/ice-review-of-death-in-aurora-immigration-detention-facility-finds-deficiencies-in-detainees-medical-care/.

2. *External Reviews and Analysis Unit Detainee Death Review—Kamyar Samimi,* U.S. Dep't of Homeland Sec. (2018), https://bento.cdn.pbs.org/hostedbento-prod/filer_public/RMPBS%20PDFs/RMPBS%20News/2018-ICFO-47347.pdf.

3. First Amended Complaint, Romero-Garcia v. CoreCivic, Inc., No. 4:20-cv-00158-CDL, at 6 (Dec. 4, 2020).

4. *U.S. Immigr. and Customs Enf't Detainee Death Review: Efrain de la Rosa*, U.S. Dep't of Homeland Sec. (n.d.).

5. José Olivares, *ICE Detainee Diagnosed with Schizophrenia Spent 21 Days in Solitary Confinement, Then Took His Own Life*, The Intercept, July 27, 2018.

6. Josh Tapper, *Scandal-Ridden Iowa Kosher Slaughterhouse Is Back in Business*, Times of Israel, Feb. 7, 2016.

7. Maggie Jones, *Postville, Iowa, Is Up for Grabs*, New York Times Magazine, July 11, 2012.

8. Robert R. Rigg, *The Postville Raid: A Postmortem*, 12 Rutgers Race & L. Rev. 271 (2011).

9. ICE, Press Release, *297 Convicted and Sentenced Following ICE Worksite Operation in Iowa* (May 15, 2008).

10. Courtney Crowder & MacKenzie Elmer, *A Decade After a Massive Raid Nabbed 400 Undocumented Workers, This Tiny Town Fights to Reclaim Its Identity*, Des Moines Register, May 10, 2018.

11. Nicole L. Novak et al., *Change in Birth Outcomes Among Infants Born to Latina Mothers After a Major Immigration Raid*, 46 Internat'l J. of Epidemiology 839, 843 (2017).

12. Efrén Olivares, My Boy Will Die of Sorrow: A Memoir of Immigration from the Front Lines 10 (Hachette Books, 2022).

13. Emergency Request for Precautionary Measures Pursuant to Article 25 of the Rules of Procedure of the Inter-American Commission on Human Rights on Behalf of Parents Systematically Separated from Their Children at the United States-Mexico Border 7, 9 (May 31, 2018), https://texascivilrightsproject.org/wp-content/uploads/2018/05/20180531-Emergency-Request-For-Precautionary-Measures_Redacted.pdf.

14. Nick Miroff, *A Family Was Separated at the Border, and This Distraught Father Took His Own Life*, Washington Post (June 9, 2018).

15. Complaint, Peña Arita v. United States, No. 7:19-cv-00288 (S.D. Tex., 2019).

16. Texas Dep't of Public Safety, Texas Rangers, Report of Investigation 22, *included as* Exhibit A, Third Amendment Complaint, Peña Arita v. United States, No. 7:19-cv-00288 (S.D. Tex., 2020).

17. Jeff Sessions, Att'y Gen., *Attorney General Sessions Delivers Remarks Discussing the Immigration Enforcement Actions of the Trump Administration*, U.S. Dep't of Just. (May 7, 2018), https://www.justice.gov/opa/speech/attorney -general-sessions-delivers-remarks-discussing-immigration-enforcement-actions.

18. @SecNielsen, Twitter (June 17, 2018, 5:52 p.m.), https://twitter .com/SecNielsen/status/1008467414235992069?s=20&t=mkkL3gAlYRS X1xbKcXFMtA.

19. Email from Gene Hamilton to Matthew Whitaker (May 21, 2018), *reprinted in* U.S. House of Rep., Comm. on the Judiciary, Majority Staff Report, *The Trump Administration's Family Separation Policy: Trauma, Destruction, and Chaos*, at A-450, Appx. AE (Oct. 2020).

20. Dep't of Homeland Sec., Interagency Task Force on the Reunification of Families, Interim Progress Report 7 (March 31, 2023).

21. Ng Fung Ho v. White, 259 U.S. 276, 284 (1922).

22. Nick Miroff, *Honduran Father Who Died in Texas Jail Was Fleeing Violence, Consul Says*, Washington Post (June 11, 2018).

23. Statement of Colleen Kraft, President, American Academy of Pediatrics, *AAP Statement Opposing Separation of Children and Parents at the Border* (May 8, 2018), https://www.aap.org/en/news-room/news-releases /aap/2018/aap-statement-opposing-separation-of-children-and-parents-at -the-border/; Yao Lu et al., *Diverse Experience of Immigrant Children: How Do Separation and Reunification Shape Their Development*, 91 Child Development e146, e158-e159 (2020).

24. Brenda G. McGowan & Karen L. Blumenthal, Why Punish the Children? A Study of Children of Women Prisoners 63 (National Council on Crime and Delinquency, 1978).

25. Jeff Sessions, Att'y Gen., *Attorney General Sessions Delivers Remarks Discussing the Immigration Enforcement Actions of the Trump Administration*, U.S. Dep't of Just. (May 7, 2018), https://www.justice.gov/opa/speech/attorney-general-sessions-delivers-remarks-discussing-immigration-enforcement-actions.

26. Amy Bracken, *No Mercy: Haitian Criminal Deportees*, NACLA Report on the Americas 6 (Sept./Oct. 2009).

27. David C. Brotherton & Luis Barrios, Banished to the Homeland: Dominican Deportees and Their Stories of Exile 204 (Columbia Univ. Press, 2011).

28. David C. Brotherton & Luis Barrios, Banished to the Homeland: Dominican Deportees and Their Stories of Exile 216 (Columbia Univ. Press, 2011).

29. Beth C. Caldwell, Deported Americans: Life After Deportation to Mexico 80–81 (Duke Univ. Press Books, 2019).

30. Oscar Martínez & Juan José Martínez, El Niño de Hollywood: Cómo Estados Unidos y El Salvador Moldearon a un Sicario de la Mara Salvatrucha 13, at 81–82 (Penguin Random House Grupo Editorial México, 2018).

31. Juan José Martínez D'Aubuisson, *The Omnipresent Business of the MS13 in El Salvador*, Insight Crime (Jan. 25, 2022), https://insightcrime.org/investigations/the-omnipresent-businesses-of-the-ms13/.

32. Oscar Martínez & Juan José Martínez, El Niño de Hollywood: Cómo Estados Unidos y El Salvador Moldearon a un Sicario de la Mara Salvatrucha 13, at 65–66 (Penguin Random House Grupo Editorial México, 2018).

33. Testimony of Alejandro N. Mayorkas, Secretary of Homeland Security, before U.S. Senate, Homeland Security & Gov't Affairs Comm., on Threats to the Homeland 14 (Nov. 17, 2022).

34. Dara Lind, *Trump Just Delivered the Most Chilling Speech of His Presidency*, Vox (July 28, 2017).

35. Oscar Martínez & Juan José Martínez, El Niño de Hollywood:

Cómo Estados Unidos y El Salvador Moldearon a un Sicario de la Mara Salvatrucha 13, at 86 (Penguin Random House Grupo Editorial México, 2018).

7. Alternative Futures

1. Jeff Sessions, Att'y Gen., *Attorney General Sessions Delivers Remarks Discussing the Immigration Enforcement Actions of the Trump Administration*, U.S. Dep't of Just. (May 7, 2018), https://www.justice.gov/opa/speech/attor ney-general-sessions-delivers-remarks-discussing-immigration-enforcement -actions.

2. Dep't of Homeland Security, *Secretary Mayorkas Remarks at a Media Availability Outlining Planning and Operations Ahead of the Lifting of the Title 42 Public Health Order* (May 10, 2023), https://www.dhs.gov /news/2023/05/10/secretary-mayorkas-remarks-media-availability-outlin ing-planning-and-operations.

3. Tom R. Tyler, Why People Obey the Law 178 (Princeton Univ. Press, 2006).

4. Kent W. Smith, *Reciprocity and Fairness: Positive Incentives for Tax Compliance, in* Why People Pay Taxes: Tax Compliance and Enforcement 223, 224–225, 246 (Joel Slemrod ed. 1992).

5. Raymond Paternoster et al., *Do Fair Procedures Matter? The Effect of Procedural Justice on Spousal Assault*, 31 L. & Soc'y Rev. 163, 190–191, 192 (1997).

6. Emily Ryo, *Deciding to Cross: Norms and Economics of Unauthorized Migration*, 78 Am. Socio. Rev. 574, 592 (2013).

7. Emily Ryo, *Deciding to Cross: Norms and Economics of Unauthorized Migration*, 78 Am. Socio. Rev. 574, 590, 593 (2013).

8. Emily Ryo, *Through the Back Door: Applying Theories of Legal Compliance to Illegal Immigration During the Chinese Exclusion Era*, 31 L. & Soc. Inquiry 133 (2006).

9. Fong Yue Ting v. United States, 149 U.S. 698, 709 (1893).

10. Paul H. Robinson & John M. Darley, *The Utility of Desert*, 91 Nw. Univ. L. Rev. 453, 480 (1997).

11. Fong Yue Ting v. United States, 149 U.S. 698, 740 (1893) (Brewer, J., dissenting).

12. Klonis v. Davis, 13 F.2d 630, 630 (2nd Cir. 1926).

13. Klonis v. Davis, 13 F.2d 630, 630 (2nd Cir. 1926).

14. Arturo Cano, *Limita EU el Trámite Digital a Migrantes Para Solicitar Asilo*, La Jornada, May 16, 2023, https://www.jornada.com.mx/notas/2023/05/16/politica/limita-eu-el-tramite-digital-a-migrantes-para-solicitar-asilo/.

15. Widlore Mérancourt & Anthony Faiola, *Deportees Land in Port-au-Prince: "Nobody Told Us We Were Going Back to Haiti,"* Washington Post, Sept. 19, 2021.

16. Padilla v. Kentucky, 559 U.S. 356, 360 (2010).

17. Tanya Golash-Boza, *The Immigration Industrial Complex: Why We Enforce Immigration Policies Destined to Fail*, 3 Socio. Compass 295, 296 (2009).

18. *Secretary Mayorkas Delivers Remarks at the U.S. Conference of Mayors*, Dep't of Homeland Sec. (Jan. 20, 2022), https://www.dhs.gov/news/2022/01/20/secretary-mayorkas-delivers-remarks-us-conference-mayors.

19. Texas v. United States, 606 F. Supp. 3d 437, 449 (S.D. Tex. 2022).

20. United States v. Texas, No. 22-58 (U.S. June 23, 2023).

21. United States v. Carrillo-Lopez, No. 21-10233, 2023 WL 3587596 (9th Cir. May 22, 2023).

22. Immigr. & Naturalization Serv., Annual Report of the Immigration and Naturalization Service 10 (1961).

23. *Immigration Prosecutions for April 2022*, TRAC Reports Inc. (June 29, 2022), https://trac.syr.edu/tracreports/bulletins/immigration/monthlyapr22/fil/.

24. Angela Y. Davis, Abolition Democracy: Beyond Empire, Prisons, and Torture 92 (Seven Stories Press, 2005).

25. W.E.B. DuBois, Black Reconstruction in America 1860–1880, at 131, 187 (Free Press ed. 1998) (1935).

26. W.E.B. DuBois, Black Reconstruction in America 1860–1880, at 674 (Free Press ed. 1998) (1935).

27. W.E.B. DuBois, Black Reconstruction in America 1860–1880, at 725, 727 (Free Press ed. 1998) (1935).

28. W.E.B. DuBois, Black Reconstruction in America 1860–1880, at 602 (Free Press ed. 1998) (1935).

29. Mariame Kaba, We Do This 'Til We Free Us: Abolitionist Organizing and Transforming Justice 61 (Haymarket Books, 2021).

30. Henry R. Luce, *The American Century*, Life Magazine, Feb. 17, 1941, 61, 64.

8. Reimagining Citizens

1. Brief and Supplemental Appendix for Appellee, United States v. Ragbir, No. 01-3745, at 15 (3rd Cir., 2002) (quoting Ragbir's July 27, 1999 confession).

2. *In re Ragbir*, 2007 WL 1180505 (BIA, 2007) (unpublished).

3. Ragbir v. Homan, 923 F.3d 53, 60 (2nd Cir. 2019) (quoting Scott Mechkowski, Deputy Director of the ICE New York Field Office).

4. Brief for Defendants-Appellees, Ragbir v. Vitiello, No. 18-1597, at 8 (2nd Cir., 2018).

5. Amy Gottlieb, *ICE Detained My Husband for Being an Activist*, New York Times (Jan. 18, 2018).

6. Rich Lamb, *Massive Protest Erupts, 2 City Councilmen Arrested, As ICE Detains Prominent Immigration Activist*, CBS News (Jan. 11, 2018).

7. Ragbir v. Sessions, No. 18-cv-00236, slip op. at 4-5 (S.D.N.Y. Jan. 29, 2018).

8. Amy Gottlieb, *ICE Detained My Husband for Being an Activist*, New York Times (Jan. 18, 2018).

9. Ragbir v. Homan, 923 F.3d 53, 70-71 (2nd Cir. 2019), *vacated on other grounds*; Pham v. Ragbir, 141 S. Ct. 227 (2020).

10. Sarah Song, Immigration and Democracy 9 (Oxford Univ. Press,

2019); Joseph Carens, Immigrants and the Right to Stay 18 (MIT Press, 2010).

11. Joseph Carens, Immigrants and the Right to Stay 43 (MIT Press, 2010).

12. Population Group, *Table 25: Percent of Offenses Cleared by Arrest or Exceptional Means*, Fed. Bureau of Investigation (2019), https://ucr.fbi.gov /crime-in-the-u.s/2019/crime-in-the-u.s.-2019/tables/table-25.

13. Alexi McCammond, *Read the Transcript of the Donald Trump Recording*, Bustle (Oct. 7, 2016).

14. John Guyton et al., *Tax Evasion at the Top of the Income Distribution: Theory and Evidence*, Nat'l Bureau of Econ. Rsch., 4, 37 (2021), https:// www.nber.org/papers/w28542.

15. Dietrich Knauth, *Revlon Creditors Say the Company's Bankruptcy Is Headed for a "Mess,"* Reuters (July 21, 2022).

16. Chris Hudgins & Michael O'Connor, *US Corporate Bankruptcy Filings Rise in August*, S&P Glob. Mkt. Intelligence (Sept. 7, 2022), https:// www.spglobal.com/marketintelligence/en/news-insights/latest-news-head lines/us-corporate-bankruptcy-filings-rise-in-august-72006667.

17. Aaron Elstein, *Revlon Executives to Get Up to $36M in Bankruptcy Bonuses*, Crain's New York Bus. (Sept. 14, 2022), https://www.crainsnew york.com/finance/revlon-executives-get-36m-bankruptcy-bonuses; Dietrich Knauth, *Revlon Gets Court Approval for $1.4 Billion Bankruptcy Loan*, Reuters (Aug. 1, 2022); Dietrich Knauth, *Revlon Creditors Say the Company's Bankruptcy Is Headed for a "Mess,"* Reuters (July 21, 2022).

18. Bordenkircher v. Hayes, 434 U.S. 357, 364 (1978).

19. Paul Butler, Let's Get Free: A Hip-Hop Theory of Justice 62 (The New Press, 2009).

20. John Cummings, *A Man of Convictions*, Newsday (July 2, 1966), at 14W, 34; *Slayer of Blind Son, 13, Is Held in $5,000 Bail*, New York Herald Tribune (Oct. 14, 1939), at 8; *Mercy Slayer of Son Is Given His Freedom*, Washington Post (Dec. 25, 1941), at 16.

21. Martha Minow, When Should Law Forgive? 4 (W.W. Norton & Co., 2019); Burdick v. United States, 236 U.S. 79, 95 (1915).

22. Immigr. and Nat'y Act, Pub. L. 414, 66 Stat. 163, § 311 (June 27, 1952); An Act to Repeal the Chinese Exclusion Acts, 57 Stat. 600, § 3 (Dec. 17, 1943).

23. Art Harris, *Louisiana Court Sees No Shades of Gray in Woman's Request*, Washington Post (May 21, 1983), at A3.

24. Frederick A. Cleveland, American Citizenship as Distinguished from Alien Status 65 (The Ronald Press Co., 1927).

25. 42 Stat. 1022 § 3 (Sept. 22, 1922); 34 Stat. 1228, § 3 (Mar. 2, 1907).

26. Pequignot v. City of Detroit, 16 F. 211, 216 (E.D. Mich. 1883).

27. Doug Wead, All the Presidents' Children: Triumph and Tragedy in the Lives of America's First Families 229–232 (Simon & Schuster, 2003); 30 Stat. 1496 (May 18, 1898).

28. Dimitry Kochenov, Citizenship 134 (The MIT Press, 2019).

29. Ming Hsu Chen, Pursuing Citizenship in the Enforcement Era 5–6 (Stan. Univ. Press, 2020).

30. Dimitry Kochenov, Citizenship 241 (The MIT Press, 2019).

31. Anna Seghers, Transit 78 (N.Y. Rev. of Books 2013) (1951).

32. Anna Seghers, Transit 178 (N.Y. Rev. of Books 2013) (1951).

33. United States Holocaust Memorial Museum, *Voyage of the St. Louis*, Holocaust Encyclopedia (July 12, 2021), https://encyclopedia.ushmm.org /content/en/article/voyage-of-the-st-louis.

34. Lisa Fittko, Escape Through the Pyrenees 48–49 (David Koblick trans. 1991) (1985).

35. Hannah Arendt, The Origins of Totalitarianism 299 (A Harvest Book Harcourt Inc. 1968).

36. Klonis v. Davis, 13 F.2d 630, 631 (2nd Cir. 1926).

37. Anthony M. Kennedy, Association Justice, Supreme Court of the United States, *Speech at the American Bar Association Annual Meeting*, Supreme Court (Aug. 14, 2003), https://www.supremecourt.gov/publicinfo /speeches/sp_08-09-03.html.

38. *Surrender Documents*, National Park Service, https://www.nps.gov /apco/learn/historyculture/surrender-documents.htm.

39. Andrew Johnson, *"Proclamation of Amnesty and Reconstruction," May 29, 1865*, Civil War Era NC, https://cwnc.omeka.chass.ncsu.edu/items /show/13.

40. Andrew Johnson, *Proclamation 179—Granting Full Pardon and Amnesty for the Offense of Treason Against the United States During the Late Civil War*, The Am. Presidency Project (Dec. 25, 1868), https://www.presi dency.ucsb.edu/documents/proclamation-179-granting-full-pardon-and-am nesty-for-the-offense-treason-against-the.

41. Frederick Douglass, The Unknown Loyal Dead, Speech at Arlington National Cemetery, May 30, 1871, *in* Frederick Douglass: Selected Speeches and Writings 609, 609–610 (Philip S. Foner ed. 1999).

42. John Reeves, The Lost Indictment of Robert E. Lee: The Forgotten Case Against an American Icon 77 (Rowman & Littlefield Publishers, 2018).

43. *General Robert E. Lee's Parole and Citizenship*, National Archives, https://www.archives.gov/publications/prologue/2005/spring/piece-lee.

44. *President Gerald R. Ford's Remarks Upon Signing a Bill Restoring Rights of Citizenship to General Robert E. Lee*, Ford Library & Museum (Aug. 5, 1975), https://www.fordlibrarymuseum.gov/library/speeches/750473 .htm.

45. Marjorie Hunter, *Citizenship Is Voted for Robert E. Lee*, New York Times (July 23, 1975), at 1, 30.

Conclusion

1. W.E.B. DuBois, Black Reconstruction in America, 1860–1880, at To the Reader (1935) (Free Press ed. 1998).

2. Liz Stark, *White House Policy Adviser Downplays Statue of Liberty's Famous Poem*, CNN Politics (Aug. 3, 2017).

3. *Matter of Jean*, 23 I&N Dec. 373, 385 (A.G. 2002); *Matter of Wojtkow*, 18 I&N Dec. 111, 113 (BIA 1981).

ABOUT THE AUTHOR

César Cuauhtémoc García Hernández is the Gregory H. Williams Chair in Civil Rights and Civil Liberties at the Ohio State University Moritz College of Law and an immigration lawyer. He has appeared in the *New York Times*, the *Wall Street Journal*, NPR, *The Guardian*, and many other venues. The author of *Crimmigration Law* as well as *Migrating to Prison* (The New Press), he lives in Denver, Colorado. For more information about his work, visit ccgarciahernandez.com.

PUBLISHING IN THE PUBLIC INTEREST

Thank you for reading this book published by The New Press; we hope you enjoyed it. New Press books and authors play a crucial role in sparking conversations about the key political and social issues of our day.

We hope that you will stay in touch with us. Here are a few ways to keep up to date with our books, events, and the issues we cover:

- Sign up at www.thenewpress.com/subscribe to receive updates on New Press authors and issues and to be notified about local events
- www.facebook.com/newpressbooks
- www.twitter.com/thenewpress
- www.instagram.com/thenewpress

Please consider buying New Press books not only for yourself, but also for friends and family and to donate to schools, libraries, community centers, prison libraries, and other organizations involved with the issues our authors write about.

The New Press is a 501(c)(3) nonprofit organization; if you wish to support our work with a tax-deductible gift please visit www.thenewpress.com/donate or use the QR code below.